Financial Secrets

Martin Hawes is New Zealand's most popular financial author. His book on family trusts, published in 1995, was an immediate success. Since then he has had a string of bestsellers on topics such as investment, mortgages, superannuation and tax.

Martin is a popular seminar presenter and keynote speaker and, together with his partner, Joan Baker, he writes regular columns for the *New Zealand Herald* and *Rural News*. Martin accepts private clients through his Wealth Coaching programme. In addition, he has a small number of independent, non-executive directorships and is President of Save the Children New Zealand.

Martin lives in Queenstown. In his spare time he runs, reads, skis, rock climbs and climbs mountains.

He welcomes comments on his books and can be contacted at: mhawes@wealthcoaches.net.

Financial Secrets

The New Zealand guide to everyday finances

MARTIN HAWES

SHOAL BAY

A Shoal Bay book
First published in 2002
This revised edition published 2004 by
Longacre Press Ltd
9 Dowling Street, Dunedin

Copyright © 2002, 2004 Martin Hawes

Cover photographs by Kurt Langer

ISBN 1 877251 16 X

All rights reserved. No part of this publication may
be reproduced, stored in a retrieval system or
transmitted in any form by any means electronic,
mechanical, photocopying, recording or otherwise,
without prior permission from the publisher.

Printed by Rainbow Print Ltd, Christchurch

Contents

ACKNOWLEDGMENTS 9

INTRODUCTION 11

1. PLANNING 15
Planning your life, then living the plan

The complete financial plan   15
The budget   18
Four steps to successful budgeting   18
What's the point of it all?   20
The five big budgeting problems   20
Budgeting can be fun   21
The financial secrets   22

2. ADVISERS 23
Seeking professional help

Lawyers   24
Accountants   25
Mortgage brokers   25
Insurance specialists   27
Investment advisers/financial planners   29
The financial secrets   33

3. BANKING & INSURANCE 34
Public businesses, not public servants

Banking services   34
Banking Ombudsman   36
Insurance services   37
Types of insurance   39
Insurance and Savings Ombudsman   44
The financial secrets   44

4. BORROWING 46
Using other people's money

Everyday borrowing   46
How lenders make money   49
Where to go for money   50
Getting a loan   53
Guaranteeing a loan   56

The monkey on your back: your mortgage   57
Saving money on your mortgage   63
Debt consolidation   65
The financial secrets   66

5. SAVING AND INVESTING   68
Making your money work

Some people shouldn't save!   68
The (only) three investments   69
Work out your financial goals   69
Diversification   71
Do-it-yourself or a managed fund?   72
Deposits   73
Shares   77
Property   84
Offshore investments   90
The financial secrets   93

6. SUPERANNUATION   94
Saving for your retirement

The demise of the surcharge   94
Planning your super   95
Ways to save for retirement   97
What super funds earn   98
The financial secrets   99

7. CONSUMER LAW   100
Know your rights

The Fair Trading Act   100
The Consumer Guarantees Act   103
Buying a car   104
Second-hand goods   106
Contracts   107
Quotes and estimates   109
Laybys   109
Hire purchase   110
Debt collection   112
The financial secrets   114

8. TAX   116
Not a penny more, nor a penny less

The role of the IRD   116
Personal tax in New Zealand   117
Investments and tax   119
Businesses and tax   120

The structure of your business   124
What can a business claim?   127
Tax audits   128
The financial secrets   130

9. RELATIONSHIPS   131
Sharing money

The Property (Relationships) Act   131
Put money on the agenda   133
Arranging income: one pot or two?   136
When it's over   137
Child support   141
Money and children   142
The financial secrets   144

10. HOUSING   146
Your home, your castle

To rent or to buy?   147
Buying a house   147
Selling a house   155
Renting a home   159
The financial secrets   162

11. EDUCATION   163
What's it worth?

The law   163
The cost of compulsory education   163
Tertiary education   165
The Student Loan Scheme   167
The financial secrets   170

12. EMPLOYMENT   171
Finding, keeping and leaving your job

Getting a job   172
Developing your job and career   175
Leaving your job   176
Taking a personal grievance claim   178
The financial secrets   180

13. GOVERNMENT ASSISTANCE   181
Getting help

Work and Income New Zealand   181
Income support   181
Finding work   185
Family Assistance   186

Accident Compensation Corporation   187
Benefits are a back-up   190
The financial secrets   190

14. RETIREMENT   191
You've earned it

Planning your income   191
Expenditure   194
Retirement budget   195
Succession planning   195
Family trusts   199
Asset testing for residential care subsidies   200
Retirement villages   202
The financial secrets   205

15. FINANCIAL FAILURE   206
When things go wrong

Insolvency: the basics   206
Going bankrupt   208
Being a creditor   210
The financial secrets   211

GLOSSARY   213

INDEX   217

Acknowledgments

This is a big book covering a wide range of financial topics, and it required the sourcing of a great deal of detailed information. My sincere thanks to the people at AMP for all the help they have given me with this project.

Introduction

Fifteen years ago few people knew what an eftpos card was, and even fewer used it. Ten years ago the Internet was a mysterious entity to most of us. We had heard of it, but didn't have the least idea how it worked or how it could possibly relate to us.

Today, few of us could manage without either. One has only to suffer a momentary crash in either system to be reduced to anything from bemused frustration to impotent rage. We are accustomed to the new technology: we expect to be able to make our cash transactions quickly and painlessly; we rely on our ability to send quick messages to family, friends or business connections, or to search an esoteric – or everyday – topic on the World Wide Web.

A similar revolution has crept up on us in the financial world. Things like revolving credit facilities, family trusts, split loans, offshore investments, student loans, web-based budgeting and hedge funds were either not available a decade ago, or only available to those in the know. Now they are a part of everyday finances.

Old certainties have faded. Where once you had to make an appointment with a formidable old bank manager and plead your case for a mortgage, today you are bombarded with slick advertising from banks imploring you to buy their wares. Insurance agents no longer call you (just as you are sitting down to dinner) to give you 12 reasons why you owe it to your family to take out some life insurance. Instead their companies recommend – through a variety of sophisticated and subtle means – that their 'financial adviser' will carry out a needs analysis and suggest some insurance covers as part of your overall financial plan.

As well, the distinction between institutions like banks and insurance companies has become blurred. Insurance companies offer many of the products and services that banks offer and banks now offer insurance. In many instances these organisations have become one-stop shops for financial services and most now refer to themselves as 'financial services providers'. There are also hundreds of other independent financial companies in the market promoting themselves, equally agressively, as the answer to all your financial prayers.

This is all very empowering for you, the customer. You no longer have to approach financial services companies as a supplicant. Now it is a business arrangement between equals. You can choose which provider you want and negotiate the best deal for yourself. You are the customer and you can buy what you want. If one provider doesn't meet your needs or provide satisfactory service, there are plenty of others.

But it can also be very confusing. Where do you go for advice? What's the best insurance package for your circumstances? Where will you invest your small inheritance? Should you buy a small rental property or pay off your mortgage? What does the Property (Relationships) Act mean for you?

This book sets out to answer questions like these. It also makes the point that despite the dazzling array of new 'products' on the market, the bedrocks of sensible financial management remain the same.

Money is important – not as an end in itself but because it pays for the things you want to do in life. The better you can manage your money, the more choices and opportunities become available to you.

The aim of this book is to give you enough information to provide a basis for you to devise a sensible and workable financial plan for yourself, and to help you come to grips with the sometimes mysterious and intimidating world of finance. It shares with you the 'financial secrets' of successful money management. Ignore them and you will fall behind while others get ahead.

As with all my books I have set out to put what are, in reality, quite complicated financial concepts into everyday terms. The book is not meant to be read from cover-to-cover; rather it is intended as a ready reference, which you can keep handy and dip into when the need arises. As such, it provides broad guidelines rather than definitive advice, but it also gives references to more detailed sources of information. I have tried to provide sufficient cross-referencing within the book – and a comprehensive index – to enable you to find readily the subject that most interests or concerns you.

This is the first revised edition of this book and the facts and figures are up to date, as far as I could confirm before we went to print, at the date below. I intend to update the information at regular intervals and if there is any topic that you think that I have missed, or if you have other comments, I would welcome them. I can be contacted at mhawes@wealthcoaches.net.

Martin Hawes
March 2004

Financial Secrets

1. PLANNING
Planning your life, then living the plan

Setting goals, then making plans to achieve those goals, is the basis of all good money management. So, fittingly, this book starts with planning and budgeting.

Money really matters. It is not the most important thing in life, but it is necessary to fund the things that are. If you are continually in difficulty with your money you will have no focus or energy left to devote to the things that really matter.

Few of us have enough money to do whatever we want. Life and money are therefore about choices – deciding what are the important things that you are prepared to spend money on, and what is less important to you.

It seems obvious that to make the best of the money you have, you need a plan. No one invites 12 people to dinner without planning a menu, then making sure there is food and drink in the house and gas for the barbeque. Living from day to day without making plans and setting goals for the future is a bit like just hoping you'll have enough food to go around when your guests turn up.

Once you have a good workable plan, money management becomes so much easier because all the choices and decisions have been made. Now you can simply get on with working the plan – and get on with your life.

THE COMPLETE FINANCIAL PLAN
A financial plan is not simply about budgeting. It is essentially taking a long-term view of how you want to live your life, now and in the future, deciding on the goals for you and your family and working out a way to achieve these goals.

Developing a plan means making your choices about expenditure calmly and rationally – mindfully. It is important that you (and your partner) sit down and work it out at a quiet time, when you are under no pressure. Together you can set your financial priorities according to how you want to live your life.

Your plan doesn't need to be some complex weighty document, beautifully typed and bound. Indeed, this is an area where less is often better. Ideally, you should be able to summarise it on a single sheet of paper so it is readily accessible and actionable. Once completed, it should not be stuck in the bottom drawer, never to see the light of day. Although the plan should be put in writing, you should also be able to carry it in your head so it can drive your daily behaviour. The plan should set goals across a range of financial issues:

- Day-to-day finance – bank accounts, use of credit cards etc
- Debt reduction
- Asset protection – insurances, and perhaps a family trust
- Savings and investment
- Retirement
- Succession – your will and/or family trust

All these areas are covered in detail later in this book.

Setting goals

Goals can be short term (being able to pay all the monthly bills and clear debts, being able to afford a hobby), medium term (saving to buy a house, planning to have children and providing for their immediate needs and/or future education, saving for an overseas trip) or long term (building up an investment portfolio, saving for retirement). Whatever they are, you have a better chance of achieving them if they are realistic and specific. For example, 'getting rich' is certainly a goal of sorts, but you might like to spend time defining what 'rich' means to you and what you would need to achieve in order to feel you've attained this goal.

It is important that your goals are committed to writing. It has been proven over and over again that goals that are put in writing are much more effective and likely to be reached.

Once you've worked out where you are going in life, it's time to sit down and work out the nuts and bolts of how you are going to get there: your budget.

THE 'NOW' SOCIETY

There's a sophisticated advertising and marketing industry out there, using all its considerable skills to persuade us that we *must* have their product – *NOW*. Clever ads, special offers and promises of easy finance all combine in an attempt to convince us that we'd be positively irresponsible not to take advantage of such an amazing opportunity ...

Having a budget (and the discipline to stick to it) can protect you against the sort of impulse buying (using money that you had no intention of spending) that is triggered by exposure to such campaigns. As well, you can remind yourself that 'special sales' are an almost permanent feature in today's retail environment. The offer will probably come around again at a time when you can better afford it.

If, on the other hand, you have already budgeted for, say, a new washing machine, and this does seem to be a genuinely good deal, then you can take advantage of the 'special offer' without blowing the budget.

CALCULATING YOUR NET WORTH

Anyone approaching a bank or financial institution for an overdraft or a loan will be asked to fill in a form to assess their net worth. This is simply a summary of what you own (your assets) less what you owe (your liabilities), and gives a snapshot of how much you would have if you sold everything and paid off all your debts. It is a measure of how 'rich' you are.

Calculating your own net worth regularly (say every year) can be a useful exercise. You can watch how it grows (or declines, if you are getting things wrong). You can even graph this growth if you want to. In the final analysis your net worth, and the changes to it, tell you how successful your money plans and management are. A net worth statement could look like this:

Assets	$
House	185,000
Superannuation	25,000
Rental property	120,000
Cash at bank	8,000
Total assets	**338,000**
Liabilities	
House mortgage	85,000
Rental mortgage	90,000
Hire purchase	12,000
Total liabilities	**187,000**
NET WORTH	**151,000**

Be honest!

Valuing things like real estate or small family businesses can be quite difficult and you don't want the trouble and expense of getting professionals in. However, to get an accurate picture you need to value things fairly and sensibly. If you inflate the value you will certainly have a higher net worth, but in reality you are kidding yourself. Strike a reasonable value for the things you own, and use the same basis for valuation every time, so you get an accurate picture of the changes.

If your net worth is declining ...

... you are getting poorer and are probably doing something wrong. While it is quite reasonable for older people in retirement to live on their capital and so reduce their net worth, most younger people want to push up their net worth and become better off each year.

A declining net worth indicates one of two problems:

1. *You own the wrong things.*
   This is especially so if you have investments that are not performing. Contact a financial adviser and get a full review of your investments and finances.

2. *You are spending more than you earn and effectively living on your capital.*
   Perhaps you have a line-of-credit mortgage or are using credit cards to borrow to fund a lifestyle that is beyond your means, or maybe you are continuously dipping into the term deposit or savings account. If this is the case you need to go back and do another budget, and then live within it. Again, if a pattern of spending more than you earn emerges, you should see a financial or budget adviser as soon as you are aware of the problem.

THE BUDGET

Some people think 'budget' is a dirty word. For them, the idea of having a budget is about living a poor, miserable life, scrimping and saving and penny-pinching. But a budget is simply a plan for your money – how you are going to balance your income and your outgoings, and deal with any shortfalls or excesses. Unattractive though the idea of a budget might sound, you cannot expect to have good and happy finances if you have not planned them.

The only 'dirty' word involved is 'discipline'. The best plan in the world won't succeed unless you make a genuine effort to stick to it. Having clear and achievable goals will help. If you are convinced in your own mind that what you are aiming for is really worth the effort, you'll find it easier to bypass the temptations you encounter on the way.

FOUR STEPS TO SUCCESSFUL BUDGETING

1. Consider your income.
2. Consider your expenditure.
3. Decide on your time-frame.
4. Monitor and adjust.

Income

A budget is not solely about reducing expenditure: many people give little thought to the income side of the equation. To balance a budget, income can and should be maximised and as much effort should go into this as into deciding where you are going to spend your money. An extra dollar earned is as good as (if not better) than a dollar saved.

Increased income can come from:

- Continuously managing your career, looking for promotions. Have you asked for a raise lately? Is there any overtime available?
- Finding a part-time job or setting up a small business. Or could you, for instance, take in a boarder?
- Benefits. Are you sure you are getting your full entitlement from the government?
- Investments. Is your money working hard?
- Tax. Are your affairs arranged tax efficiently? Is there any way you could reduce your tax?

Expenditure

Planning and controlling expenditure is the other side of the budget. There are 12 main categories to consider:

- Groceries
- Housing (rates or rent, maintenance, garden)
- Debt repayments (mortgage, hire purchases etc)
- Utilities (phone, electricity, gas etc)
- Transport
- Insurance
- Children (childcare, school fees, uniforms etc)
- Clothing/grooming (hairdresser, chemist etc)
- Medical
- Entertainment (movies, shows, pay TV, magazines)
- Holidays
- Sundry (appliance repairs, gifts, pets)

In addition, you should budget for the occasional purchase or replacement of capital items, such as a new washing machine or lawnmower (and hope that both don't die the same week!).

Budget time-frame

Are you going to budget on a short-term or long-term basis – for the next week or the next year?

While it is probably simplest to set your budget according to when you get paid – i.e. if you are paid fortnightly, you budget your expenditure on a fortnightly basis – this doesn't take into account those bills that come in monthly, quarterly or annually (car registration, insurances). You will need to work out an accurate idea of your total annual expenses so that you can put aside a proportion of this every fortnight and have money available to pay those big bills.

Monitoring

No one ever gets a budget perfectly right. Don't get depressed and stop the process just because your actual income and expenditure don't match the plan. In fact, it is likely that the first time around you will be well out – over on some items and under on others.

Budgeting is an ongoing process: you need to monitor your income and expenditure and make the necessary adjustments (and keep making them) until you start to get some accuracy.

BUDGET TIPS

Budget tip #1

Buy things with cash – even the groceries. For many people, handing a piece of plastic over the counter does not really feel like spending money. People who pay for their groceries with cash are often a lot more careful in what they buy because $20 notes seem so much more real.

Budget tip #2

Never make your budget too tight, because you won't stick to it. The psychology of budgeting is much like that of dieting – once you have blown it there's a temptation to throw in the towel. Make the budget realistic, with a bit of fat, and not something that is so strict you are bound to fail.

Budget tip #3

Write down your budget, and any other financial plans and goals. Committing these things to paper makes them much more likely to be achieved.

Budget tip #4

Spend a couple of months carefully monitoring where you spend your money. Carry a notebook and write down everything you spend so you know where your money goes. After two or three months you might get quite a shock to find that comparatively large amounts of money are being spent on things that don't really give much satisfaction.

Budget tip # 5

Buy quality. You are better to buy one thing that will last and give you a lot of pleasure, even if it is expensive, than a whole lot of shoddy things because they are cheaper. For example, one nice (albeit expensive) jacket is cheaper in the long run than several items you don't really much like and therefore hardly wear.

FIVE THINGS THAT CAN BLOW THE BUDGET

House
People often buy a far more expensive house than they need. A house is not an investment – it is somewhere to live. You may be able to afford high mortgage repayments, but there is an ongoing cost that can strain the budget and limit your lifestyle. Moreover, people often spend far more on the house and garden than they ever think they will – it is easy to spend a few hundred dollars to paint a room or to put in some plants and shrubs. However, these costs add up, often to a level much higher than you would imagine.

Car
People often buy a more expensive car than they need. If you really enjoy your car and spend a lot of time in it, have an expensive car. But if your car is simply a means of getting from A to B, then buy a good-quality budget vehicle.

Holidays
Have the holiday you want, but be aware that it is likely to cost you more than you think. If you are taking an expensive holiday, ask yourself if that is truly what you want to do, or whether there is something else that would give you greater satisfaction for your money.

Hire purchase
Many people buy things because the retailer makes the purchase seem so easy by providing the necessary finance. The decision to buy things is often based on the fact that they will cost only $15 per week. Yes, you may be able to find that money easily enough, but those payments add up over a year or two to hundreds or thousands of dollars. Before you buy, look at the total cost, then ask yourself whether you would still go ahead with the purchases if you were paying cash.

Credit cards
Credit cards make spending and buying easy, but with the high interest charged there is a very real cost. If your card is a problem, cut it in half.

Compare how you are earning and spending your money with what you have planned to do. If there is a great deal of difference, you will either have to change the way you live and spend, or earn more. It may be that you have to do both.

Your budget should drive your daily spending behaviour. There's not much point deciding how much money you will have and how it is going to be spent and then forgetting or ignoring these decisions.

WHAT'S THE POINT OF IT ALL?

Remember that the reason you are budgeting is not just to make sure you have enough money to cover your outgoings and the occasional emergency. Your aim should be to have something extra left over to put aside as savings and investments for your future.

You can do this in which ever way feels right for you. Some people decide how much they want to save and adjust their lifestyle according to what is left over. This is called the 'pay yourself first' approach and entails putting aside a certain amount of your income into some sort of savings plan and pretending that you never had the money – it simply never existed. This is a kind of enforced discipline and is particularly suitable for people who find the whole idea of budgeting too hard. If the money is siphoned off into some other account, you never see it and therefore don't miss it.

Others find they are able to spend their money on the lifestyle they want, but don't allow their expenditure to rise to the point where there is nothing left at the end of the month. By keeping their long-term goals in sight they are able to make regular savings.

THE FIVE BIG BUDGETING PROBLEMS

A range of reasons can cause people to stop using their budget to guide their financial decisions. The big ones are:

- *The budget is too tight*
  If your budget is unrealistic, you may keep to it for a few weeks or months, but eventually it will be broken, and then discarded in disgust. Do your budget honestly.
- *Unexpected expenditures*
  Something like major car repairs could mean the budget no longer works. The answer to that is to get the car fixed, pay the bill and then redo the budget.
- *Life changes*
  A new baby comes along or you are transferred to another town. The old budget is no longer valid – do another one.
- *Only one member of the family was involved in the budget planning process*
  It is critical that everyone who makes income and expenditure decisions shares in and owns the decisions that have been made. (This can cause difficulties in itself: *see* Budget Stress).
- *Boredom*
  The budget may be exciting to draw up, but slowly other things in life take precedence and the budget spends more and more time in the bottom drawer until eventually it disappears completely. Those who manage their finances well use budgeting *all* the time and for ever.

> **BUDGET STRESS**
>
> Both partners need to be involved in drawing up the family budget. However, this can cause stress within a relationship. Making decisions about money can show up differences in attitude and precipitate disagreements. It transpires that she always thought he should do more overtime, while he always thought that her yachting hobby was too expensive. Budgeting is a time when these things come out into the open and disagreements arise, sometimes becoming heated.
>
> The budget won't work if you're pulling in different directions or one partner resents the imposition of another's view, so any fundamental differences need to be addressed.
>
> Choose a time when you are both feeling calm and relaxed, and be prepared to *listen* and *negotiate*.
>
> Remember, the aim is to strike a balance that will satisfy you both.

BUDGETING CAN BE FUN

Impossible? It's true. Doing your budget on-line on an interactive programme makes the whole process much more enjoyable because you can quickly see the difference that adjustments to your income or expenditure make to your financial position. There is an excellent New Zealand web site where you can do this for free:
   www.sorted.org.nz

Get some help

Starting off can be difficult, as can maintaining the process and staying on track. Budget Advice Services are available in most centres or you can consult a financial planner or adviser. Many people find that having an objective 'outsider' helping with their budgets makes a big difference.

THE FINANCIAL SECRETS

- You need some goals and a plan to reach your goals.
- Commit your goals and your plans to paper.
- Focus on your income – getting money in – as well as your expenditure.
- Know where your money goes – information is the first step to managing your expenditure.
- Commit to spending money only on what matters to you. Stop spending on what doesn't matter.
- Don't spend your life dreaming about winning lotto. Start a savings and investment plan NOW.

CONNECT

- Budget Advice Service (see your local phone book)
- Sorted, a web site maintained by the Retirement Commission www.sorted.org.nz

BOOKS

- *Keep Your money Working : How to Maximise Your Dollars in Retirement*, Consumers Institute, 1997
- *A New Zealand Guide to Living Well in Retirement*, Noel Whittaker & Roger Moses, Hodder Moa Beckett, 1995

Both contain useful information about budgeting.

2. ADVISERS
Seeking professional help

Financial matters can be complicated and few of us can do without the services of a trusted and competent adviser at some stage in our lives. However, nothing costs more than bad advice. Make sure any adviser you consult knows his or her stuff.

Be it a lawyer, accountant, mortgage broker, insurance specialist or investment adviser, the best way to choose any professional is through personal referral – from family, friends, workmates etc. But in the final analysis it comes down to using your judgment. Shop around, visiting several before committing yourself to any one. Most advisers will give you some free time to meet and chat about your requirements without any obligation. You can use that time to gather information to help you make your judgment.

There are several points to explore in the first interview with any adviser:

- Ask about his or her training, qualifications and experience. You may like to ask how many clients the adviser has (though you may not get an answer!). What you are really looking for here is to find out whether he or she is qualified and successful.
- Look at the state of the adviser's office. (It's good to have this first interview there – you can get some sort of impression of the degree of efficiency.) Don't be taken in by flashy addresses and smart support staff. Rather, look for signs of organisation. Even before the first interview you may be able to tell a lot by their telephone system and manner. Is this firm efficient and capable of giving you the level of support you need?
- Watch for the adviser's level of engagement and focus. If he or she appears distracted or uninterested, perhaps this is not the right person to attend to your affairs. If, for example, the adviser is late for your meeting or takes phone calls during it, you should look elsewhere.
- Is the adviser a specialist or a generalist? If a generalist, then what sort of support and backup does he or she have?
- Find out how the adviser charges – not just what will be charged for a particular piece of work, but the basis of the charging. In

dealing with a financial adviser, ask if he or she receives any commissions from banks or insurance companies.
- Also with financial advisers, ask if the firm buys in research from one of the investment or insurance research houses. If not, how do they keep up with all of the investment possibilities?
- Discuss the number of suppliers that an adviser has access to and who the main ones are. Can they place your insurance, investments or mortgage needs anywhere, or are they tied to just a few companies? Does the advising firm have a close arrangement with one particular company? (This is not necessarily a bad thing, provided the arrangement is disclosed to you.)
- Explore the nature of an ongoing relationship. Service often falls off over time, as a complacency sets in and the adviser starts to treat new clients better than existing ones. To avoid this you should agree the level of service that is required from the start and be sure that the adviser sticks to it. This may mean getting a service level agreement in writing.
- Above all, use your intuition. If you don't like the individual or have some sort of bad feeling, go somewhere else – there are plenty of others around. Don't deal with someone you're not comfortable with.

LAWYERS

Choosing a lawyer is bit like choosing a doctor. While some run a general practice and deal with wide areas of the law, others specialise in quite narrow areas such as property matters, family law, tax, commercial law, criminal law, trusts and wills, intellectual property etc. In the same way that your GP would not do a heart transplant, you probably would not use the same lawyer for your divorce and your tax audit.

As with a GP, a general practice solicitor will meet most people's needs for the things that crop up in the normal course of life – property conveyancing, drawing up a will etc – and it can be useful to build up a relationship over time with someone who is familiar with your circumstances. Your lawyer will refer you on to a specialist, such as a barrister for criminal court work, should the need arise.

How lawyers get paid

Lawyers usually get paid on a time and attendance basis. This means that they bill you for any time they spend working for you, usually in blocks of 6 minutes. The rate can vary from $100 per hour to $300 per hour (and occasionally even more). For some matters (eg property conveyancing or remortgaging your house) you can get a fixed price quote for the work that needs to be done.

Who controls lawyers?
The New Zealand Law Society controls lawyers. The society has strict rules regarding who can practise law and can bar them from practising. If you have a problem with your lawyer, you can (and should) make a complaint to the society.

ACCOUNTANTS
Accounting firms vary greatly both in size and range of expertise. Some are little more than book-keepers, while some of the large ones do everything from tax planning and accounting through to human resources and financial planning. Obviously, you need to choose an accountant who will provide the level of service you require.

How accountants get paid
Accountants usually charge an hourly rate which can vary from $60 per hour to $250 per hour (and occasionally more for very specialist work).

Who controls accountants?
Anyone can practise as an accountant and hold themselves out as one. However, most accountantcy firms are members of the Institute of Chartered Accountants (ICANZ). Being a member means that the accountant must adhere to a code of ethics and keep up their skills and currency through on-going training. The institute has dispute resolution procedures which includes disputes regarding fees.

MORTGAGE BROKERS
Mortgage broking in this country has grown rapidly in recent years. Around 30 per cent of mortgages now originate through brokers and this is growing strongly, although we have a fair way to go to catch up with the US, where some 85 per cent of mortgage deals are done through brokers.

What they do
- Arrange finance for you by identifying a likely lender, assembling information and documentation from you and presenting that to the lender.
- Help to structure your borrowings effectively.
- Negotiate with the lender on your behalf.

How they get paid
Mortgage brokers usually get paid a percentage of the loan amount,

ADVISERS/INTERMEDIARIES/BROKERS

A number of names are given to people who sell and provide financial services, which usually define them in terms of the legal relationship between a company and its distribution force. The three main groups are:

Employees

These are employed by a company and represent only that company. They will generally sell only the branded products from their company. Employees are usually paid a salary with a performance bonus component.

Agents

Agents are largely contracted to one company and represent that company. The main difference between an agent and an employee is that the agent is self-employed. His or her income is derived from sales commission, ongoing servicing income (a small percentage paid every year) and fees charged for advice. Agents may have access to a variety of suppliers but are usually expected to put most of their sales through the primary company.

Brokers/advisers

Brokers and advisers usually have relationships with a number of suppliers and no particularly strong ties to any of them. This means the product supplier does not carry liability for the broker's actions.

The distinction between agents and brokers is becoming blurred, and many work across the whole range of financial advisory services. Some will do you a financial plan, help with your investments, sell you some insurance and arrange you a mortgage. This can be good and it can be bad. There is no doubt that it is convenient to go to a one-stop shop but there is always the risk that there might be gaps in the adviser's knowledge in some specialist areas. If you have one person helping you with all your financial arrangements, make sure it's someone with all the relevant skills and knowledge, or who can either call on specialists within his or her firm, or call on outsiders.

often around 0.6 per cent. That means that a loan of $100,000 will attract a commission of $600 – paid by the lender, not you. This commission may vary between lenders, giving an incentive for the broker to place more business with one lender than another.

In addition, mortgage brokers sometimes receive trail fees. This is a fee, perhaps (0.2 per cent) which is paid to the broker every year the loan continues, providing an incentive for the broker keep in touch with you and discourage you from switching.

What's good about mortgage brokers?

They know all the main mortgage lenders, their lending criteria, their rates and the different loan types on offer. They are well placed to advise you on the best loan for you.

They should be able to target your loan application to the right lender. For example, if you have a loan proposal that many lenders would not accept, a good mortgage broker should be able to find one who might.

You don't usually have to pay them (although a fee is built into the transaction by the supplier).

What you need to be careful about

- The broker is paid by the lender. Make sure he or she is really on your side and not in reality a salesperson for the lending organisation.
- Make sure the broker is not especially keen on one lender simply because that lender pays the best commission.
- Be wary of brokers who call a couple of years after you have taken a loan suggesting you switch lenders. Switching may or may not be a good idea for you, but it will definitely be a good

idea for the broker because he or she will get paid again. (This is called 'churning'.)
- Mortgage brokers may not attend to your other risks associated with having a mortgage, e.g. house, contents, life or income insurance.

Who controls mortgage brokers?
No one. The New Zealand Mortgage Brokers Association (NZMBA) has a code of ethics and promotes standards, educational and qualifications criteria. However, this association is quite new, membership is not compulsory and there is ultimately no sanction on brokers' behaviour, provided it is not fraudulent. If you have any complaints you should go to this body or you could try complaining to any banks involved with the broker, because they are usually fairly sensitive to adverse publicity.

INSURANCE SPECIALISTS
Some of these go under the guise of financial planners or financial advisers: there are many people who can sell you insurance.

What they do
- Identify your insurance needs and advise on appropriate solutions.
- Help choose the right insurer for your needs.
- Help make up a proposal to an insurer, present it and negotiate it through the acceptance process.
- Act as the go-between for all of your dealings with the company, including claims.

How they get paid
Almost always by commission paid by the insurer, except if they work for a bank, where they are likely to be on a salary plus bonus. The commission they receive will vary hugely, depending on the type of insurance sold. Advisers often receive trail fees from the insurance company if you continue to renew your insurance. This has the benefit of making them keep in touch with you to ensure you are happy.

What's good about insurance specialists?
They know about insurance: which companies offer the best insurances according to type, where the best deals are, what you should have and what you don't really need. Insurance is a complex issue and there are many different types of each available. It is nearly a full-time job keeping up with this and a good insurance adviser should save you a lot of time and trouble shopping around.

If you need to make a claim your adviser will be your first point of contact and will help you. This works quite well because the adviser has every incentive to keep you happy and so will do his or her best to get the claim through as quickly as possible.

What you need to be careful about

- Insurance advisers get paid according to how much insurance you take. It is important that you are able to question the advice and be shown which needs are actually being covered and why.
- They get paid by the company who provides your policy and this may be where their true loyalty lies. Although nearly all insurance advisers are free to place insurance with a range of companies, they do have special arrangements with particular companies. A bias may arise when an adviser either gets a greater commission or must place a certain percentage of its business with a particular company.
- Insurance advisers sometimes get involved in financial matters they don't really understand. It pays to ask an adviser who is offering investments what his or her relevant qualifications and experience are.
- Make sure your adviser passes on your premium payments to the company! Any money you give them should be placed in a trust account and passed on to the company within 50 days. While it seldom happens, there have been odd cases of agents simply taking their clients' money and running. You should receive confirmation from the insurance company that your insurance is in place within a few weeks – if not, chase it up.

Who controls insurance specialists?

There are no formal qualifications required but various industry bodies set standards for membership. Make sure your adviser is a member of at least one of them.

The Financial Planners and Insurance Advisers Association (FPIA) is the largest and leading industry body. It drives the ethics, education and qualifications framework in the industry as well as consulting with government. The FPIA administers the insurance qualification Certified Life Underwriter (CLU). To obtain a CLU an adviser must have undertaken a formal course of study at university and have been supervised for two years.

Other industry bodies include:
- Corporation of Insurance Brokers (CIBA) (general insurance only)
- Independent Insurance Brokers Association (IIBA) (general insurance only)

- Life Brokers Association (LBA)
- Million Dollar Round Table (MDRT)

It is worth remembering that while the formal qualifications required and the controls on insurance advisers are not particularly great, insurance companies are very sensitive about their reputations and are unlikely to deal with anyone who is incompetent or untrustworthy.

INVESTMENT ADVISERS/FINANCIAL PLANNERS

Strictly speaking, these are two separate groups because the process of financial planning is different from giving investment advice. However, in practical terms the two are intertwined: investment is always involved in financial planning and you cannot properly give investment advice without doing a financial plan first.

Most financial advisers work for companies set up to do financial planning and advisory work. Some of these companies are franchise operations with offices around the country. It is this company that will have a relationship with the various investment fund managers; it is the company to which you are giving your money. Your primary relationship as a client is with this company – if something goes wrong, you will sue the company (although you may also sue the individual adviser).

Having said that, the individual adviser is important: this will be the person with whom you are dealing directly. If you find a good one, stay with him or her – even if he or she leaves for another firm.

What they do

Financial planning covers a broad range of issues including risk analysis, debt management, investment and tax advice and estate planning. The basics of money management (e.g. a budget) should be in place first, so make sure your adviser covers this. A good financial planner will be able to gather the information necessary to complete an analysis of your needs and then either provide the solutions or recommend you to someone else who can.

The Financial Planners and Investment Advisers Association recommends a six-step process. According to this, an adviser should:
- Establish your present position.
- Establish objectives – not just financial but also what you want to achieve for yourself and your family in the short, medium and long term.
- Analyse and recommend solutions.
- Communicate.
- Implement.
- Monitor and review.

How they get paid
There are many alternatives:
- From commissions on the financial products they sell. This commission is often directly related to the fee charged for lodging money. For example, if you were going to invest $10,000 in a fund that had an up-front fee of 2 per cent, your $10,000 would effectively buy only $9800 worth of units. The 2 per cent (or $200 in this case) would go to the intermediary who arranged the investment.
- By taking a flat percentage of all money they invest for you (and then returning the commissions received back to you). This fee might be 1 per cent, paid annually.
- By charging you an hourly rate for work done. In many ways this is the best for you because when there is no commission there is no chance you will be advised according to what fees might be earned.
- By charging you (say, $1500) for writing a financial plan but reducing the fee if you proceed with some of the recommended investments.
- By taking 'trail fees' – a fee paid by fund managers etc if you remain with the investment. These fees range from 0.2 per cent to 0.5 per cent of the funds invested and vary from fund manager to fund manager.
- By a combination of any or all of these.

Always ask what fees will be charged and also what up-front fee there is for any particular investment. You should also find out what you get in return for the fee (e.g. regular review, investment information).

What's good about investment advisers/financial planners?
The best advisers know a great deal about financial planning, money management and all aspects of personal financial services. A good financial adviser will be able to set a workable plan for you and advise you in detail on how to meet your financial goals.

Good financial advisers should have knowledge of a wide range of investments and access to commentary on those investments. (This is no mean feat: there are hundreds of different funds available in New Zealand alone.) The best advisers buy in research from one of the specialist research houses (Fund Source and Morningstar are the two main ones), which provide historical returns and ratings for various funds. If in doubt, question why a particular supplier is recommended and ask to see independent product comparisons, available from most advisers through their computer systems.

What you need to be careful about
- The quality of advice – be sure that a structured process is followed and documented.
- The credentials of the adviser – always ask to see their disclosure statement (see below) and check the substance of the firm they represent.
- Promised investment returns that seem to be too good to be true.
- Some investment advisers, although they say they are independent and not tied to one company and its products, have quotas whereby they are required to place a certain percentage of their business with that firm.
- By taking a commission, the adviser is an interested party. He or she has an apparent incentive to make sure a transaction happens and no financial incentive to make sure the transaction is right for the client.
- The quality of investment and financial advisers has risen in this country over the last decade but there are advisers out there who are neither trustworthy nor competent. For example, there are some advisers who still do not suggest the repayment of debt to their clients who ask what to do with a lump sum. This always arouses the suspicion that the adviser is aware there's nothing in the repayment of debt for them.
- The fees and charges – seek a full explanation before you sign anything.

> **PLAY SAFE**
>
> When making an investment through an adviser, never make the cheque payable directly to the adviser or the firm. At the very least make it payable to the adviser's trust account. Even better, make it payable to the company you are investing in (fund manager, insurance company, bank etc).

Who controls investment advisers and financial planners?
Anyone can hold themselves out either as an investment adviser or a financial planner. However, there are two controls that help to protect the public:

The Investment Advisers (Disclosure) Act 1996
This Act of Parliament is designed to protect the investing public by stating that anyone who offers investment advice must disclose (to you) certain information:
- Any convictions for dishonesty offences.
- Any bankruptcy.
- Any prohibition from managing a company.
- Their money-handling procedures – will your money be held in a trust account? Are there records and audit procedures? Could the adviser use the money for anyone else's (including his or her own) financial benefit?

In addition you can require them to disclose within five working days:
- Their qualifications and experience.
- The organisation with which they have a relationship (and the nature of that relationship).
- Whether they have a financial interest that might reasonably influence their advice, i.e. whether they would receive any money from anyone other than yourself (e.g. commissions) in connection with the advice being given.
- The types of securities and investments on which advice is offered. If it is not the full range, why not?

Financial Planners and Insurance Advisers Association (FPIA)

This is a voluntary organisation but has over 1200 members. Most good investment advisers belong to the FPIA and anyone you are thinking of approaching for advice would need to have a good reason for not belonging. There are a few good, quite high-profile advisers who refuse to join for their own reasons, but the vast majority of good advisers are members.

Members of the FPIA are bound by the organisation's ethics and professionalism, agreeing to maintain certain levels of competence, money-handling systems and client confidentiality. Ultimately this is no guarantee that all members of the association will be competent and ethical, but it is better than having no association and no rules at all.

Some members of FPIA are Certified Financial Planners. If someone has CFP after their name it means they have completed an academic course (usually at Massey University), have had supervised practical experience in financial planning and have presented some sample financial plans for review. CFPs are usually the best-qualified and best people in the industry (although there are plenty of exceptions).

In the final analysis no one controls financial planners and investment advisers. Anyone can promote themselves as one and although the Investment Advisers (Disclosure) Act and the FPIA help, neither is a guarantee that the person you approach will be competent or ethical. While a number of companies have standards equivalent to or better than those set by the industry bodies, there are plenty of ratbags still out there 'advising' on investments. Always be careful.

THE FINANCIAL SECRETS

- ❏ Good advice is not cheap – but poor advice is even more expensive.
- ❏ Find out how your advisers are being paid. Be sure they are working in your best interests, not theirs.
- ❏ Make sure you get what you are being paid for, and complain loudly if you don't.
- ❏ Anyone can offer advice in most areas of finance. It is up to you to check out the adviser.
- ❏ Check out your adviser the way you would any service – qualifications, credentials, previous experience, references etc.

CONNECT

- ❏ Consumers' Institute, phone 0800 266 786 (0800 CONSUMER)
  www.consumer.org.nz
- ❏ New Zealand Law Society (see your local phone book)
  www.nz-lawsoc.org.nz
- ❏ Institute of Chartered Accountants (ICANZ) (see your local phone book)
  www.icanz.co.nz
- ❏ Financial Planners and Insurance Advisers Association
  www.fpia.org.nz
- ❏ Banking ombudsman, phone 0800 805 950
- ❏ Insurance and Savings Ombudsman, phone 0800 888 202
  www.iombudsman.org.nz
- ❏ Mortgage Brokers Association, phone 09 486 5456
  www.mba.co.nz
- ❏ Other useful web sites:
  www.LawFind.co.nz
  www.sorted.co.nz
  www.goodreturns.co.nz

3. BANKING & INSURANCE
Public businesses, not public servants

Banks and insurance companies used to be seen as arrogant and inflexible – they told you the rules and you either liked it or lumped it. But in today's competitive climate their marketing, advertising and selling has changed greatly. Now banks and insurance companies advertise heavily, seeking your business. They know that unless you are completely satisfied with their service you can readily go elsewhere. You are a valued customer, not a supplicant.

The roles and functions of these institutions have also changed – to such an extent that each now offers many of the products and services that were once the sole domain of the other: banks can provide you with insurance and insurance companies can perform many of the functions of a bank.

From the consumer's point of view it is convenient to able to deal with a single institution, saving both time and money, but there are two questions to bear in mind:

1. Is the individual you are dealing with competent in all of the services offered? Can an insurance specialist competently advise you about your mortgages and investments? Does your banker know about the full range of insurances that are available?
2. Are you getting the best deal? 'Financial services providers' often offer discounts if you have all your business with them, but this could be a discount from a very high base. You may get a better, more cost-effective deal by using a bank for banking, and an insurance company for insurance. It's worth getting quotes and making comparisons – there may be a lot of money involved.

BANKING SERVICES
Banks offer the following services:
- Transaction accounts – i.e. a cheque account
- Savings accounts
- Credit cards
- Foreign currency
- Investment advice
- Loans – mortgages, overdrafts etc
- Insurance

Of all of these services, the only one that banks have to themselves is the provision of transaction accounts – you can get any of the others elsewhere – so it is transaction accounts and their fees that we will discuss here.

Transaction account fees

Nothing riles people more than the fees they are charged for the transactions on their everyday bank accounts. These have risen sharply over recent years as banks have tried to recover their costs, ceased to cross-subsidise services and encouraged people to use electronic transactions rather than visiting branches. Manual transactions (e.g. withdrawals at the counter) cost the banks more, so they charge higher prices for them both to recover their own costs and to encourage you to change your banking habits.

Bank fees are here to stay. It does no good to get angry at bank staff – put your energy instead into trying to identify how you can reduce your fees. Some banks will assist you to do this by recommending a combination of accounts that best suits your needs.

Most banks charge fees on transaction accounts according to the type and number of transactions you make.

> **WHAT PRICE LOYALTY?**
>
> Many of us bank as a matter of course with the bank our parents used, or the one where we opened our first account, perhaps as a student.
>
> There can be many advantages in this. Building up a good track record often means you can get loans readily, without having to go through the time-consuming business of proving your creditworthiness over and over again. It may also put you in a position to negotiate fee reductions and other concessions.
>
> But could you do better elsewhere? It can do no harm to check out the sevices and offers of other banks – and it never hurts to remind your present bank that it can't take your custom for granted.

Type of transaction

Manual transactions are much more expensive than electronic ones (eftpos, telephone or Internet banking).

Number of transactions

Most accounts give you a certain number of free transactions each month (perhaps five), then you pay for each transaction thereafter. However, some banks allow you to choose between a high monthly base fee (perhaps $15) with unlimited free transactions and a low monthly base fee (perhaps $3) but with a charge for every transaction. Your job is to work out how many transactions you usually make each month and choose the cheapest option for you.

Other charges

Banks charge for just about everything they do – they are businesses, not public servants. You should work to avoid as many of these costs as you can. Before you use any bank service, ask what it will cost. The following list is indicative only:

Bank cheque	$10
Replacement of card	$10
Telegraphic transfer	$25
Dishonour fee	$25
Stop payment	$25
Voucher copy	$15
Special answer	$20
Bill payments set-up	$4
Withdrawal from overseas ATM	$5
Automatic payment fee	$5
Alteration to auto payment	$5
Travellers cheques	1 per cent
Using another bank's ATM	50 cents

If you overdraw your account the banks may charge either a fee for dishonouring a cheque or a fee for honouring the payment – i.e. they won't bounce the cheque but will charge you $15, say, for not bouncing it.

SAVING MONEY ON BANK FEES

To compare one bank with another, the first step is to know your pattern of usage. The second step is to shop around to find the bank and the option that suits you best. This is a time-consuming process but it is worth the time. If you save $10 a month on bank fees that's $120 a year, which is better in your pocket than the pockets of the bank's shareholders. Other ways to reduce bank fees are:

- Cut down on the number of transactions you make by using your credit card whenever you can. There is no charge per transaction on credit cards so you can consolidate all your monthly purchases on your card and pay it off in one transaction a month.
- Get your cash when you make a purchase using eftpos – and carry cash for all of those little purchases.
- Stay away from bank branches – the bank doesn't want to see you and you don't want to pay to stand in a queue.
- Use the telephone and the Internet when you can.
- Make regular payments by automatic payment or Internet. They cost to set up (perhaps as much as $5) but they are then usually cheaper to run.

Fee reductions

Some banks will reduce or even eliminate fees in certain circumstances and for certain people:

- Children under 18.
- Superannuitants.
- People who maintain a certain minimum balance in their accounts (variously from $500 to $5000).
- People who have a mortgage with the bank.
- Anyone who asks may be able to negotiate themselves a reduction – a bank is a business like any other and will move to accommodate you if the extent of your business is worthwhile.

THE BANKING OMBUDSMAN

This office was established in 1992 to help protect bank customers' rights and assist in resolving any complaints and difficulties that arise from the provision of banking services. It is an office that is kept quite busy!

Only an individual can complain to the banking ombudsman. No claim can exceed $100,000 and you must first have approached the bank to try to resolve the issue and reached deadlock. The Ombudsman will try to resolve the dispute informally at first, but if no settlement is possible a judgment will be made.

The judgment is binding on the bank, but not on you – you can pursue your claim through the courts if you wish. The judgment the ombudsman makes will be based on:
- The law.
- Fairness.
- The Code of Banking Practice.

> **THE CODE OF BANKING PRACTICE**
>
> This is a booklet produced by the Bankers Association which sets out the standards to which its members should comply. Its purpose is to promote good banking practices and good bank/customer relationships. It should be available from any bank branch.

INSURANCE SERVICES

Unfortunately, insurance is not one of those things you can go out and buy when you need it. Insurance concerns what *might* happen, and so needs some forward planning.

Insurance is always about 'what if?'. What if my car is stolen? What if my house burns down? What if I get sick? If the answer to any of these questions is painful, then you need to insure against it. If the answer is not painful, don't bother.

The odds are not in your favour

Insurance is concerned with risk – the chances of some event happening or not. Insurance companies employ actuaries – experts in statistics – whose jobs involve working out the likelihood of some event happening (e.g. a house fire, car accident, illness or injury). Insurance companies use these statistics to set their prices. If they are right the company will make money and be able to pay claims as they arise.

Most insurance companies have been around a long time and have many customers, which means their statistics and pricing work for them. You as an individual, however, don't know how likely it is that any particular event will happen to you. Life is a series of gambles. Insurance allows you to decide which bets you are prepared to take and which ones you are not. Where the risk is too great it is appropriate for you to insure. You know it is likely to cost you more than you are ever likely to claim, but you are covered for a risk that would be a disaster for you.

Too much or too little?

Many people get their insurances wrong: they over-insure or under-insure. Neither is desirable. The key principles involved are to cover yourself only for the risks you cannot afford to carry yourself.

TEN TIPS FOR SAVING ON INSURANCE

1. Don't over-insure (don't under-insure either!).
2. Raise the level of your excess.
3. Pay your insurance in one lump sum each year.
4. Install burglar and smoke alarms – you may get a premium discount.
5. Name the drivers of your car – there can be discounts, especially if they are not under 25 years.
6. Roll all your insurances together with one provider (but make sure it is the right one).
7. Be careful when making a claim – you will probably lose your no-claims bonus (which can be as much as 50 per cent).
8. Some companies offer big discounts for older people.
9. Choose your type of cover carefully. For example, if you have an older, inexpensive car you might be happy with third-party cover, which only covers damage to the other person's car.
10. Review your insurances when your lifestyle changes – e.g. the children leave home or you get a bigger mortgage. You may have more or less than you need.

PAYING THE PREMIUM

The premium is the amount you pay for your insurance – annually, monthly or fortnightly. Sometimes an annual payment will be discounted, recognising that this option costs the insurance company less to administer. Go for this option if you can.

Some examples of ways you can do this:

- With house and contents insurance a higher excess will reduce the premium cost – you may be willing and able to cover the first $1000 of any claim.
- A medical insurance policy that covers surgical or hospital events only costs significantly less. Could you pay for routine doctor's visits yourself?
- With income-replacement insurance a longer voluntary stand-down (the period between being off work and the insurance company paying out) will reduce the cost and in many cases this will be covered by sick leave.
- Why take out life insurance when you have no dependants and no debts?

If there is a level of loss that you can afford without significant impact, you should take that option to reduce your premium. (In essence you are providing your own insurance for this amount.) To do otherwise is over-insurance and a waste.

Although over-insurance is bad, under-insurance can be even worse. Nearly every time there is a natural disaster (e.g. a flood) you see people on television up to their knees in water telling us they have no insurance. Similarly, there are people with dependants and debts who have no life insurance, and many people who have no income-replacement insurance when they really should have.

The key to getting your insurance right is to ask those 'what if?' questions – and insure when the answer would mean a lot of pain.

Price isn't everything

People usually want to buy the cheapest, but with insurances you need to be careful of three things:

1. That the insurance company is financially sound

There is little to stop any company setting up in the insurance business and there have been cases of companies collapsing and taking their customers' money with them. One major event (e.g. a big flood) to which the company is greatly exposed can see huge losses and the failure of the business. Make sure that you choose a well-established company with a good credit rating.

2. *That the prices you are comparing are for the same policies*
While basically covering the same event, some insurance policies will have more features and benefits than others. For example, some car insurance policies automatically cover the windscreen and other glass and this is included in the price; others consider this an optional extra for which you will have to pay more. There are a great many of these kinds of variations and this is one reason to seek advice: a good financial adviser will know how to compare apples with apples. If you don't use an adviser, at least be wary of policies that are significantly cheaper than all the others.

3. *That the company has sound underwriting practices and a reputation for paying*
Some companies make it very easy to purchase insurance but, come claim time, it is almost impossible to get money out of them.

TYPES OF INSURANCE

House insurance

There are two types of house insurance:

1. *Indemnity cover*
This pays an amount equivalent to the market value of your house, which is likely to be quite a lot less than it would cost to replace the house. Although this is the cheapest home insurance, it is not often used because it can still result in major financial loss.

2. *Replacement cover*
This replaces your house regardless of cost. The insurance company will either rebuild the house for you or will give you an equivalent amount in cash.

You then choose between a defined-risk policy, which covers you only against a particular event (e.g. fire), and a general 'accidental risk' policy, which covers nearly every event except wear and tear, damage from war, riot etc.

The cost of house insurance depends on:
- The age of the house.
- The size and construction materials.
- The amount of excess you choose.
- Its location – a house in the country far away from fire services may cost more than one in a city.

- Whether it is your home, rental accommodation or a holiday home.
- Whether you have smoke alarms installed.

> **EARTHQUAKE COMMISSION (EQC)**
>
> If your home and contents are insured, you will automatically be covered for natural disasters such as earthquakes, landslips and volcanic activity by the Earthquake Commission. Part of the premium you pay your insurance company goes to the EQC to cover this.
>
> The EQC covers your land, your home and contents. There are limits, however. You will receive a maximum of $100,000 for your home and $20,000 for its contents, although you may be able to arrange more cover from your insurance company.
>
> There is also a great number of exclusions: land is covered only if it is within eight metres of your house, for instance, and small excesses apply.

Contents insurance

Cover for the contents of your house and other belongings is generally a combination of replacement and indemnity insurance: in the event of loss some things will be replaced, while for others you will receive their market value. Usually your belongings are only covered while they are in your house or temporarily somewhere else in the country. Belongings that are out of the country are not covered.

It is usual to insure your contents for an overall sum. Make sure that this sum would replace all your household items if you lost the lot (say, in a fire). You may be surprised by how much you do actually own, when you sit down to add it all up. Expensive items such as jewellery may need to be valued and itemised separately within your policy.

The cost of contents insurance depends on:
- The total value of the belongings you insure.
- Whether they are in a house you own (i.e. not in a holiday home or rental premises).
- The amount of your excess.

Car insurance

Every car owner needs car insurance. Even if you could cover the loss of your own car, the damage to someone else's Mercedes could be catastrophically expensive. There are two basic types:

- *Third-party cover*

  This covers damage to other people's cars and property. It is the most basic level of insurance and does not cover your own car at all. The premiums are, therefore, quite cheap. It may be possible to add cover for fire and theft of your own car to your third-party policy without too much of an increase in premium.

- *Comprehensive cover*

  This insures your own car in the event of an accident, as well as other people's. Generally the cover for your own car will be only indemnity (or market) value. However, there are now insurers who will offer you 'agreed value' cover, meaning that if your car is written off, the insurance company will pay the amount that you have agreed at the time you took out the policy.

See also ACC, pp.188-89

The cost of your car insurance depends on:
- The age, make and model of the car – particularly powerful cars can attract high rates.
- The region you live in.
- The age(s) of the driver(s) – those under 25 years have high premiums.
- Your driving record, including previous claims.
- Your excess.
- Whether the vehicle is garaged.
- Whether you have a car alarm.
- Gender – some insurers offer lower premiums for women.

Life insurance
There are two basic types of life insurance:

Whole-of-life and endowment policies
These policies give you life cover and at the same time an investment fund. The premiums are high because only a part of this is for insurance cover; the rest is investment. Most of these policies are for the long term – you pay into them for, say, 20 years and if you do not die in that time, the insurance pays out a lump sum. The premiums remain the same throughout the life of the policy.

The policy can be cashed in at any time ('surrendered' is the term usually used). However, if you try to surrender it in the early years you won't get much for it because most of the establishment costs (and sales commission) are loaded on at the beginning. In fact, if you try to cash in the policy within the first three years there is usually no surrender value at all.

Sometimes this type of policy is relevant, especially for succession planning where, for example, the policy will provide for an amount of money to go to some beneficiaries of a will, allowing one member of the family to take over an asset such as a farm. However, they are not common because most people today prefer to buy their life insurance and make their investments separately.

Beware of advice recommending cashing in this type of policy: seek a second opinion. If the policy has been in place for some time you may be giving up a lot for a little and it may not be easy to get the same cover elsewhere.

> **INSURANCE OR ASSURANCE?**
>
> Many people wonder what the difference is between these two terms.
>
> Quite simply, assurance covers things that are *certain* to happen (mainly death). Life cover should more correctly be called life assurance. Insurance, on the other hand, covers things that *might* happen (e.g. theft of a car or destruction of a house).
>
> The distinction between the two is being more and more blurred and it is now common for people to talk about life insurance.

Term insurance

This life insurance is similar to insuring your house or car: you pay a premium for the insurance to cover you while you need it (i.e. you have dependants and/or debts such as a mortgage), then when you no longer need it you cancel it and stop paying. There is no investment component, no lump sum (unless you die) and no surrender value. This is the most straightforward type of life cover and, because the premiums are low, it is the most popular.

There are several ways in which premiums can be structured:

- Premiums rise as you age.
- Premiums rise as your age increases and are also adjusted for inflation to maintain the real value of the cover.
- Premiums remain the same – generally higher at the start of the policy in comparison to the other options but comparatively less later in life.

The cost of life insurance depends on:

- Your age.
- Your medical history – sometimes cover for existing medical conditions will be excluded.
- Whether you are a smoker.
- Gender – women live longer and so get lower premiums.
- Whether you engage in any hazardous activities (e.g. mountaineering).

Income-replacement insurance

Income-replacement insurance replaces your income (or at least a part of it) if you are unable to work through illness or injury. It is true, of course, that if you were incapacitated you would receive some income from a benefit or through ACC, but for many of us this would simply not be enough.

There are many types of income-replacement insurance:

- The disability you suffer may mean you can do some kinds of work but not work at your usual profession. Your policy will stipulate under what circumstances you may make a claim.
- Some policies pay you a percentage of your normal income for life, while others will cease at age 65 years or some other time.
- You may opt to have a stand-down period of 30 or 90 days, meaning you cannot claim for short-term disabilities.

This is an area where you need to be sure you're getting what you think you're getting.

The cost of income-replacement insurance depends on:
- The amount of income you are insuring (the amount you earn and the percentage of it that you would want to receive).
- The length of time that income will continue in the event of permanent disability.
- Whether your payment is inflation indexed and so will increase with time.
- Your age and health.
- Whether you are a smoker.
- Your gender.
- Your occupation.
- Whether you engage in any hazardous activities.
- How long a stand-down period you are prepared to accept.

> **YOUR GREATEST ASSET**
>
> The loss of your income can be the greatest financial disaster that can befall you, for your income is the thing you can least do without. Your ability to earn is your biggest asset. Think about it: an average income of $40,000 pa for 40 years comes to $1.6 million.

Trauma insurance
This is insurance that covers you against a particular event. It pays a lump sum or a monthly payment if you suffer a heart attack, stroke, malignant cancer and a few other conditions. It is often offered with life insurance, although it can be purchased as a stand-alone product.

The cost of trauma insurance depends on:
- Your age.
- Your health.
- Whether you are a smoker.
- Your gender.
- Whether you want comprehensive or limited cover.

Health insurance
There are two basic kinds of health insurance:
- *Comprehensive cover*
  This covers you for a whole range of medical conditions, from going to the doctor with a sore throat to a major operation in a private hospital and just about everything else in between. You can choose the level of cover you want, agreeing to exclude various things with corresponding reductions in your premiums.
- *Hospital-only cover*
  This covers you for the cost of an operation in a private hospital. Obviously the premiums are much cheaper than for a comprehensive policy.

> **NO WAITING LISTS**
>
> Health insurance is like any other insurance – you should buy it to the level that you need. If you can afford to pay for your own routine medical care (e.g. visits to your GP) then you should not have one of the high benefit/high cost policies.
>
> However, many people are alarmed by the frequent stories in the media about the long waiting lists for public hospitals and like the idea of having relatively cheap 'hospital only' policies. With one of these, the insurance company will pay for any operation you might need and you'll avoid having to join a waiting list for public care.

The cost of health insurance depends on:
- Your age.
- Your health – existing conditions may be excluded.
- Whether you are a smoker.
- Your stand-down period – you may not be able to make a claim for three months from the time of starting your policy.
- Previous claims – some insurers offer no-claims bonuses.
- The percentage of costs you agree to meet – i.e. you may decide that the insurer will pay only 80 per cent of the costs of any treatment.

Health insurance premiums have risen steeply over the last few years, so before you sign up:
- Be certain you really need health insurance.
- If you do, shop around and make sure you are comparing like policies with like.

INSURANCE AND SAVINGS OMBUDSMAN

The Office of the Insurance and Savings Ombudsman (ISO) exists to help people resolve disputes with their insurance companies involving sums up to $100,000. It is an independent and impartial service and most insurance companies come under its jurisdiction. It works in a similar way to the banking ombudsman and its services are free.

If you have a complaint you must first contact the insurance company. If you receive no satisfaction you may take it to the ISO, which will try to resolve the dispute and may make a ruling. Such a ruling is binding for insurance company, but if it goes against you, you may take the matter to court.

THE FINANCIAL SECRETS

- ❏ Banking and insurances are services – purchase them like any other.
- ❏ Shop around – banks and insurance companies are businesses and want your custom.
- ❏ Don't complain about bank fees – they are here to stay. Work to reduce them.
- ❏ The rule for insurance is to cover risks you cannot afford to take.

CONNECT

- Banking Ombudsman, phone 0800 805 950
- Earthquake Commission, phone 04 499 0045
  www.eqc.govt.nz
- Insurance and Savings Ombudsman (ISO), phone 0800 888 202
  www.iombudsman.org.nz
- Consumers' Institute, phone 0800 266 766 (0800 CONSUMER)
  www.consumer.org.nz

BOOKS

- *Banks, Banking and Bankruptcy*, Keith McIlroy, Shoal Bay Press, 1997
- *The Code of Banking Practice*, a booklet available from all bank branches.
- *Keep your Money Working*, Consumers' Institute, 1997

4. BORROWING
Using other people's money

Nearly all of us borrow money at some time or other. Rather than waiting and saving until we have enough money to buy something we want, we borrow so we can have it *now*.

There is a cost for this instant gratification – the interest you pay. Money has a value over time and if you want to use someone else's money, you have to pay for it.

There are three types of things you can borrow for. One makes good sense; the other two are poor financial practice:

1. *Value-builders*

   These are things that are likely to grow in value – your home, investment property and some other investment types. It makes sense to borrow to buy these things because they should at least maintain and could quite likely increase their value. If you wait until later to buy them, they are likely to be more expensive.

2. *Value-losers*

   The problem with borrowing to buy things like cars, home appliances, boats etc is that they will diminish in value while the loan you took out is still there. It makes little sense to borrow for these things, but if you are determined to do so you should set the loan repayments high enough so that you pay it off before the item loses all its value.

3. *Consumption*

   Borrowing for such things as holidays, clothing, a night out etc is usually done with a credit card. This sort of borrowing makes no sense whatsoever: after the consumption is over, the debt remains. Letting this sort of debt accumulate on your credit card account – borrowing for consumption – is a sure sign that you're in financial trouble. Avoid it like the plague!

EVERYDAY BORROWING

Taking on a loan is not just about approaching the bank for thousands (possibly hundreds of thousands) of dollars to buy a house or finance a business. There are also small, everyday loans, two of which are very common. (A third, hire purchase, is covered in Chapter 7.)

See also Hire purchase, pp.110-12

Credit cards

Used well, credit cards can significantly help your money management and save you money. Used badly, they are quick way to the doss-house. More people get into more financial trouble with credit cards than with just about anything else.

The main benefits of credit cards are:

- You can take advantage of free credit for up to 55 days (for a purchase made on the first day of the billing cycle).
- The free credit can be taken on even your mundane, everyday expenses such as groceries, power and phone bills. This is especially advantageous when you have a mortgage on a line-of-credit account because you can use the cash that has been freed up by paying by credit card to reduce your mortgage temporarily and so save interest.
- You save on bank fees. There is no transaction charge for credit card use and so you can put as much of your day-to-day spending as you like on your card and then pay it off in just one transaction.
- Convenience – buying goods by phone or on the Internet often requires a credit card.
- For overseas travel. Most credit cards can be used in most countries.
- Some credit cards provide a good alternative to hire purchase. There are cards that attract a relatively low rate of interest (around 12 per cent) provided that you purchase an item of $1000 or more. Using such a card to buy, say, a washing machine is quite attractive because the interest rate is significantly lower than hire purchase and these are no up-front fees. Furthermore, the flexible nature of credit cards means that you can pay back the debt faster if you are able.

> See Line-of-credit accounts, pp.62-63

Convenience

Credit cards are probably the most convenient way of borrowing money. Once you have applied and got your card you can use it as and when you want, either to buy things or to draw down cash. The monthly bill can be paid by telephone or Internet transfer from another account, cheque, automatic payment or direct debit.

Flexibility

Credit cards are a very flexible way of borrowing – you can draw down (within your limit) and pay back whenever you can.

> Not all plastic cards are created equal. Some, like Visa or MasterCard, allow you to spend and then pay off over time. As such, they are extending you credit. Others (e.g. Diners Club and most American Express cards) are charge cards. You must pay these off immediately or incur some steep penalties. There is no credit extended.

Cost

Credit cards demand that you pay back a minimum amount every month. However, unless you pay in full every time you pay a very high interest rate on the built-up debt.

There are two ways in which credit cards cost:

1. The annual fee. This is usually something like $10-$20 each six months and is payable regardless of use. For many people this is worth paying even if they don't actually use the card: an annual cost of around $40 is worthwhile simply for the comfort of knowing you could borrow some money if you had to.
2. The interest charged if you do not pay your card off in full or if you draw down cash. This interest can be huge – over 20 per cent in some cases. It is essential that you pay the card off every month in full. If you don't, everything you buy attracts that high rate of interest. Moreover, you should withdraw cash on your card only if you absolutely have to – cash withdrawals attract interest from day one.

Should you cut up your card?

The convenience of credit cards and their high interest rates get a lot of people into trouble. Good use of credit cards requires financial discipline – if you don't have it, get rid of the card.

Periodically card companies write to you, extending more credit, and it's hard for some to resist the temptation of spending to the limit. Remember always that this is a very expensive way to borrow money.

See Debt consolidation, pp.65-66

If you find you have hard-core credit card debt try to consolidate it onto your mortgage. If you can't do that, make the repayment of the card your top financial priority, putting any spare money towards it. Perhaps most important of all, make sure you don't make the position worse. Cut your card in half and send it back to the provider.

TIPS FOR CREDIT CARD USE

- Shop around for the best card – it might not necessarily come from a bank.
- Select the best card for you. If you are likely to buy big-ticket items on it and pay it off slowly over a year or two, get a low-interest card.
- Don't have too many cards – you pay an annual fee for each.
- Have a card that you can use overseas.
- Pay off your card every month.
- Avoid borrowing for consumption.

Overdrafts

Sometimes you might be able to arrange an overdraft with your bank which allows you to go into debit on your everyday account. An overdraft will be to an arranged limit and will be for a limited period of time. Generally that period of time will be quite short, and at the end of it you will either have to get your account back into credit or renegotiate the overdraft. Most businesses and some individuals will have long-standing overdraft arrangements with their bank, which the bank will regularly review. If it is unhappy with the arrangement, it may withdraw it.

Overdrafts are not as common as they once were, because most people have credit cards or a line of credit with their mortgage, which provide funds for extra borrowing needs. These are generally more convenient to use because they are a longer term arrangment and save having to approaching your bank to negotiate a new facility at regular intervals.

See Line-of-credit accounts, pp.62-63

For any substantial overdraft facility your bank will require some security if it does not already have it, although if you have a good record with the bank, it might provide a small overdraft without it.

HOW LENDERS MAKE MONEY

Charging interest

Most lenders are not lending their own money. They borrow from other sources, add a profit margin and then lend it to someone else. The price you pay for your loan is therefore influenced by two things:

1. The rate at which the lender can borrow. This varies widely. A bank will take funds from depositors at a relatively cheap rate; a second- or third-tier finance company will attract depositors only if it offers a higher rate. So, in effect, a bank 'borrows' from its depositors or from other institutions at, say, 6.5 per cent, while a finance company might have to pay 9.5 per cent.

TOTAL COST OF A LOAN: THE FINANCE RATE

Comparing one loan with another is difficult. Do you look at its term? The interest rate? The fine print?

The best way is look at the total cost of credit over the course of the loan. This includes the total interest payable, the up-front fees and any mortgage insurance required. The lender must disclose this total credit cost in your loan agreement. The figure is annualised and given as a percentage, called the finance rate. The finance rate is usually higher than the interest rate – sometimes by a long way.

It is the finance rate that represents the total cost of borrowing.

2. The profit margin the lender puts on. This largely depends on who the lender is lending to and what the loan is for. For example, home loans, which have good security (safe as houses), usually have a profit margin of 1.5 to 2 per cent while credit card loans, which are unsecured, might have a profit margin of 12-15 per cent. A bank borrowing funds at 6.5 per cent might lend on a house at 8.5 per cent (a 2 per cent margin) while its credit card rate is 18.5 per cent (a 12 per cent margin). The finance company borrowing at 9.5 per cent might put on a 5 per cent margin for car hire purchase and charge 14.5 per cent.

'Junk fees'

These are more politely known as 'application fees', 'documentation fees' or 'establishment fees'. They are the fees most lenders charge at the beginning of a loan. While they do cover true costs – staff time is required to approve and document the loans – they are also another way lenders try to make profits. It has become an established practice for them to ask for an up-front fee – and most of them get it. Of all aspects of a finance deal, the establishment fee is the most negotiable. Most lenders will reduce this fee (or even waive it) if you threaten to take your business elsewhere.

WHERE TO GO FOR MONEY

While you might use one lender for all your requirements (such as a bank), if you need a one-off loan you should target the right lender for your requirements. Many providers target particular

---

YOUR RIGHTS AS A BORROWER

Your rights as a borrower are largely set out in the Credit Contracts Act 1981. There are some areas of lending where the Act does not apply but these mostly concern commercial borrowings (e.g. loans over $250,000).

Lenders must disclose to you:

- The amount of credit (i.e. how much is being borrowed)
- The total cost of credit
- The finance rate (see box, p.49)
- How, when and where payments are to be made

The penalties for lenders not complying with the Act can be tough. If a court case results from a breach of the Act, the court may reduce the liability of the borrower by as much as the total cost of the credit. Where the lender has acted in a harsh or oppressive manner, it may be required to re-open the loan agreement and remedy the situation.

Perhaps the most important part of the Act for borrowers is the requirement for the lender to disclose the total cost of credit. This is designed to (and often does) make the borrower think again.

markets with particular loan types, so it makes sense to go to the best provider for the type of loan you want.

The main sources of finance are banks, finance companies, retailers' finance companies, and family and friends.

Banks

Most of the major banks will do nearly all types of lending: home loans, credit cards, line-of-credit accounts, hire purchase-type loans, unsecured personal loans, foreign currency loans etc.

Pros

- There will be a branch (fairly) near you – or at least the bank will be easy to reach by telephone or Internet.
- You can have all your borrowings with one institution.
- You can consolidate all your borrowings onto your home loan if you have sufficient equity in your home.

Cons

- Banks are not very flexible – they have their rules and are reluctant to break them.
- They may not lend to a very high proportion of the value of some items (e.g. cars).
- They can be expensive.

Finance companies

Finance companies come in all shapes and sizes. Some are very big and specialise in commercial property lending or lending on large pieces of equipment (e.g. bulldozers or fishing boats). Others are very small and perhaps focus on hire purchase for home appliances.

Pros

- Specialisation makes them very good in some areas (e.g. specialist providers of car hire purchase).
- Many have a flexibility not often found in banks – they may be prepared to bend the rules to get a deal.
- They often have easier lending criteria than banks.

Cons

- Finance companies are generally more expensive than banks.
- They often have few branches.

Retailers' finance companies

Many retailers have their own finance companies set up to provide hire purchase finance. This is most common for whiteware, computers, stereos and other appliances, as well as motor vehicles.

Pros

- They're easy and convenient to use.
- They have fairly easy lending criteria.

Cons

- They can be very expensive – with the up-front fees, the finance rate can be as high as 25 per cent.

Family and friends

Generally, people borrow from family and friends because they cannot get the money from elsewhere, though this is not always the case. One of the big advantages of borrowing from family and friends is that you cut out the middle man (the bank). For example, parents with cash in the bank for which they have no immediate need might lend money to their adult children to, say, buy a house. The parents get a slightly better rate than the bank would give on a deposit, while the children get a slightly cheaper home loan. However, you need to be careful about two things:

1. That the loan is properly documented. Verbal agreements between friends and family can lead to misunderstandings and unpleasantness. As well, always bear in mind that you might not always be dealing with the friend or family member directly – if that person should die you would be dealing with the executor of the estate.

2. That the lender gets his or her investment time-frame right: it can be a disaster if parents lend their children money to buy a house but find that they need it back after a year or two.

Pros

- You get cheaper money because there's no middle man.
- You may be able to borrow money when no one else would lend it to you.
- There are unlikely to be strict rules and penalties regarding things like early repayment.
- The lender may get a better investment rate and the borrower a cheaper loan.

Cons
- There's plenty of scope for falling out with family and losing friends if the loan goes bad.
- Either the borrower or lender could die and so change the nature of the relationship.
- You have to be very nice to Auntie.

GETTING A LOAN

Clearly a lender will not simply hand over money to anyone who asks. It will make an assessment of you and your application to make sure you are likely to meet the obligations to which you have agreed. After all, it needs to look after its own interests: bad loans are not only costly to the bank or finance house but often create adverse publicity for them.

You need to know how lenders assess borrowers, not just so you will pass the test, but so that you will pass with flying colours. If you are seen by lenders as someone they really want to do business with, you will be in a strong position to negotiate the best deal. You may get a reduction in the up-front fee, your lawyer's costs subsidised, a waiving of the requirement for a registered valuation of your house etc. If you have a strong proposal, shop around and ask the lender to make concessions.

Lender assess borrowers in terms of the three Cs:
1. Character
2. Cashflow
3. Collateral

Character

The first thing a lender does is assess you personally. This is the most important part of the whole process.

This assessment is partly subjective and partly objective. The subjective part is about considering your reliability and honesty and whether you are the kind of person who will meet obligations. In order to make this judgment a lender will usually want to meet you, particularly where large amounts of money are involved (e.g. commercial property or business loans). For smaller loans the subjective assessment of you as an individual is often less important. Nor do some banks bother much about a subjective assessment when it comes to making a housing loan. First among these are the direct banks, which will approve and make loans over the telephone or via the Internet. In many cases lending on people's own homes is regarded as so secure that there is no need to meet them.

The objective part of the character assessment involves running a credit check. Most lenders are linked directly on-line to credit

> **CATCH-22**
>
> Sometimes a lender will ask for references from organisations you have borrowed from in the past. This can create difficulties for people who have never before had a credit card, a hire purchase agreement or a mortgage. They cannot provide these references and find themselves in a Catch-22 position.

> **YOUR OWN CREDIT CHECK**
>
> Under our privacy laws you have a right to know what information is held on you. You can write to one of the credit reporting agencies (e.g. Baycorp) asking what they have on file about you and they must tell you within 21 days. This is a useful thing to do, especially if you have a fairly common name and believe there might be something incorrect on your file.

reporting agencies such as Baycorp or RMG and can run a credit check on you quickly and easily. If you have anything untoward in your financial past you may find that your loan or credit application is declined – or at least you'll be asked a lot more questions.

Factors in your favour are:
- A clean credit history.
- A stable work history.
- A stable place of residence.
- Having repaid previous borrowings on time (especially if they were with the same lender).
- The prospect of your bringing plenty of business to the bank.

Factors against you are:
- No previous borrowings.
- A history of bounced cheques.
- A record of bad debts or court judgments.
- A previous bankruptcy.
- A conviction, especially for dishonesty or fraud.

Cashflow

No lender will approve a loan if it can't see how it's going to be repaid. You have to prove you have sufficient income to meet the repayments. In addition, for a home loan, you may have to show that you have the deposit you say that you have, by providing statements from your savings account. The lender considers two factors:

1. The size of your cashflow

This is usually fairly straightforward: most people simply state their salary and give proof of this through a payslip or a letter from their employer. Those who are self-employed or in business need to furnish copies of their annual accounts. Some lenders may find these accounts difficult to interpret, particularly if they have been adjusted for tax purposes, and the self-employed often have to explain their business accounts to a lender.

Most lenders, especially when looking at mortgage applications, will apply a formula. For example, a mortgage lender may require that the repayments make up no more than 30 per cent of household income. Other lenders will look at your income, calculate your usual out-goings (perhaps from a budget provided by you) and from these figures satisfy themselves that you can afford to make the loan repayments. If you have some big expenses you cannot alter (e.g. hire purchase repayments) you may have problems.

Work bonuses and overtime may be taken into account provided there is a reasonable pattern of these being earned. Some lenders will take child support payments and benefits into account but others will not.

If you have a marginal income it pays to shop around for your loan because these income criteria are applied differently by different lenders.

2. The security of your cashflow

The lender wants to be sure your income will continue so you can meet all your payments throughout the life of the loan. To this end, you may be asked about your employment history, as well as its nature. Clearly, someone who has worked in the same, safe job for a period of years will be viewed more kindly than someone who changes jobs and employers every few months. Someone who has 20 years in the public service, steadily moving up the ranks, may be regarded more kindly than a Member of Parliament on a three-year term! The self-employed may also find this aspect difficult, as income is less secure for those in business. Lenders will often want to see business accounts going back several years as they look for a pattern of ongoing profitability.

Factors in your favour are:
- Your loan repayments are easily covered by your income.
- A history of job stability.
- Good professional qualifications.

Factors against you are:
- Your loan repayments are only just (or not) covered.
- A poor work history.
- No professional qualifications.
- High fixed expenses.
- Being close to retirement age.

Collateral

This is another word for the security you are providing. Lenders like security – if you default they can seize whatever it is you have given as security, sell it and recover at least part of their money.

Generally, the security will be the item you are borrowing to buy – house, car, home appliance etc, although they may also ask for security over assets you already own. The security is the lender's last line of defence.

REPOSSESSION

Repossessing your item of security may not be the end of the story. If there is any shortfall in money outstanding on your loan (i.e. if the item cannot be sold for the full amount) the lender can still continue to pursue you. For example, suppose you borrowed $15,000 to buy a boat for $20,000. With $14,000 still outstanding on the loan you default and the boat is repossessed and sold for $12,000. The lender can approach you for the $2000 shortfall. You would also be liable for any of the lender's costs (e.g. legal fees).

LOAN SHARKS

Sometimes you see newspaper ads for 'fringe lenders' who offer unsecured loans to the desperate. These are loan sharks and are to be avoided at all costs: their interest rates are horrendous and the handling of defaults likely to be less than gentle.

See also Becoming a guarantor, p.207

Secured loans

Usually, the level of the interest rate on a secured loan is set according to the nature of the security taken. Some items are regarded as good security (e.g. houses, cars), while others will attract a higher interest rate (e.g. computers and stereos).

The reasons for this difference are:

- Some items hold their value better than others.
- Some items are easier to repossess: a house will be there if the lender needs to repossess it; a stereo may not be.

Unsecured loans

Not all loans need collateral. Some are 'unsecured', which means that the lender is relying on your word you will repay it and has nothing specific to repossess if the loan goes bad. The most common unsecured loans are on credit cards, although at times banks will promote unsecured personal loans up to $10,000 or $20,000. In these cases the lender will make sure that your 'word' is good and scrutinise the application carefully.

Loan-to-security ratio

The size of the loan you want compared with the amount of security you have is called the loan-to-security ratio (LSR) or the loan-to-value ratio (LVR). Although it is called a ratio it is often expressed as a percentage. Thus, a loan of $150,000 on a house worth $200,000 is said to have an LSR of 75 per cent.

A bank might accept an LSR of 60 per cent on a boat but 90 per cent on a house. Lenders will go to 100 per cent on some items for some people but this is relatively rare. Generally a lender will want to see you put up at least a part of the purchase price as your deposit. Different lenders have different policies concerning the LSR and it pays to shop around.

GUARANTEEING A LOAN

Quite often a lender will ask for a guarantor for a loan. This is someone who is prepared to provide a guarantee that the borrower will meet all the loan repayments and who will make up any shortfall if the loan goes bad.

Usually a lender will ask for a guarantor if:

- The borrower is under the age of 18. This is because it can be difficult to enforce a credit contract against someone who is under this age.
- There seems to be some risk that the borrower will not pay.

As a borrower, you don't have to agree to find a guarantor, but you may not get the loan without one.

Agreeing to be guarantor is a big step and you should always seek independent legal advice. You can try to persuade the lender to limit your guarantee, but generally it will be for 'all obligations', which means that you can be made to step into the shoes of the original borrower. If the borrower defaults on the loan you will be responsible for the full amount plus any unpaid interest and costs. You can try to get back what you have paid from the borrower, but given that he or she has defaulted on the loan, that is unlikely to get you very far.

You must be even more careful if you have been asked to put up some security to support the guarantee. If the borrower defaults and you cannot meet the guarantee, the lender may repossess the items you have put up as security.

There is some protection for you as guarantor. The lender must act 'reasonably' towards you. You must be given a copy of the loan document and a document setting out the obligations you have under the guarantee. You must receive any demands or notice of the borrower's default and possible repossession. This will tell you what the borrower owes and what you have to do to avoid further action.

Guarantees can sometimes be set aside. If the lender had deceived you, by assuring you that the borrower would be able to pay the debt or misrepresented the amount of the guarantee, the Fair Trading Act will apply and the guarantee may be set aside. Furthermore, the lender cannot act in a harsh or oppressive manner, pressure you to sign the guarantee or take advantage of you in any way (for example, if your English was not good).

THE MONKEY ON YOUR BACK: YOUR MORTGAGE

Although people talk about their mortgage they should, more accurately, call it a home loan. The mortgage is really the security for the home loan. A mortgage is put on the title, which means that when you sign a mortgage document you are assigning certain rights over your property to the lender, including the right to possess it if you default on your loan.

New Zealand follows the Torrens system of land registration. This is one of the most efficient land registration systems in the world, which, compared with many other countries, works quickly and at a reasonable cost. Any mortgages over a property are recorded on the title, where they stay until they are discharged. The mortgagee will allow the mortgage to be discharged only when any loans are repaid and any other obligations are met.

Copies of the title are held at the Land Transfer Office and are available to the public so that anyone can look to see if a property is secured. The first mortgagee (lender) will usually hold the true title and any subsequent lenders would have to approach the first mortgagee in order to have their interest registered. Sometimes the first mortgagee will not allow any further lenders to take security because the loan agreement specifies that they hold the first and only mortgage.

The process of putting a mortgage on a title (and taking it off again) costs. Your lawyer will probably charge about $500 for putting the security in place and perhaps $300 for taking it off again. This includes a fee of around $50 to the Land Transfer Office. Note that your bank may also charge something like $50 for the discharge of your mortgage.

Banks like home loans

Although their margins on home loans are not particularly good (around 1.5-2 per cent), banks really like to lend on housing. This is because:

- Home loans are safe. Houses almost always retain their value. As well, the bank knows that the property it has taken as security will be there if it needs to move on it (whereas the car it has taken as security might not be). Banks also know that people will do whatever they can to meet their mortgage payments – the house is important to them and they will do what they must to keep it.
- Making a loan on a house gives the bank's staff an opportunity to sell you other products and services. They will offer transaction accounts, savings accounts, insurance of all types, a credit card, investments and superannuation, automatic payments etc – all things they make money from. Getting you to take a home loan is a good way to begin a profitable relationship for the bank.

This is very empowering for you. If you know that someone really wants to sell you something, you can approach them with confidence. A bank is a business like any other. It needs to sell to survive and you should make sure you are treated as you would be as the customer of any other business.

How much can you borrow?

Most lenders will lend to around 80 per cent of the value of your house. This of course assumes that your character and your cashflow are good – no one will lend if they are not. Loans over 80 per cent of the LSR are likely to require mortgage insurance.

A few lenders advertise that they will lend to 90 per cent or even 95 per cent of your house value, but you would need to have a very good credit history and a good, secure income before it would be considered. Moreover, the house you are borrowing on would need to fairly good and the lender might ask you to provide a guarantor for the loan. A lender would look very carefully at all aspects of your application before agreeing to make a loan at this level.

Some lenders set different levels of the LSR depending upon what area of the country that you live in. For example, they might lend to 85 per cent on a house in Auckland, but only to 60 per cent on a house in a small town on the West Coast.

The lender will want to see some sort of valuation on the house. This may be:

- Rating valuation (RV). This is the old government valuation (GV) and some lenders will accept this if you are borrowing to a low LSR (below 50 per cent) and the valuation is recent.
- Registered valuation. An independent report from a registered valuer will cost you $200-500. When you are switching lenders over the course of a mortgage the lender will rely on a valuation because there is no actual purchase price to be considered.
- Purchase price. The lender will still want a registered valuation but will also want to know what you have paid for the house. In most cases lenders will use registered valuation or purchase price, whichever is the lower.

The *positive* factors for good home-loan collateral are:
- A low LSR
- A good, well-maintained property
- It's in a large, growing city
- A guarantee is available

The *negative* factors for collateral are:
- A high LSR
- A poor, high-maintenance property
- It's in a small town
- There's no guarantee available

Types of home loan

There are two types of loans defined by the way the interest rate is fixed: variable-rate loans and fixed-rate loans.

Variable-rate loans

Sometimes called floating-rate loans, these are loans where the interest rate varies (or floats) according to the market, i.e. the cost of the bank's funds. While the bank can change its rate during the loan to whatever it likes, it knows that if it is significantly out of line with all the other home lenders, you will switch to another bank. Competitive pressure and your ability to switch at any time keep the rate down. You can pay off this loan at any time, in whole or in part.

Advantages of floating-rate loans:

- You can repay all or part of the loan at any time, meaning you can switch lenders or use any spare cash you have to repay the loan.
- You benefit when interest rates fall.

Disadvantages of floating-rate loans:

- You are exposed to the vagaries of the interest-rate market – a big increase in rates could see you in trouble.
- Generally, floating-rate loans have been more expensive than fixed-rate loans in the last few years.

Fixed-rate loans

These are loans where the interest rate is fixed for a period of anything from six months to five years. They have become hugely popular in New Zealand over recent years – for good reason. As mentioned above, in recent years fixed-rate loans have generally been cheaper than floating-rate ones. This is because for most the last decade longer-dated money has been cheaper than short-term money. However, it is also because banks have tended to use certain fixed rates as specials, creating a good headline for marketing purposes. Many people have taken advantage of these special rates and done very well out of them.

The main problem with fixed rates is that they are not flexible – you cannot pay them off whenever you want. Because lenders match the term they lend for with the term they borrow for, you will be charged a penalty for early repayment. This may be as much as three months' interest – a considerable incentive to

---

WARNING! FIVE-YEAR FIXED LOANS

Sometimes lenders offer particularly attractively priced loans that are fixed for five years. For most people, this is too long to fix a loan. The chances of your wanting to sell a house within that time, or getting some sort of lump sum or extra income that you will want to put towards the mortgage, are high. If you do so, you will likely be hit by penalty interest. Generally, a period of one to three years is the right time to fix for.

stay with the loan. This is disadvantageous, not only if you decide to sell your house, but also if you get a lump sum or some extra income and want to pay it off the mortgage. Some lenders will allow you to pay small extra amounts off a fixed-rate loan – it pays to check the policies of individual lenders.

Advantages of fixed-rate loans:
- You know exactly what you are going to pay for your chosen loan period.
- Fixed rates have generally been cheaper in recent years (though they may not remain so, of course).

Disadvantages of fixed-rate loans:
- They are inflexible.
- They carry a penalty for early repayment.

To fix or to float?
This is something everyone struggles with. There are two factors to consider:

1. The likely trend for interest rates. This is of course hard to pick, as most of the known information in the interest-rate markets will already be built into the price. Clearly you will want to get the cheapest rate possible but there is no certain way to know this, apart from listening to economic commentators, who are not always a reliable source! If your fixed rate is a special offer it is likely to represent the best deal. Even if it is not, experience has taught us that in recent years, at least, fixed rates have been cheaper.
2. How much extra cash you are likely to get that you could use to pay off the mortgage. If there is likely to be none you could have everything on a fixed rate, but if you do anticipate some sort of windfall then that amount at least should be on a floating rate.

Methods of loan repayment
Some types of loans are defined by the way you pay them off.

Table loan
This is by far the most common type of loan in New Zealand. It is sometimes called a principal and interest (P&I) loan. Part of your regular monthly payment goes towards paying off the principal and part goes towards paying off the interest. Your monthly payments will be the same every month but the interest and principal components vary with each

> **SPLIT LOANS**
>
> Most people should split their loans: part fixed and part floating. Generally it's best to have the bulk of the loan at a fixed rate because of the certainty this gives. It is true that you may miss out if rates fall, but you also avoid the risk of a sharp rise. Getting rid of that risk is more important for most people than profiting from a possible fall in rates.

payment. This is because your repayments of principal lower the balance you owe and therefore the interest due becomes less. At the start of the loan, the biggest part of the monthly payment goes towards interest but towards the end of the loan nearly all of your payment is reducing the balance.

Reducing loans

This loan type is now seldom used. Every month you make an interest payment on the outstanding amount owed, and at the same time you make a payment of an agreed amount of principal (perhaps $1000 each month – more if you can afford it). Your monthly payments will reduce over time as the principal owing falls and the interest is calculated on the reducing monthly balance. Although this type of loan is now seldom offered, it could suit some people who know they are going to have high income for a period but expect it to fall.

Interest-only loans

With this loan type you make no principal repayments until the end of the loan. (This final payment is sometimes called a 'balloon payment'.) The principal is then repaid in full either through the sale of the house, refinancing with another lender, or agreement with the lender to roll the loan over for another period. These loans are seldom offered because lenders would rather see you reduce the sum owed every month than rely on your finding a way to repay it in one lump sum. Sometimes, however, lenders will offer a loan that is initially interest only (say, the first two years), then the loan converts to a table loan.

Line-of-credit loans

Sometimes called a revolving credit facility, these are becoming very popular in New Zealand. A line of credit is like a big overdraft – you can draw down on it and pay it back whenever you want to.

Some people use their line of credit as their main (or only) bank account, having their salaries paid into it (which reduces indebtedness temporarily) and then using it to pay their bills and living expenses.

Rather than having spare cash in a savings account (at a lower interest rate) you can use your line-of-credit account to reduce your

---

LACK OF PROGRESS?

People are often disappointed when they decide to repay a P&I loan early and find that in spite of all the payments they have made the amount required to repay the loan in full is still quite large – often only a little less than the amount originally borrowed. This is because most of their repayments have gone towards paying interest.

Some get into financial difficulty with this, especially when they have borrowed to buy a depreciating asset like a car or a home appliance. Very often the price the item will fetch does not repay the loan.

LENDERS CALCULATE INTEREST DAILY

Nearly all lenders calculate interest on a daily basis. For example, a $100,000 loan at 10% will attract interest of $27.40 per day. If payments are made monthly, the interest charged at the end of the month (31 days) will be $849.32.

Understanding this helps to explain why it is to your advantage to keep your line-of-credit account topped up. The more money you can keep in the account – even for a short period – the less interest you will pay.

mortgage while retaining the freedom to draw money out again when you need it.

Some lenders offer a variation on this, in which the amount of credit you have reduces over time, along with your ability to draw on it, until it is repaid. The loan usually requires interest payments only.

If you don't think you have the discipline to manage a line of credit, you should use either an ordinary variable-rate loan, which you can pay off at will, or one of the line-of-credit loans that reduces the level to which you can borrow.

SAVING MONEY ON YOUR MORTGAGE

Because your mortgage is usually so big and for such a long period, it is critical for your overall financial standing that you take what steps you can to reduce its total cost.

Many people are surprised to discover just how much interest they will pay in total over the term of a loan. Here's a fairly standard example:

Loan size	$100,000
Term	25 years
Interest rate	7.5 per cent
Total interest	$121,400

With this loan you would pay out a total of $221,400 (principal and interest) over 25 years. This is a huge amount of money and gives great scope for savings. It is worth making managing your mortgage a high priority. Here are four ways to save money on your mortgage:

1. Understand the arithmetic of loans

Interest rates

It is obvious that a loan at a lower interest rate will cost you less, but you could be surprised that what seems like a small difference in the rate can make a big difference to the total cost of the loan. If you could get the loan above at an interest rate of 7 per cent, rather than 7.5 per cent, the figures would look like this:

Loan size	$100,000
Term	25 years
Interest rate	7 per cent
Total interest	$112,100

This is a saving of $9300 in total interest repayments. It's worth aiming for the lowest rate possible!

MORTGAGE TIP #1

A fall in interest rates during the course of a floating-rate loan will present an opportunity to get ahead. You could lower the payments to reflect the lower interest rates, but if you leave the payments at the same level, a greater proportion of each one will be devoted to reducing the principal, which means that you will pay the loan off more quickly.

Size and frequency of payments

Interest is the cost of borrowing money over time: the more quickly you can pay back your loan, the more money you will save. Consider these two examples:

Loan size	$100,000
Term	25 years
Interest rate	7.5 per cent
Monthly payment	$738
Total interest	$121,400
Loan size	$100,000
Term	15 years
Interest rate	7.5 per cent
Monthly payment	$927
Total interest	$66,860

An enormous saving of $54,540 is achieved by paying the loan off more quickly (but note that this involves making a much higher monthly payment).

2. Split your loan

This means splitting your mortgage between fixed and variable interest rates to your best advantage. For most people that will mean having the bulk of your loan on a fixed rate and the balance on either a line-of-credit or some sort of variable-rate facility, which you can pay off whenever you like. Having the greater part of the loan on a fixed rate gives you certainty, safety from difficult interest rate rises and often the lowest rate. Having the balance on a floating rate means that if you sell an asset (e.g. a car), receive a work bonus, tax refund or some other lump sum you can use that to reduce your mortgage without incurring a penalty.

3. Negotiate the best deal

Many people are surprised to learn that the lenders' rates and fees are negotiable. A bank is a business like any other and wants your custom – so make it work to get it. You can negotiate the interest rate and the application fee. We recently had a client whose bank wanted to charge a $3800 application fee, but reduced it to zero to get the business! You can also negotiate lower insurance premiums, lower bank fees (if you have your mort-

---

> **MORTGAGE TIP #2**
>
> It has often been suggested that making your mortgage payments fortnightly instead of monthly will save money. There is a small saving in interest to be made by repaying the principal at shorter intervals. The reason for any further saving is purely mathematical: if you halve your monthly payment and pay this amount fortnightly you will, in fact, be paying more in total over the course of the year because there are 26 fortnights in a year but only 24 half months!
>
> The general principle of paying back your loan as quickly as possible to save money applies here, as ever.

> **DISCHARGE THAT REPAID MORTGAGE**
>
> When you have paid off your home loan, your bank may suggest that it is a good idea to leave the mortgage security over the house in place. The pitch goes that if the mortgage is there, it will be easier for you to borrow again in the future. By leaving the mortgage on your property, you will save in lawyer's fees if you want to borrow from the bank in the future.
>
> This is a reasonable cost-saving thought, except that some people have found it has come back to bite them. If you leave the mortgage in place and enter into any arrangement with the bank whereby you have an obligation (say, guaranteeing one of your children's loans), the bank can move on its security (i.e. your house) if something goes wrong with one of those loans. Tempting though it may be to save some money and leave it in place, you are much better advised to have the mortgage discharged and re-mortgage if you need to borrow again.

gage with the bank) and reduced credit card fees. Obviously the bank has to really want your business to make concessions like this. Few people try to negotiate with their bank, but of those who do, most are successful.

4. Keep your borrowings under review

The world of home loans (and other loans) is constantly changing. New products and services are being introduced all the time and new players are always coming into the market. Your home loan is too big and too important for you to simply take it out and forget it. Review your mortgage position regularly to check that what you have is still the best deal around, and that it still suits your circumstances.

DEBT CONSOLIDATION

If you have one or more high-interest loans and a modest mortgage, you could consolidate all your debts onto the house loan. The idea is to shift all the high-interest debt (hire purchase or credit cards) onto the loan that attracts the lowest interest rate (almost always the mortgage).

This means having to refinance the mortgage – effectively borrowing cheap money to repay the expensive money. (You may have to pay a new fee to adjust your mortgage in this way. And, of course, you have to have enough equity in your home to take the extra mortgage. If you have already borrowed to 90 per cent, forget it.)

For example, John and Sue have a mortgage of $125,000 over 25 years at 7.5 per cent, and a car hire purchase of $20,000 over five years at 14 per cent.

	Loan	*Payment*	*Total interest*
Mortgage	$125,000	$923 per month	$152,000
Car HP	$20,000	$465 per month	$ 7900
Totals	$145,000	$1388 per month	$159,900

John and Sue borrow an extra $20,000 on the house (at 7.5 per cent) and use these funds to repay the car hire purchase. They will save interest of $3850 over the next five years.

Warning!

Note, however, that Sue and John now have a debt of $145,000 against the house. If they simply adjust their monthly payments to pay off the new mortgage over the same term (25 years) the figures will look like this:

	Loan	*Payment*	*Total interest*
Mortgage	$145,000	$1070 per month	$175,000

While they might be pleased with the savings in their monthly outgoings of $318, they have actually *increased* the total amount of interest payable over the term of their mortgage! This is because the extra $20,000 is attracting interest over 25 years rather than over 5 years (albeit at a lower rate). There are two ways John and Sue can avoid this:

1. Keep their monthly outgoings at the same level as before ($1388) for the next five years, which will ensure that the additional $20,000 is paid off early and they will get the advantage of the lower interest rate on this amount.
2. Take the super-saver route by keeping their monthly outgoings at the same level for the duration of their mortgage.

	Loan	*Payment*	*Total interest*
Mortgage	$145,000	$1388 per month	$90,700

By doing this they will actually save $69,000, compared to the total amount of interest they would pay in their original situation.

There's nothing magical about this. By increasing the amount of their monthly payments they will pay off their total mortgage nearly 11 years earlier than they would otherwise have done.

Summary

- Consider consolidating high-interest, short-term debts with your low-interest, long-term mortgage.
- Remember, though, that time is money. Don't swap a big short-term debt for an even bigger long-term debt. Keep your monthly payments as high as possible, so that you can repay the principal on your combined loans as quickly as possible.
- Be disciplined! Don't keep on tapping into the equity of your house to buy more and more things. The aim is to reduce your interest bill, not to increase your overall indebtedness.

THE FINANCIAL SECRETS

- ❑ Borrowing is smart if you borrow for the right things – value builders.
- ❑ Borrowing is dumb if you borrow for the wrong things – consumption and value losers.
- ❑ Credit cards can be very convenient and help your financial management, but you *must* pay them off every month.
- ❑ Your financing deal is not carved in stone: negotiate, negotiate, negotiate.
- ❑ Remember that interest is what you pay for money over time. Reduce your interest bill by paying back loans as quickly as possible.

CONNECT

- Consumers' Institute, phone 0800 266 786 (0800 CONSUMER)
  www.consumer.org.nz
- Banking Ombudsman, phone 0800 805 950
- Other useful web sites:
  www.sorted.org.nz
  www.goodreturns.co.nz

BOOKS

- *Five Ways to Save More Money on Your Mortgage*, Martin Hawes, Penguin, 1999
- *The Code of Banking Practice*, a booklet available from all bank branches.

5. SAVING AND INVESTING
Making your money work

Your financial security will ultimately depend on the amount of money you are able to put aside for savings and investments. Most of us invest for one (or more) of four reasons:

1. To save for something we want in the near future – e.g. a holiday, a car, a deposit for a house.
2. To have security in the form of 'rainy day' money. None of us likes to live in fear of running short; we all want to have something put aside if we can.
3. To be able to earn money while we sleep. Most wealthy people don't have to work for their income. Their money keeps coming from their business or investments.
4. To have money for retirement or some other time when income from work ceases.

SOME PEOPLE SHOULDN'T SAVE!

Elimination of debt should be your first financial priority. If you have a mortgage or other debts you should divert any spare cash (from work, inheritance, sale of an asset etc) towards paying off those debts first.

After all, a bank will pay you significantly less interest on a savings account than it will charge you on your mortgage. As well, your investment income is taxed, making the difference between interest earned and interest paid even greater. It makes no sense to invest money for an after-tax return of 3 per cent when you are paying 7 per cent on your mortgage.

This is even more important if your debts are on credit cards or hire purchase agreements where the interest rate is even higher.

This is the case even if you know you will want the money again soon. A line-of-credit mortgage is designed for just this sort of use. It allows you to pay off debt (temporarily) and then draw it again when you need it.

It is possible you might find an investment that gives an after-tax return of over 7 per cent, but this will almost certainly mean taking considerable risk.

See Line-of-credit accounts, pp.62-63

THE (ONLY) THREE INVESTMENTS

People often find investment confusing because there seem to be so many options. However, when you boil it down, there are really only three investments:

1. Interest-earning deposits
2. Shares (sometimes called equities)
3. Property

Only these three things give income and a cash return: deposits pay interest; property gives rent; and shares pay dividends. Every other purported investment is either:

- *A means of investing.* Unit trusts, property syndicates, superannuation funds etc are vehicles through which you invest.
- *Speculation.* Art, antiques and collectibles are not true investments because they give no income. To get a 'return' on your 'investment' in these things, you are relying on (hoping for) an upward shift in price. This is speculation, not investment.

WORK OUT YOUR FINANCIAL GOALS

The most important part of saving and investment is working out your financial goals and knowing when you want to achieve them. Ask yourself what you're saving for and when you'll want the money. The answer to these questions will dictate your saving and investment strategies because different goals call for different types of investment. There are three main factors to consider:

1. Time-frame
2. Risk
3. Return

Investment time-frame

Are you looking for a short-term or a long-term investment? Shares, and to a lesser extent property, are volatile investments – their returns are good but generally only in the long term. They make unsuitable short-term investments.

Deposits, on the other hand, are much better for short-term savings: the returns (the agreed interest rate) are known at the time you make the investment and your money will be there when you want and expect it. (Of course deposits will not normally produce such good returns as shares or property over the long-term.)

As a rule of thumb:

Type of investment	*Ideal time-frame*
Deposits	Less than 3 years
Shares	3-5 years minimum
Property	Minimum of 5 years

The purpose of your savings will also influence the mix. Save for the overseas trip or for the deposit on the house through interest-earning deposits, probably at your bank, but save for retirement by putting most of your money in shares and property.

Purpose	*Type of investment*
Short-term savings	Deposits
Rainy day	Mostly deposits
Money while you sleep	Shares/ Property
Retirement	Shares/Property

Risk and return

The higher the return you are seeking, the greater the risk you must take. This rule of investment is immutable.

This means if you want high returns you must take some risk, and if you want less risk you must put up with lower returns. Anyone whose investment has produced great returns has taken a risk (or has possibly been lucky).

There are two kinds of investment risk:

1. *Performance risk.* This is simply the chance that your investment will fail to perform or even collapse in value. This tends to happen more to shares and property, but deposits are not entirely immune.

2. *Volatility risk.* This is the amount of thrashing around – up and down – an investment does while it performs. Shares have a high volatility risk, property somewhat less, and deposits least of all. Volatility risk is what makes some investments unsuitable for

---

SCAMS

If an investment you are offered seems too good to be true, it probably is. Every day there are people offering investments that are 'certain' to give very high returns. But either these offerings are not 'certain', or they will not give high returns – you can't have both.

Some are complete scams - the promoters are out to take your money, and a good many succeed. There are three ways to recognise a scam:

1. The promoters promise very high returns.
2. They tell you you have to invest now - you need to write a cheque immediately.
3. The minimum requirement keeps falling. At the beginning they might say you have to invest $100,000, but if you are reluctant this might fall to $50,000, then $25,000 ...

Every year dozens of people (many of them surprisingly astute business people) get ripped off by scams. Remember: if it sounds too good to be true, it probably is.

The Securities Commission web site (www.sec-com.govt.nz) offers useful advice for investors, particularly with regard to fraudulent practices (and practitioners) operating in the marketplace. See their page 'Scamwatch' for details of all the current scams doing the rounds.

the short term. If you want your money back while that investment is on one of its periodic down ticks, even though overall it might be performing well, you'll take a loss.

	Performance risk	Volatility risk
Deposits	Low	Low
Shares	High	High
Property	Medium-high	Medium

DIVERSIFICATION

Diversification is the best way to reduce both performance risk and volatility risk, although it will also cut your returns.

Diversification simply means spreading your money around a range of investments. A bundle of sticks is stronger than a single log; a bundle of investments is stronger than one by itself. When one or two of your investments are languishing and not performing, some of the others may be going well. This reduces the effect of the sharp ups and downs, smoothing out the returns over time. It means you won't get the possible great returns that you might from a single or small number of investments, but your money will be safer.

To diversify properly you should spread your money across all the asset classes: deposits, shares and property. This is especially important for long-term savings (e.g. retirement savings). Those saving for the short term (e.g. for a holiday) will probably not diversify at all, saving solely through term deposits.

Those who want greater returns and are able to take the risk have more of their money in shares and property, while those who like to play safe have more in deposits and only a little in shares and property. Here are examples of three different portfolios for people who are prepared to take different levels of risk:

Aggressive/Growth	Balanced	Conservative
10% deposits	35% deposits	60% deposits
20% property	15% property	10% property
70% shares	50% shares	30% shares

Some of the factors you should consider in choosing your risk/return mix:

- Age. Older people will generally take a more conservative approach as they cannot afford negative returns.
- Investment skill. Those with greater investment skills can adopt a more aggressive approach.
- Time horizon. Those saving for the long term can have a more aggressive portfolio.

- Personality. Those who worry a lot should be more conservative.
- Dependent family. People with a dependent family should invest more conservatively.
- Other income. Those not reliant on their investment income can invest more aggressively.

You can diversify by building a portfolio by yourself, or you can buy into a ready-made fund that is already diversified. Fund managers offer a range of diversified funds for long-term saving, in which you can choose to take a growth, balanced or conservative approach.

DO-IT-YOURSELF OR A MANAGED FUND?

Many people do make and manage their own investments, but there are some advantages in investing through managed funds. Most will have at least a part of their investments in a fund.

Direct investment

The advantages of investing directly yourself are:

- There are no fees or other costs to reduce your returns.
- It's more tax efficient – fund managers often have to pay tax on their capital gains while you may not.
- You have a sense of control over your money, rather than giving it to a manager you've have never met.

Managed funds

Managed funds involve three parties:

1. *Investors:* the people who want to put their money into a particular investment area
2. *The trustee:* the company that holds the investments (shares, cash, bonds etc) in its own name and makes sure the fund is managed according to the rules set in its trust deed. The trustee is usually paid a small percentage of funds under management as its annual fee.
3. *The promoter and manager.* This is the company that sets up the fund, makes the investment decisions and looks after the paperwork. The fund manager usually gets a fee when units are sold and also an ongoing management fee, although there has been a trend in recent years for reduced or even no up-front fees. (Note also that there is no fee payable for listed funds (e.g. TeNZ or WiNZ), although you will pay some brokerage.

See Index funds, p.80

Who are managed funds for?

Most New Zealanders have at least some of their investment money in managed funds of some sort or other. Their advantages are:

- Easy access to difficult markets such as offshore shares or commercial property. Few of us can afford to buy a good-quality commercial property, but by pooling our money and investing through a managed fund we can at least own a little bit of one. Similarly, few of us have the ability to pick good individual shares in unfamiliar countries.
- Easy diversification – a lot of funds are already diversified by holding a spread of investments.
- You spend less time involved in managing investments.
- You can invest small and regular amounts (e.g. $100 per month)
- Professional fund managers may be better informed and more skilled in this complex area, with better contacts and more discipline.

See Offshore investments, pp.90-91

How to choose the right fund

This is one of the most difficult decisions, and an area where you should get help from an investment adviser. There are hundreds of funds available and no one person could keep up with what is going on in all of them.

Most good financial advisers buy research from the likes of Fund Source or Morningstar, which are specialist research houses. Research houses check out and rate funds, advising the advisers. Of course even they are largely judging funds by their past performance and present position, neither of which is any guarantee for the future.

There are two steps in choosing a fund:

1. Choose the area in which you want to invest (e.g. shares in emerging markets, Australasian retail property, Asian shares or whatever). With most funds, most if not all of the money goes into that area. Sometimes funds are more diversified, particularly those set up for superannuation investment.
2. Choose the manager you want, and therefore the specific fund, preferably having spoken to an investment adviser.

> **THE PAST IS NOT THE FUTURE**
>
> Don't buy into a fund solely on the basis of past returns. It's easy to cast an eye down newspaper lists and see which funds have performed over the last few years. But if a fund has performed exceptionally recently it is because the markets it invests in have probably boomed. Bust often follows boom, and the fund is likely to normalise fairly soon (maybe just after you have put your money in). Investment is about the future, not the past.

DEPOSITS

Deposits are the least risky investment you can make (and therefore usually the least profitable). This is because giving your money to someone else to earn interest is not an ownership (or equity) investment in the way shares and property are. Ownership investments are more risky because if the investment becomes insolvent, it is the owners who are last to get their money back. On the other hand, people who have lent their money to get interest (i.e. depositors) will get their money repaid before those who are owners.

However, all investments carry some risk. You are giving your money to someone else and there is always a chance you won't get it back. Even bank deposits or government stock, though they carry very little risk, do carry some – banks have been known to fail; governments sometimes do not meet their obligations.

Other deposit investments can be quite risky – for example, a third-tier finance company offering 15 per cent at a time when banks are offering 6 per cent. If you are going to save and invest through deposits, it pays to have your money in good solid institutions such as banks, good finance companies or government or local authority stock, rather than in some high-yield finance company of doubtful quality. If you want a bit more risk and a higher return you are better to think of shares and property rather than third-grade finance companies.

For a low-risk investment with low volatility, you can't beat good quality deposits. They are ideal for short-term savings (less than three years) and your money will be there when you want it. They can also form a part of your long-term savings through the purchase of bonds. Good short-term deposits include:

See Bonds, pp.76-77

Bank deposits

Banks are generally the safest and most convenient places to park short-term money. They are safe because banks are required to conduct their businesses within certain ratios, which are checked and supervised by the Reserve Bank. It has been a long time since a major bank defaulted in New Zealand. Your deposit can be:

1. *At call.* This means your money is available whenever you need it. Generally 'at call' accounts don't attract very high interest rates, although many banks increase the rate as you hold more money in the account.
2. *Term deposits.* These are for a set term – anything from 30 days to three years. Term deposit rates vary according to the term you choose and are generally significantly higher than 'at call' savings accounts. If you decide you need to break a term deposit before the expiry date, however, you will be paid less interest.

RESIDENTS WITHHOLDING TAX (RWT)

When you invest with a bank, finance company or other institution to earn interest, the borrower will make a deduction from the interest it pays you and pass that on to the government. This is Residents Withholding Tax and is applied at your personal tax rate (19.5, 33 or 39 per cent) if the interest payer has your tax number, or at 45 per cent if it does not. A credit for the tax that has been withheld is accounted for in your tax return.

Bank bills
These are wholesale deposits used by banks, corporate and private investors with large amounts of money. Bank bills start at $100,000 and are for 30 days through to 180 days. There is a very busy market in bills – banks and corporates buy and sell them every day. Because they are for larger amounts of money, the interest rates on bills tends to be higher than for smaller term deposits.

Unit trusts
Many fund managers (insurance companies, trust companies etc) offer unit trusts based on deposits. The two main ones of these are:

1. *Mortgage income trusts.* These are unit trusts holding a range of mortgages as investments, providing unit holders with income from the interest earned. Generally, unit holders earn higher interest than they would through a bank term deposit. However, because there is usually an up-front fee for a mortgage income trust, they tend not to suit people who may want their money back within a year as the higher return is negated by this fee.
2. *Cash management trusts.* These are unit trusts that invest in short-term investments (e.g. bank bills, deposits etc). Because investors' funds are pooled the unit trust has a lot of money, allowing it to invest in the wholesale money market and so achieve higher returns. Some return as much as 1 per cent more interest than banks, with little additional risk. Money invested in cash management accounts is available at any time, making them a good alternative to 'at call' bank deposits.

Finance companies
Finance companies usually pay higher interest rates than banks – they have to, to attract investors.

Finance companies come in all shapes and sizes – and all degrees of financial standing. The biggest and probably the most sound are the ones owned by the major banks (AGC, UDC and BNZ Finance), although your deposits are not guaranteed by the parent company.

The others are a mish-mash of varying degrees of quality, with interest rates reflecting the risk incurred. Be very careful about chasing high returns if you want your investment money to be safe.

Secured or unsecured?
Many finance companies offer deposits that are secured by way of a debenture. This means that if the company becomes insolvent you will be paid in priority to any unsecured creditors. This can give a margin of safety. Sometimes a finance company will offer deposits with second-debenture security, meaning some other lender has

already taken the first debenture. This is still better than having an unsecured loan.

Credit unions
Credit unions and friendly societies (and various other organisations) will also accept your deposits. These are largely to be avoided unless you have some personal or other reason to make an investment. Credit unions can offer worthwhile benefits to members, but occasionally they do go broke and take their depositors with them.

Contributory mortgages
These are another pooled investment promoted by some firms. The idea is that the promoter raises funds from investors and lends it to someone on mortgage security. The attraction is that they usually pay a higher return than bank or finance company deposits.

However, many people have lost money on contributory mortgages. The name sounds so safe – the word 'mortgage' has connotations of security – but the investment is only as good as the borrower and the security provided. Unfortunately some of the borrowers are property developers and the only reason they are borrowing from the fund is because banks have turned them down. That is why the interest rate offered is higher. Remember, the higher the return offered, the higher the likely risk.

Bonds
Bonds are a fixed-interest investment – they pay a fixed rate of interest for a fixed period of time. Bonds are quite often known as 'stock' in this country (although in many other countries 'stocks' are what we call 'shares').

Bonds can be among the safest investments – for example, government stock is money the government has borrowed from the public for a period of five or 10 years and, being the government, it is most likely to give it back when the time comes! Bonds issued by local authorities and state-owned enterprises are also likely to be very safe.

But company-issued bonds will be less safe. In the US such bonds are called 'junk bonds' – they pay a fairly high rate of interest but for good reason.

Advantages of bonds
Being fixed-interest investments, bonds offer some good advantages to investors:
- They bring stability to a portfolio – the interest rate and term are fixed so you know what return you will get and when.

- They are generally (although not always) safe.
- They provide good protection against falling interest rates.
- They give sure returns for those who need income.

Disadvantages of bonds
There are some negative features of bonds:
- They are not a high-growth investment.
- They can show capital losses if interest rates rise and you need to sell (see below).
- They are not tax efficient (see below).

Bonds should not make up too much of a portfolio. Most people should own some fixed-interest investments, but probably not more than 10-20 per cent of their total investment.

Secondary markets
There is a secondary market for most bonds so you can usually sell them before the maturity date and cash up if you need to. It is quite common to make profits and losses on the sale of bonds because the market price is set by prevailing interest rates. If rates rise purchasers will only pay a price that reflects this higher interest rate. Conversely, if rates fall, your bonds will be more valuable because people will pay more for them.

The formula for calculating the price of bonds is quite complicated and most people don't bother learning to use it. However, it is important to understand that there can be capital profits and losses on bonds.

Tax and bonds
Capital profits on the sale of bonds are treated as assessable income and taxed accordingly. This contrasts with capital gains on the sale of shares, which are not taxable.

See also Investments and tax, pp.119-20

SHARES
Shares can be all things to all people. There are people who speculate and trade shares on a daily basis, while others see shares as a long-term investment, buying and holding for years or decades. Where you fit and what you do on the market is very much a matter of individual choice, and will depend on such things as:
- Your financial goals.
- Your investment and finance skills.
- The amount of time you want to devote to your investment.
- Your interest in the subject.

> **THE NEW ZEALAND STOCK EXCHANGE**
>
> The buying and selling of shares is organised by the New Zealand Stock Exchange, a company listed on its own market and which makes sure that anyone who wants to buy shares can 'meet' everyone who wants to sell. To enter this market you must use a sharebroker – you cannot yet buy and sell shares on the sharemarket without the intervention of a middle man.

> **SHAREBROKERS**
>
> There are two sorts of brokers:
>
> *'Full-service' brokers* will discuss your investment options and advise you whether and what to buy or sell. These brokers usually charge 1 per cent of the value of your trade, depending on the size of your order and your negotiation skills.
>
> *'No frills' brokers* do not give advice but will simply take your order and fulfil it by buying or selling for you on the market. These brokers are cheaper, sometimes offering a flat rate that might be as low as $30, but you need to know exactly what you want to do on the market and tell them.
>
> The choice of which sort of broker to use really comes down to your confidence in your own ability to make buy and sell decisions. Certainly new investors are likely to be much better off using a full service broker and even those who are quite experienced will benefit from another opinion before they buy or sell.

However, whichever way that you decide to deal in the market, you must own some shares. Shares are a key part of any investor's portfolio as they give you exposure to that most important money-making activity, business. Over time, shares generally give the best return of all investments, provided you are not unlucky enough to buy just before one of the periodic crashes!

The most important thing to keep in mind is that shares and the sharemarkets only exist so that investors can buy a small part of a business. None of us could afford to buy all of Telecom or Coca-Cola, so the ownership of these businesses is split into small parts (or shares), which can be bought and sold by investors of all sizes. Remember always that you don't own 'shares'; you own part of a business and the success of your investments depends wholly on the performance of that business.

Returns from shares

The returns you will get from your investment in shares comes from two sources:

1. *Dividends*

   Each year the company pays out part of its profits as dividends. Typically it will pay out 30-50 per cent of its after-tax profit to shareholders and retain the rest to fund growth. Usually you will receive this in cash, although some companies offer their shareholders more shares instead.

2. *Capital growth*

   The value of your shares will broadly track the profit performance of the company. If the business performs well and continues to make good profits (and increase those profits), the share price will rise. This means that as a shareholder you hold shares that someone else would pay more for.

Most studies have shown that the people who do best from the sharemarket identify good businesses and hold shares in them for several years. It is difficult to predict the short-term ups and downs of the sharemarket generally, and of individual shares in particular, though there are people who have managed to profit from short-term price changes.

Share contracts

When you buy or sell shares you receive a contract note from your broker. This will tell you:
- The number of shares you have bought or sold.
- The price paid or received.
- The amount of brokerage payable.

When you are buying shares you must pay the amount due immediately. Some people hold cash with their broker so that he or she can simply take the necessary funds from the account. If there is any mistake with the contract note make sure you contact your broker immediately.

The risks of shares

Shares produce high returns over time, but over the short term they are risky. That risk takes two forms:

1. *Performance risk.* Companies do fail and when they do, they can take your money along with them.
2. *Volatility risk.* While a company's shares might perform well in the long term, in the short term they may go down in value and stay down for a considerable length of time before starting to rise and find their true value.

There are two ways of managing this risk:

1. *Buy shares as a long-term investment.* Plan to hold on to them for at least five years.
2. *Buy a spread of shares.* The more you diversify, the less risk you will have.

These two things reduce greatly both performance risk and volatility risk. Buying just one or two shares and planning on owning them for a few months is very risky. Buying a basket of shares and planning on holding them for 10 years is not very risky at all.

Sharemarket managed funds

Most fund managers (insurance companies, banks and others) offer unit trusts based on shares to the public. These funds may be based on a particular market (e.g. New Zealand or Australian shares) or on regions (Asian or European shares), or may specialise in smaller companies or even particular industries.

Sharemarket unit trusts are particularly useful to get you into markets you would find difficult to invest in yourself. It makes

---

SHARE REGISTRATION

When you have bought and paid for your shares, you will be registered as the owner of them. There are specialist share registration firms who specialise in this (e.g. BT Registries, Computershare) and they will write to you within a week or two of purchase and advise you of the registration. They will also provide you with a holder number and FIN. This last stands for 'Faster Identification Number' and works like the PIN on your eftpos card.

The Stock Exchange runs a system called FASTER, which replaced the use of share certificates. Instead of receiving a certificate proving your ownership of shares, the registration is stored electronically and you need your FIN and holder number to sell your shares. These numbers should be kept safe and secure.

overseas share investment easy, for example, often with little currency risk (the managers hedge the exchange risk).

There are two main types of sharemarket managed fund:

Active funds

These are unit trusts where the manager goes out and trades shares actively, trying to pick the best performers through company analyses and good timing. In effect these unit trusts are doing your job for you as they play the market trying to get the best return possible. Two things work against them:

1. The funds are classified as share traders and therefore taxed on all of their profits – both capital profit and dividends.
2. The fees are generally quite high. The managers have to spend a lot of time identifying the right companies to buy and sell and someone has to pay for their time.

There are some very well-performing active New Zealand share funds, but most struggle to beat the market overall. A financial adviser should be able to point you towards a good one.

Index funds

An efficient way of buying a spread of shares is to buy into an index fund. These are funds that passively track a share index, which is why they are sometimes called 'tracker funds' or 'passive funds'.

Index funds own shares in exact proportion to a particular sharemarket index. The managers don't try to buy shares they think will perform spectacularly well but instead buy the shares that are in the index. This is all done by computer – as the index changes, so too do the shares that manager holds.

Because this type of fund is easy to manage, the management fees are very low. Even better, because there is no trading of shares, there is no tax on capital profit – the IRD has ruled that these funds are for investment rather than trading purposes.

Buying into an index fund is a cheap and easy entry into the market, giving you exposure to the index of your choice. There is TeNZ, which is based on the top 10 New Zealand companies, which you can buy on the sharemarket itself, or a whole range of other index trackers offered by fund managers.

Many investors have most of their share funds in an index tracker and perhaps a small percentage in a few individual shares they think will do particularly well.

The disadvantage of passive funds is that the fund manager cannot sell out when there is a downturn either in the market overall or in particular shares. Nor can he or she heavily weight the portfolio towards one or two shares that look like performing well.

'The index'

You hear a lot of talk about 'the index'. However, there is not just one index – there are lots of them. There are indices based on our biggest companies, on smaller companies, on industries (e.g. technology), and of course lots more based on other markets offshore. You can even buy into an index that represents the performance of shares globally – the World Index.

An index is an artificial or synthetic portfolio of shares, weighted according to each company's size. It is designed to give an average for a particular investment area – a benchmark so that people investing in a particular area (e.g. American tobacco companies or New Zealand small companies) can measure their performance.

For example, the NZSE 50 index contains New Zealand's 50 biggest companies, each with an amount in the index according to its size. This might mean that Telecom (New Zealand's biggest company) makes up 25 per cent of the NZSE 40 while Steel & Tube (a much smaller company) makes up 1 per cent of the index. The performance of Telecom will therefore make a much bigger difference to the movements of the index. This could be problem in New Zealand if you own a passive fund because you are dependent for investment performance on just a few companies.

The index represents the average of the market's performance. Many investors try to beat the index, while others are quite happy just to match it – shares give pretty good returns overall and many investors are happy to stick with being average.

There are two types of indices:

1. *Gross index*
   The value of the shares includes dividends received. It is as if the portfolio took each company's dividends and re-invested them.

EMPLOYEE SHARE PLANS

Some large companies with shares listed on a stock exchange offer their employees the chance to buy shares in the company. There are various schemes, some of which have tax breaks and are therefore quite attractive. There can be a tax exemption up to $720 pa on some schemes, while others allow you to defer tax on the money you use to buy the shares until such time as you leave the company and sell the shares.

The schemes are generally attractive, but there are three things to be wary of:

1. The company offers these schemes as an incentive to employees, but being a good employer does not necessarily make the company a good investment. Most of the companies offering these schemes are multinationals and the effect your work can have on their profitability, and therefore their share price, is minimal. Make an objective assessment of the investment potential of such a scheme if it's offered.

2. Some of these schemes work by the company effectively lending you the money to buy the shares. If the shares fall in value, you must still repay the loan when you leave. Other schemes, which are far more attractive, allow you to forgo a part of your salary to buy shares. If you can afford to do this without any adverse effect on your family budget, they may well be a good deal.

3. You may not have much diversification if you end up with a large investment in the company for which you work. Worse still, if your company struggles or fails, you may lose your investment – along with your job.

2. *Capital index*

This index ignores dividends and measures on the change in value of the shares within it.

Shares and tax

See also Investments and tax, pp.119-20

The two returns from shares, dividends and capital gain, are taxed differently:

Tax on capital gains

Generally there is no tax to pay when you sell your shares at a profit – New Zealand has no capital gains tax. This is provided you have not purchased the shares with the intention of trading them. If you have bought the shares for holding long term, for their dividends and the growth in those dividends over time, you will have no tax to pay on their sale.

However, if you bought them in order to trade them – i.e. with the intention of selling them quickly for a profit – you will be deemed by the IRD to be a share trader and will be taxed on your capital profits.

The line between being a share trader (and being taxed) and a share investor (and not being taxed) is blurred. Ultimately it comes down to your intention at the time of purchase, which can be difficult to prove either way. To decide whether you are an investor or a trader the IRD will look at:

- The length of time you owned the shares.
- Any pattern of buying and selling shares on a short-term basis.
- A history of stagging (buying new shares before they list and selling them shortly after listing).
- Any short-term financing arrangements that you have, in particular margin trading facilities (see opposite).
- Written material showing recommendations from brokers etc as to whether a share is a good long-term investment or a short-term trade.
- Any written financial plan you might have.

Each case will be judged on the facts and on its merits.

Tax on dividends

Dividends are taken as capital income in the hands of the recipient, the shareholder. However, the good news is that New Zealand has a dividend imputation system, which means that provided the company in which you are invested has paid tax, the tax on your share of the dividends is credited to you. This means the old system of double taxation, whereby the company paid tax on its profit before it paid out dividends and then investors paid tax on it again, no longer applies.

Your dividends will come with imputation credits. These credits are at the rate that the company has paid tax. If the company has paid tax at the rate of 33 per cent, the dividend will come with an imputation credit of 33 per cent. If you are also on the tax rate of 33 per cent, you will have no tax to pay on the dividend. If you are on the top rate of 39 per cent, you will have a little tax to pay, and if you are on a lower rate you will get a refund. In effect, the company is passing on as a credit the tax that it has already paid.

Other countries have systems similar to ours – the Australians call them franking credits. However, if you invest in overseas companies (including Australian ones) you cannot use the credits – the dividend will be taxed in your hands with no credit for the tax the company has already paid.

Borrowing to buy shares

Borrowing to buy shares works in exactly the same way as borrowing to buy property – it magnifies your gains but also your losses. Shares are a volatile investment, so gearing up your share purchases by borrowing is risky and must be done with care.

Generally, borrowing to buy shares should be contemplated only by experienced investors. Nevertheless, for those who are prepared and able to take risks, geared share purchases can increase returns dramatically.

There are three main ways of borrowing to buy shares:

Margin trading

Margin trading facilities are usually arranged through sharebrokers or specialist finance companies. You provide a deposit (called a 'margin') of 20-50 per cent of the total price of purchase, and the financier provides the rest, on which it charges interest. The size of your margin depends on the quality of the shares you are buying. The lender will want a higher margin for riskier shares, but will allow a lower margin for what it regards as better-quality shares.

Once you have bought the shares you must keep your margin at its original percentage. If the shares fall in value, it is your money that is lost first. For instance, suppose you bought $5000 worth of shares with a deposit of $1000 but the value of the shares fell to $4000. Your broker will call you and ask for another $800 to restore your margin to its original 20 percent. This is the dreaded margin call. If you are unable or unwilling to provide more cash to meet the margin the broker will sell the shares immediately.

When there are a lot of people margin trading in a market, a moderate fall can become a rout. This was one of the reasons the crashes of 1929 and 1987 were so severe.

Warrants and options

These are securities that are listed on the sharemarket. A warrant gives you the right to buy a share for a certain price on a set date. You are not, however, obliged to do so. For example, if you buy a Telecom warrant for 50 cents, giving you the right to buy Telecom shares in two years' time at 600 cents, you can throw the warrant in the rubbish bin if the shares don't reach that price. Your risk is limited to the price of the option.

However, if Telecom shares rise to 900 cents, your warrant may now be worth around 300 cents – a great gain on your initial purchase price of 50 cents. This is effectively borrowing, because you have to pay only a small percentage of the value of the shares at the beginning and the balance if you exercise your option later.

Endowment warrants

These are a long-term means of gearing into shares. You provide a deposit to buy shares and a bank provides the balance by way of a non-recourse loan. A non-recourse loan is one where the lender will not approach you for repayment if there is a shortfall after the shares are sold; your loss is limited to the deposit you have paid. The dividends from the shares go to the bank to repay interest, but you may have to put in more money on a regular basis if there is an interest shortfall.

When the warrant falls due in, perhaps, seven years, the shares are sold, the loan repaid and the balance is yours. Endowment warrants are a good form of gearing up to buy shares because they are long term, there is no margin call and your risk is limited. The best-known provider of endowment warrants is Macquarie Bank.

PROPERTY

Investment in property has been a key strategy for many Kiwis. It is seen as way of becoming wealthy, and indeed many people have become rich through investing in and developing property. It is also seen as a store of wealth – an investment for the long term that protects against or even beats inflation. In fact, in New Zealand property investment is almost iconic, with many people doing it simply because it is seen as the thing to do.

Property can be a very good investment but not everyone succeeds at it. There are many pitfalls, which are exacerbated by the big dollars involved.

As an investment, property has a number of advantages:
- Tax benefits.
- Hedge against inflation.
- Sense of control – you own something that seems real and tangible.
- Low volatility – unlike shares, you do not follow the value of your holdings on an hourly basis.
- Ability to borrow.
- Ability to add value by alterations, additions or redecoration.

However, against these are some difficulties:
- Low returns from some property types.
- Borrowing increases the investment risk.
- High costs of buying in and selling out of investments.
- Difficult to cash up quickly – a very illiquid investment.
- The large amounts of money involved mean that many people end up with property as their only investment in an undiversified portfolio.

Most of these difficulties can be alleviated to a greater or lesser extent by going about property investment in an intelligent way.

Here are some basic rules:
- Make property only a part of your investment strategy, buying into other investment types as well.
- Treat property as a long-term investment so that the costs of buying and selling are spread over a number of years.
- Calculate and allow for all of the costs involved.
- Keep your borrowings low, gearing up to no more than 60-70 per cent of the value of your purchase. Many people use the equity in their own house as the deposit to purchase an investment property, which means they are effectively borrowing 100 per cent of the purchase price. This can create big problems if the investment does not perform.
- Buy property that gives a good return from rents. This means not buying another house in the suburbs but rather flats or commercial property, probably through a managed fund.
- Don't buy solely for tax purposes. The investment must stack up in its own right. You are always better to make some profits and pay some tax than to make losses and pay no tax.

Property investment types

There are four major property investment types, each of which has its own advantages and disadvantages.

	Advantages	Disadvantages
RESIDENTIAL	Low dollar value allows easy entry Plenty available so it's an easy place to start Easy to finance Low vacancy rates	Requires a lot of management Subject to political interference Often low-yielding Short leases can leave you without tenants – or income
INDUSTRIAL	Easy to manage Good tenants High-yielding Long-term leases	This investment type is unfamiliar to most people It can be hard to find a new tenant
COMMERCIAL	Prestigious Good tenants Long-term leases	The high dollar value of property makes it a hard market to enter Difficult to finance Unfamiliar to new investors Lower-yielding
RETAIL	High growth rates in good areas Long-term leases	Must invest in top locations Often a high dollar value Difficult to finance Tenants can be difficult

It should be noted that investment in industrial, commercial (office) and retail property often involve a great deal of money and most people achieve these investments by way of managed funds.

Cost of property ownership

Many investors don't take into account the full cost of property ownership when deciding whether to buy a property. There are costs to buy, costs to manage and costs to sell:

Costs to buy:
- Lawyer's fee
- Valuer's fee
- Maintenance report
- Financing costs

- Mortgage insurance
- Furniture/whiteware
- Your time

Cost to manage:
- Rates
- Insurance
- Maintenance
- Advertising costs
- Vacancy
- Accountant's fees
- Obsolescence factor (new kitchen and bathroom every few years)
- Your time

Costs to sell:
- Agent's fee
- Lawyer's fee
- Depreciation recovered (*see* p.89)
- Valuer's fee
- Your time

These costs vary greatly from property to property and according to the investor's circumstances. If the property is a commercial one, the tenant will pay some of the ongoing costs for you. Nevertheless, it is essential to calculate the costs of ownership accurately before committing to the purchase.

Yield

In judging whether a property is a good investment or not, you first need to consider the question of its yield – its annual income expressed as a percentage of its cost. This allows you to compare your prospective purchase with other investments.

The yield of a property is always calculated before any borrowings, because the amount of interest you pay is likely to vary over time. It factors rent received and purchase price only; it takes no account of any capital gain that might accrue.

The biggest investment mistake is to buy low-

COSTS OF RESIDENTIAL PROPERTY MANAGEMENT

There are no unit trust or major property syndicates based on residential property for a very good reason: the cost of management is too high. Professional fund managers must cost in their time fully, and this means residential trusts don't work.

Most residential property investors work hard to make their investments successful. They spend a lot of time doing their own maintenance, finding and managing tenants, collecting the rent, dealing with the bank and looking for new property bargains. To get a decent return, residential property investors put in a lot of hours, which are never added up and properly costed.

In some cases at least, those managing their own properties could put this time into other things (e.g. running a business, doing some overtime) just as profitably, perhaps more so. Residential property investment requires a return on both time and capital. If you are not getting a return on both, think again.

If you don't want to put in the time, you can get the property professionally managed. This will cost about 7-8 per cent of rents.

GROSS YIELD/NET YIELD

The *gross* yield of a property is the amount of total rent paid in a year compared with the value of the property. It takes no account of any of the direct costs.

The *net* yield takes account of the costs of ownership: rates, insurance, vacancy and maintenance in particular. The net yield is the amount you will actually receive, so this is the important figure for you as an investor. Be wary of real estate agents who promote properties with a gross yield. You'll have to do some sums to work out the net figure yourself.

yielding property, usually a second house. Tens of thousands of Kiwis have done this, at great detriment to their financial position. A low-yielding property is one for which the rental received is a low percentage of the purchase price.

Example

An investor buys a property for $220,000. The rent is $240 per week, which is $12,480 pa. After costs (rates, insurance, maintenance) and an allowance for vacancy periods (e.g. four weeks empty) the net annual rent is $9800 pa. The yield is: 4.45 per cent.

$$\frac{\text{Net rent}}{\text{Property value}} \quad \frac{\$9800}{\$220,000} \quad \times 100 = 4.45\% \text{ yield}$$

This yield is far too low. The investor is very dependent on capital gain for a decent return. The investor would be better to look for a higher net yield (7 per cent would be the minimum) and so not be so reliant on capital gains.

Negative gearing

Negative gearing is one of the reasons so many people have gone into property investing. Being negatively geared gives a tax benefit and that is, of course, very attractive to most of us.

Negative gearing is based on the concept that you can afford a cashflow deficit, provided you make a profit on the capital gain. The idea is that you buy a lot of property, to the extent that your cost of borrowing (i.e. interest) is greater than the income you receive your rents. The loss is (you hope) made up for by the increase in the value of your properties – that is the gamble you are taking.

For example, you buy a property for $220,000 that has a net annual rent of $10,000. To fund the purchase, you borrow the entire amount of the purchase ($220,000) at 8 per cent interest, using both the new property and your own home as security.

The numbers look like this:

Rent	$10,000
Interest	$17,600
Loss	$7600

This looks like a crazy thing to do – and yet thousands of people have done it, hoping that:

1. The loss will be made up by an increase in the value of the property.
2. A tax benefit alleviates the loss – the loss of $7600 is deductible against the owner's other income (salary etc). Someone on a tax rate of 33 per cent will get a tax refund of about $2500.

The trouble with negative gearing is, of course, that the capital gain might not be there. Even worse, rent rates might fall (or even cease) at times, but the interest still needs to be paid. Many people have come unstuck with negative gearing.

You should only negatively gear if you are certain that:

- The value of your property will rise.
- You can meet the interest costs, even at reduced rental levels.
- You are buying towards the bottom of the market cycle.

Property investment and tax

Many investors go into property because it is a tax-efficient investment.

There are three major tax advantages of property investment:

1. You can claim any losses you make from your properties against other income if the loss is because expenses (income, maintenance etc) are greater than rental income. But you are better to make a profit and pay tax than make a loss and get a refund.
2. You can claim depreciation on the properties, meaning you might make a tax loss on your property even though you have positive cashflow. Depreciation is a non-cash expense – it is something you claim through your books even though no cash changes hands. You can claim depreciation on the building and its chattels (light fittings carpets, appliances etc) but not on the value of the land. However, when you sell, you will have to repay some

---

WHAT DRIVES UP PROPERTY VALUES?

Over long periods of time property values have increased. However, property values can also fall. There are four things that have a strong effect:

Inflation
At times of high inflation the replacement cost of a building is greater, pushing up the value of existing stock

Low interest rates
Property values will tend to rise when interest rates are low because more people can afford the financing costs and there is a greater demand for property.

High immigration
When there are a lot of people moving to this country to live (and few leaving), the demand for property both to live in and work in is enhanced.

High economic growth rates
When the economy is going well, people have more money and more confidence to buy. Note that this can be regional – a well-performing province or area will see good growth in property values; at the same time a poorly performing one might see a decline in values.

depreciation if you sell the buildings and chattels at a value greater than what you have depreciated them down to. This is called 'depreciation recovered' and gives some property investors an unpleasant surprise when they sell.
3. Property investors can claim some previously private and therefore non-deductible expenses against their income. These are things such as the daily newspaper (to follow the property market), some motor vehicle expenses (to view their properties), some home costs (as an office to run their rental property businesses), telephone (to talk to tenants, agents etc) and travel costs (to look at properties or attend conferences).
4. Interest is another deductible expense for property investors. If you still have a home loan when you buy an investment property, pay this off ahead of your investment loan because this is not deductible.

Most property investors benefit from hiring a good tax accountant. Such a person should be able to save you more in tax than is charged in fees.

Property developers and tax

For tax purposes, property developers are treated differently from property investors. Property development is the act of buying land or buildings with the intention of selling it at a profit. Usually this involves doing something to the land to increase its value – perhaps putting a building on the land or subdividing. However, whatever is done (or, in a few cases, not done) it is the *intention* at the time of purchase that is important. Investors buy their properties for the rental income and any sale at a profit is simply a happy coincidence; property developers buy their properties in order to sell them at a profit.

Property developers must pay tax on their profits because buying and selling property is their business. Once you are deemed to be a developer or trader you must pay tax on all your property sales except for:
- The sale of your own home.
- The sale of your business premises.
- The sale of property you have owned for more than 10 years.

The news gets worse for property developers. Any person who is closely related to a property developer (spouse and children) will also be deemed to be a developer, as will any trust settled by the developer or company of which the developer owns 25 per cent or more. These rules regarding 'associated persons' are complicated and very difficult to circumvent.

OFFSHORE INVESTMENTS

All investors should own some offshore investments. They give greater diversification and exposure to the world's best economies and companies. One of the most cost-effective options is to invest in WiNZ, which is a passive fund tracking the World Index. This can be bought on the New Zealand Stock Exchange and it gives exposure to a spread of shares in most major countries around the world. Because it is a passive fund, the capital gains are not taxable.

A few people buy shares directly themselves through a broker, but this is difficult to do, apart from in a few places like Australia, England and Hong Kong, so most people get their offshore exposure through managed funds.

In recent years tens of thousands of Kiwis have put billions of dollars into offshore investments. Many profited as overseas markets boomed and the New Zealand currency weakened, although there have also been losses as many markets crashed and the Kiwi dollar rose.

Some unfortunate individuals have been persuaded by high-pressure sales techniques and some tax incentives to put their money into very ordinary Queensland property investments, while others have been ripped off by brokers calling from Bangkok or Manila.

Everyone should have some of their investments offshore, but stay in the mainstream and don't be tempted by offers with extraordinary promises.

> **DON'T FALL FOR IT**
>
> Be very wary of brokers calling out of the blue from places like New York, Manila or Bangkok offering you the latest 'hot' investment. They are persuasive – but don't touch them.

See Scams, p.70

Why invest offshore?
There are a number of advantages in making offshore investments:
- Greater diversification.
- More opportunities (New Zealand makes up less than 1 per cent of the world's sharemarkets).
- Access to other industries – New Zealand has a limited number of industries in which you can invest. Going offshore lets you invest in many other industries such as textiles, pharmaceuticals, banking and finance etc.
- Access to major global brands such as Coca-Cola, Disney, American Express etc.

What are the risks?
There are disadvantages of going offshore, with corresponding risks to your investments:
- *Currency.* While your investments might perform well, a rise in the New Zealand dollar means you could show a loss when you sell up and bring your money back to New Zealand.

- *Lack of information.* It is harder to keep abreast of what's happening in other countries (although the Internet helps).
- *Different laws, cultures and ways of doing business.*
- *Tax.* There can be tax disadvantages for offshore investors. In particular, there is the double taxation of dividends because overseas dividends do not come with imputation credits and the Foreign Investment Fund regime means that capital gains on investments overseas may be taxed even though the investments have not yet been sold.

See Tax on dividends, pp.82-83

How much offshore?

See Offshore investments, p.120

Most people should have 40-60 per cent of their investments offshore, perhaps a little more or a little less depending upon individual circumstances. People who travel a lot will want more money overseas, as will those who regularly send money offshore to relatives or to import goods. Having overseas investments will act as a natural hedge against the New Zealand dollar falling, making overseas travel or purchases very expensive.

Foreign investments and tax

If you invest $50,000 or more in a company or trust outside New Zealand you may be caught by the FIF regime. This scheme is very complicated and this is an area where it certainly pays to get good advice.

THE FINANCIAL SECRETS

- ❏ Most people should repay any debts *before* they start to invest.
- ❏ One immutable law of investment is that the higher the expected returns, the greater the risk.
- ❏ The way to manage investment risk is to diversify.
- ❏ You can't best interest-bearing deposits for short-term savings.
- ❏ New Zealand's tax law is friendly to investors: there is no capital gains tax.

CONNECT

- Securities Commission, phone 04 472 9830
  www.sec-com.govt.nz
- Other web sites:
  www.sorted.org.nz; www.goodreturns.co.nz; www.sharechat.co.nz

BOOKS

- *The Bemused Investor's Guide to Company Accounts*, Bill Jamieson, Shoal Bay Press, 1997
- *Buffettology*, Mary Buffett, Fireside, 1999
- *Eight Secrets of Investment Success,* Martin Hawes, Penguin, 1998
- *The Investment Jungle*, Duncan Balmer, HarperCollins, 1998
- *Property Investment in New Zealand – A Strategy for Wealth (rev. ed)*, Martin Hawes, Shoal Bay Press, 2001
- *Rich Dad's Guide to Investing*, Robert Kiyosaki, Tech Press, 2000
- *Real Estate Riches*, Dolf de Roos, Tech Press, 2002
- *Shares: Seven Ways to Beat the Market,* Martin Hawes, Penguin, 2001

6. SUPERANNUATION
Saving for retirement

Superannuation has been a major political issue in this country for years. The problem has often been stated: as the baby boomers age there will be a big increase in the number of older people. With better health care, people will also live longer and, being in better health, will expect a good lifestyle. However, there will be fewer people of working age to pay taxes and a reasonable level of universal superannuation will be less affordable for any government. Government has started to build a fund (the 'Cullen Fund') which is designed to ensure that NZ Super can continue to be paid. This scheme, however, remains controversial and there is still no consensus about what should be done.

One thing seems clear: whatever level of superannuation is paid in the future, and whatever age it starts from, it won't amount to much. Government-paid superannuation will never provide much more than a minimal lifestyle. If you rely on it your 'golden years' will seem more like the years of the brass farthing.

This is an area where you must take control of your own destiny – you cannot rely on the government. To enjoy a good lifestyle, to pay for any expensive habits in retirement (a round of golf, a bottle of wine, the odd day's skiing, some travel etc) you will have to make provision for yourself. The government may meet your basic living expenses, but it will be up to you to find the money for the extras.

THE DEMISE OF THE SURCHARGE

The superannuation surcharge was abolished in 1998. This was a surtax of 25 per cent on income above a certain level from sources other than New Zealand Superannuation, and effectively meant that many retired New Zealanders did not get any government super. This caused outrage, particularly among older New Zealanders who believed they had paid for their super through their taxes.

Political agitation eventually led to the abolition of this surcharge and there is now no abatement regime for New Zealand Super. At present everyone gets it on reaching the age of 65 years (although there are complex rules for couples where one partner is not yet 65).

Many people believe some form of asset testing will return, however. After all, it's hard to see that a government will continue to pay what is effectively a benefit to wealthy people simply because they reach a certain age. One of the legacies of the surcharge is that few people now trust politicians on the topic of superannuation. In the absence of a consensus among politicians and experts, and the enshrining of that consensus in legislation, that distrust will continue.

The only solution is to make your own plans: to manage your finances well, to invest well and to work out how you are going to live when you are no longer working. You need to be able to be self-reliant.

It is never too late to start saving: every little bit helps. No one is suggesting that you should try to save so much that you live a poor lifestyle now. But saving does require that you give up something today, so you can have more in the future. This is a balance that only you can decide upon.

PLANNING YOUR SUPER

The logical way to plan your super is in two steps:

1. Work out how much you will need in retirement.
2. Work out how much you need to save to get that amount.

As with any long-term plans, there are many variables and plenty of scope for things not to work out as planned. The Office of the Retirement Commissioner has produced material to help with these calculations. This information is free, so why not use it?

How much will you need in retirement?

There's not always an easy answer to this one. There are many unknowns, about which you need to make educated guesses, such as:

- The age at which you will stop working (many people can and wish to continue working beyond age 65).
- The age you will live to.
- The lifestyle you will want. It may be cheaper to live in retirement but you may want to continue some expensive habits.
- Your health-care needs.
- The amount of government assistance.
- Investment rates of return while you are in retirement.
- The rate of inflation between now and retirement.
- The degree to which you will be comfortable spending your capital – if you spend everything there will be no inheritance for your children.

See Annuity mortgages, p.194

- Whether you will use the equity in your house to live on.

If you can calculate how much you will want each month to live, there are financial tables to work out the amount of capital required to give that amount. There is plenty of scope for these calculations to be inaccurate, but it is still an exercise worth doing. As a benchmark, it is generally thought that most people need about 70 per cent of the income they required before retirement.

How much should you save?

Once you have calculated the capital sum you need to produce a reasonable income, it is relatively easy to work out how much you must save. There are two main variables:

1. The time you have before you are likely to retire. Remember this plan may change: some people decide to retire sooner; some have retirement forced on them by ill-health or redundancy; others decide to work longer.
2. The returns you get on your savings. This is harder to predict, but over time a good diversified portfolio should earn at least 5 per cent after tax and fees.

If you know these two things, and the capital sum you require, it's relatively easy to calculate the amount you must save weekly. A financial planner can make this calculation or you can use the Retirement Commission's web site at www.sorted.org.nz.

If you can't afford to save the amount you have calculated, don't despair. Save what you can, within your budget and lifestyle. As time goes by you will probably be able to save more: your salary may rise, you may pay off the mortgage, your partner/spouse may go back to work etc. Even a little saved now helps – it provides a base and will grow as the returns compound over the years.

Start early

See Some people shouldn't save! p.68

Most people should pay off their mortgage before they start to save. However, as soon as you can, start saving and investing. Time makes all the difference:

1. The more time you have, the more you can tuck away. If you start at age 45, you have 240 months to make regular payments into a fund before reaching age 65; if you start at age 35, you have 360 months.
2. The more time you have, the better compound interest will work for you.

Age 45 years	saving $200 per mth (6%)	at 65 years: $92,800
Age 35 years	saving $200 per mth (6%)	at 65 years: $201,900

The difference is obvious. Start saving as soon as you can!

WAYS TO SAVE FOR RETIREMENT

The key to saving for retirement is to diversify your portfolio. You need a mix of shares, property and deposits, some of which will be offshore. This is most important for long-term savings because diversification will carry you through any adverse events that might happen over the decades.

In addition, there are some savings plans designed specifically with retirement in mind.

Superannuation funds

Superannuation funds are diversified managed funds. Nearly all are now defined-benefit contribution schemes: you put your money in and receive a lump sum at the end. They all own a spread of investments and the tax treatment is little different from other investments: you buy into the funds with money that has already been taxed, the funds are taxed at 33 per cent, and when you withdraw your funds they are free of tax.

The difference with some super funds is that you cannot withdraw them at any time: your money is locked in until you reach a certain age. This is a kind of enforced discipline. There are a few exceptions to the 'lock in' rule – you may be able to withdraw if you leave permanently for overseas or suffer a disability.

Employer-subsidised schemes

Although these are not as common as they once were, quite a lot of employers still offer to subsidise their workers' superannuation savings. If you are lucky enough to be offered one you should almost certainly take it.

Usually the employer will offer to match, in part at least, any superannuation savings you make into the scheme yourself. This may mean that for every dollar that you put into the scheme, the employer will also put in a dollar. Not all schemes are so generous but the employer's contribution will probably increase in proportion to yours the longer you stay with the firm. The 'vesting date' is the time when the employer's contribution becomes yours. If you leave before the vesting date, you do not get the employer's contribution but what you have put into the fund will be yours, along with the returns on your contribution.

The schemes usually give you a lump sum on retirement, but some give monthly income in the form of an annuity. As an addi-

---

MONEY MAGIC

Over a number of years compound interest will multiply your money over and over again. The amount that builds up can be so big that it seems like magic. But compound interest is simply interest earned on interest. Your capital earns interest, which is then added to the original sum and thus earns interest as part of the new total. This virtuous circle feeds on itself and your investments will build up, slowly at first but gathering pace over time.

For example, if you invested $4000 at 6% for 40 years (and allowed the interest to compound), you would have a total of $41,143 in interest. If you withdrew the interest every year, you would receive a total of just $9600.

See also Chapter 5

tional benefit, they often also offer life or disability insurance at cheaper premium rates than individual policies.

Most employer schemes are professionally managed and the costs of the scheme are usually met by the employer. Even if the employer does not meet the costs, the fees in employer schemes should be less than if you purchase an individual superannuation plan.

Superannuation policies

A traditional form of retirement savings was through a superannuation policy. These were sold by skilled salespeople on behalf of insurance companies and usually came with life insurance attached. You paid into them for a few decades and at the end you received the benefits.

The trouble with these policies was the cost at the beginning; if you withdrew from the policy you got virtually nothing because the person who had sold it to you got the first year or two's premiums.

Because so much of the cost is paid up front, superannuation policies are very inflexible: they are only for those who are sure they are going to continue it right to the end – in some cases 30 years or more.

Defined-benefit contribution schemes

There are also few of these left. Defined-benefit schemes are offered by some employers and require you to pay in a part of your salary. On retirement you receive a percentage of your finishing salary as a pension for life. These worked quite well when people took a job for life but with so much employee mobility they are no longer particularly useful.

WHAT SUPER FUNDS EARN

Do not expect very high returns from your super funds: they are not designed for that. Rather they are designed for long-term steady growth with relatively low volatility and little risk. The diversification that these funds have means that they are steady performers without the wild ups and downs of other investments. Generally, over long time periods, super funds will return around 2-4 per cent (after tax and fees) over the rate of inflation.

The returns will depend on two things:

1. *The type of fund you choose.* A growth fund should earn more than a conservative one but will show more volatility.
2. *The skill of your investment manager.* The returns the manager can get on the investment markets are yours – after they have been taxed and the manager's fees have been paid. Some managers are better than others at picking future market trends and allocating assets accordingly.

A good independent financial adviser should be able to recommend a fund that is likely to perform well.

THE FINANCIAL SECRETS

- You cannot rely on the government for a decent standard of living in retirement.
- The key to having enough in retirement is to start planning and saving early.
- Compound interest is your 'best friend'.
- Employer-subsidised super schemes are great if you can get them.

CONNECT

- Web sites
  www.sorted.org.nz
  www.goodreturns.co.nz

BOOKS

- *A New Zealand Guide to Living Well in Retirement,* Noel Whittaker & Roger Moses, Hodder Moa Beckett, 1995
- *The Realities of Retirement*, Bill Jamieson, Shoal Bay Press, 1998
- *Successful Super,* Martin Hawes, Penguin, 2000
- *Your Retirement Action Planner* (a booklet produced by the Office of the Retirement Commissioner)

7. CONSUMER LAW
Know Your Rights

Consumer law in New Zealand is advanced and robust. On the whole, it protects us well.

Yet too many people do not complain when they receive shoddy goods or services. Even fewer take the next step when they fail to receive satisfaction from their complaints and go to the Disputes Tribunal or the Tenancy Tribunal or an ombudsman. They just drop the complaint, grumble to themselves for a while, and leave someone else to face the same problem at some future time.

You should never be afraid to complain or to take action to get satisfaction. Your rights under law were put in place by society to protect you. Making a complaint, formal or otherwise, does not make you a whinger. These are your rights; it is your money.

To be able to exercise your rights, you must know what they are.

There are two main pieces of law designed to protect your rights as a consumer: the Fair Trading Act and the Consumer Guarantees Act.

In general, the Fair Trading Act covers problems regarding the sale of goods and services *before* a purchase is made, while the Consumer Guarantees Act covers the quality of goods and services *after* the purchase.

THE FAIR TRADING ACT

The Fair Trading Act has been with us since 1986 and covers the advertising, promotion and selling of all goods and services. It covers all traders and businesses (companies and individuals), as well as government agencies and state-owned enterprises. It also covers anyone who has aided and abetted any offence (if, for example, a wholesaler and retailer connived to mislead).

The Act stops those who provide goods and services from:
- Misleading and deceptive conduct.
- Making false representations.
- Unfair trade practices.

It also provides for consumer information and product safety standards.

Note that no one actually has to suffer a loss for the Act to apply. The Act can target conduct that is *likely* to mislead or deceive.

The false representations may occur in any form. It may be what the trader said as you were considering a purchase, or through any advertising or promotional material: TV, radio or print advertising, brochures, fliers, point-of-sale materials or even pictures. The Act also covers traders omitting to give you important information. The more common breaches occur in these areas:

- *Origin of goods*
  The label that indicates where goods are made must be true. Misrepresentation can extend to include symbols; for example, the picture of a kiwi on the label could be construed as meaning the item was made in New Zealand. If it is not, then the trader has breached the Act.

- *Availability of goods*
  Often traders will advertise something very cheaply, but when you get there to buy it you are told they have sold out. The trader must have a reasonable supply of the goods advertised, taking into account the size of the business, likely demand and the extent of the advertising and promotion. If they have run out, ask for a 'rain check', allowing the trader to get more stock to supply you.

- *Description of goods*
  This must be accurate. A computer retailer was fined $50,000 for advertising computers with 256k motherboards, when in fact they were less powerful.

- *Comparative pricing*
  Traders cannot say things like 'was $150, now down to $99' when the product or service had not been available at the higher price for some time. It is not good enough to make a comparison with some hypothetical 'manufacturer's price'.

- *Goods and Services Tax*
  When you see a price advertised, you are entitled to assume it includes GST unless it clearly states otherwise.

- *Special offers*
  What is being offered must be truly special, and any limitations or qualifications must be clearly spelt out. When a special offer says 'buy one and get one free', the free item must be as good as the one being purchased.

- *Packaging*
  Packaging is not allowed to mislead you into thinking the goods are bigger than they really are.

- *Inertia selling*
  This means sending you something you have not requested and implying it is yours unless you expressly reject it. Your silence does not constitute acceptance of an offer, whatever the trader tries to tell you.

- *Quotes and estimates*
  You should be able to rely on a quote or an estimate. A quote is an agreed price: the work must be done at that price. An estimate is a 'best guess'. A trader cannot mislead you by giving an estimate that is a long way from the final price. Generally, the final price should be within 10 per cent of the estimate.

  See also Quotes and estimates, p.109

- *Interest free*
  A price that is offered with free credit should be the same as one without free credit. Any additional insurance charges or booking fees must be clearly shown in advertising material.

- *Claims that goods or services are needed*
  A trader cannot claim that something is required when it is not. For example, a pest control company cannot claim that you need borer control when you do not; a motor mechanic cannot tell you something is required for a warrant of fitness when it is not.

- *Debt collection fees*
  You do not have to pay any fees for debt collection that are over and above the original amount owing, unless you have been made aware that non-payment will incur these costs. Debt collection letters and demands must not be similar to any court or official notices.

The fine print

Fine print in an advertisement, contract or offer will not necessarily save a trader from breaching the Act. If the fine print conceals important information that could have changed your buying decision, the trader has probably breached the Act. Important conditions must be shown in advertisements clearly and boldly.

Making a complaint

The first step for most people is to go to the trader and see if he or she will put things right. If you cannot get satisfaction, you have two options:

1. *Take a civil case against the trader.*
   This may mean you go to the Disputes Tribunal, or, if a larger sum of money is involved, to court. You may also seek an injunction against the trader, stopping them from continuing to advertise or promote the product in a particular way.

See Disputes Tribunal p.113-14

2. *Complain to the Commerce Commission*

The commission may not take on the case, but it does log all complaints and is much more likely to take up a case if there have been a number of complaints against a particular trader. Remedies available through the Commerce Commission include hefty fines and compensation to the consumer.

You can of course do both: take a civil case against a trader and at the same time make a complaint to the Commerce Commission.

THE CONSUMER GUARANTEES ACT

This Act gives you protection as a consumer, forcing traders to sell you goods and services that are of reasonable quality and giving you remedies if they are not.

The Act covers nearly all goods and services that might be purchased by a private consumer – some goods and services usually purchased by businesses are not covered. The Act covers only vendors who are 'in trade', so you are not covered if you buy something privately. However, most things you would buy from a business are covered: professional services, electrical goods, clothing, the services of tradespeople etc.

The assumption of the Act is that the trader from whom you buy is making some guarantees:

> **REMEDIES**
>
> If something goes wrong, you have the right to insist the trader puts it right. Usually this means the retailer or tradesperson you dealt with, but you may go to the manufacturer as well. (You may have no choice if the retailer has gone broke or out of business.)
>
> The trader should fix the problem – either by repairing the goods or giving you a replacement. In some circumstances, you can have the problem fixed elsewhere and claim the cost of the repair from the trader.
>
> If the problem cannot be put right you are entitled to a full refund, and this means cash, not just a credit note.

Guarantees for services

- The service must be provided with reasonable care and skill.
- The service must be fit for the purpose.
- It must be completed within a reasonable time.
- It must be provided at a reasonable cost if no price is agreed beforehand.

Guarantees for goods

- The trader has the right to sell the goods.
- The product is not being used as security for a loan and so cannot be repossessed.
- The goods are of 'acceptable quality', fit for the purpose for which they would usually be used. The goods must be free of minor defects (unless you are told about them).
- The goods must do what the trader says they will do.

- The goods must be the same as any sample or demonstrated model, and mail-order goods must be true to descriptions in a catalogue.
- Spare parts and repair facilities must be available (unless you are told otherwise).
- If no price is agreed, the price must be reasonable.
- Any guarantees that the trader gives must be honoured.

Note that the Act often uses words like 'reasonable' and 'acceptable'. These are hard to define precisely – in the final analysis, what is reasonable or acceptable may be decided by a judge, who will take into account all factors and circumstances.

Traders cannot 'contract out' of the Act by saying they will not guarantee their goods and services. However, there are exceptions to this. For example, if a dry cleaner warns you that if she tries to remove a stain the garment could be ruined, but you tell her to go ahead anyway, you may have no comeback if the garment is ruined.

Enforcement

Unlike the Fair Trading Act, there is no official government body to help enforce the Consumer Guarantees Act. Enforcement of your rights under the Act is up to you.

If you do not get any joy from the trader concerned, you have three options:

1. *Complain to the industry association* if there is one and if the trader is a member. For example if a builder has done some shoddy work, you could try complaining to the Master Builders' Federation.

See Disputes Tribunal p.113-14

2. *Go to the Disputes Tribunal.*
3. *Go to court.* This will involve a lawyer and considerable expense.

BUYING A CAR

When you buying a car from a dealer, both the Fair Trading Act and the Consumer Guarantees Act apply. In addition you have some protection from the Motor Vehicle Dealers Act.

However, if you buy a car privately, you are on your own. You can check that the car has a warrant of fitness, you can have it checked out by the AA or a local garage, but if it breaks down you will have little or no comeback against the seller.

Licensed dealers

All car dealers must be licensed. To be a licensed dealer, the person must be a member of the Motor Vehicle Dealers' Institute. However, there are a few people who trade illegally as unlicensed dealers.

> **DO YOU OWN YOUR NEW CAR?**
>
> If you buy your car through a licensed dealer you are guaranteed title to it. However, if you buy privately there is a chance that the car belongs to someone else: perhaps it has been stolen; or there is still money owing on it under a hire purchase agreement, in which case the car is still owned by the finance company.
>
> If you are buying a car privately you need to check this out.
>
> The easiest way to do this is to call Baycorp on 0900 909 777. There is a cost for making this call. You can also check with the Companies Office (www.companies.govt.nz) to see if there is any money owing on the car, but this service also costs and may not tell you if it is stolen.
>
> From May 2002, when the Personal Property Securities Act comes into force, there will be an on-line register where you can check if there is security on any item you are buying. The web site for this will be www.ppsr.govt.nz.

You can check whether you are dealing with a licensed dealer by calling the MVDI on 0800 108 106.

Buying from a licensed dealer gives you considerable protection:

- The dealer will have the right to sell the car – i.e. it will not be stolen or have money owing on it.
- The car will come with minimum warranties (see below).
- The dealer must give some basic information on the history of the car, for example the odometer reading, number of previous owners, the year it was first registered etc.
- The MVDI has a fidelity fund to reimburse people who have lost money through the actions of a licensed dealer.

Car warranties

The Consumer Guarantees Act covers the sale of motor vehicles. This means a car you buy from a dealer (whether licensed or not) must be of 'acceptable' quality – it must be safe, have no small defects unless they are pointed out to you, be in reasonable condition taking account of its age and price, and be able to do what it is made to do. In addition, the Consumer Guarantees Act means that the car must be fit for the purpose that you have told the dealer about (e.g. to tow a boat), and any new car you buy must have spare parts available.

However, buying through a licensed dealer gives you further minimum warranties. The Motor Vehicle Dealers Act sets out four categories:

- *Category A*. If the car is less than four years old and has done under 50,000km, the warranty is for three months or 5000km (whichever comes first).
- *Category B*. If the car is between four and six years old and has done less than 75,000km, the warranty is for two months or 3000km.

- *Category C.* If the car is between six and eight years old and has done less than 100,000km, the warranty is for one month or 1500km.
- *Category D.* This covers all cars. The car must have a current warrant of fitness, be in reasonable condition, be of merchantable quality and be fit for the purpose for which vehicles of its type are usually used.

When selling a car, a licensed dealer must tell you which category the car fits under. Note that not all things on the car are warranted. For example, tyres, the battery, paintwork and interior trim are excluded.

Although all dealers must give these minimum warranties, some will extend them. In addition, remember that the Consumer Guarantees Act applies. This gives you two further protections: first, the Act has no time limits, and second, it covers things like batteries and tyres.

Motor Vehicle Disputes Tribunal

If you have a dispute with a dealer that you cannot resolve, you may take the case to the Disputes Tribunal or to the more specialist Motor Vehicles Disputes Tribunal (MVDT).

The Motor Vehicle Disputes Tribunal can hear cases for up to $12,000 worth of compensation, and can cancel contracts on cars worth up to $30,000. It can also hear a case for compensation for more than $12,000 if both you and the dealer agree. You must complain to the MVDT within three months of the expiry of a warrant (or six months after the purchase of a Category D car).

There are only four MVDTs in the country and you may not have your case heard quickly. If your complaint is for an amount less than $7500 you may be better to go to the Disputes Tribunal.

Both bodies hear cases in private and lawyers are excluded.

SECOND-HAND GOODS

If you buy second-hand goods from a dealer, a range of consumer protection laws apply, including the Fair Trading Act and the Consumer Guarantees Act. A second-hand dealer cannot contract out of the Consumer Guarantees Act by offering goods 'as is, where is'. They must be of acceptable quality.

If you buy at auction the Fair Trading Act applies – an auctioneer cannot mislead or deceive you regarding your possible purchase. However, the Consumer Guarantees Act does not apply to auction sales, meaning you don't have the same protection as if you bought the goods from a dealer.

When you buy privately, neither the Fair Trading Act nor the Consumer Guarantees Act applies. You should check goods over thoroughly before you buy, and ask for a receipt. The only comeback you are likely to have is under the Contractual Remedies Act. If the seller made a false or misleading statement, you may be able to sue or cancel the contract. However, this is likely to be difficult, especially if the seller has left for Queensland in the interim!

CONTRACTS

For a contract to be legally binding you must have three things:

1. An offer.
2. Acceptance of that offer.
3. Consideration (some form of payment, usually money but sometimes other things).

Without these three things a contract is not enforceable.

Not all contracts have to be in writing, but contracts regarding the sale and purchase and leasing of real estate, hire purchase, loans, and motor vehicles purchased from a licensed dealer must be in writing for your contract to be enforceable.

Just about every other contract can be made verbally. In fact we all make contracts verbally just about every day: buying items from shops, taking a taxi ride, getting clothes dry-cleaned, filling the car with petrol ...

Once you have a contract with an agreed consideration, you must complete the contract – i.e. fulfil your side of the bargain. That means, for instance, that when you have accepted the offer of a meal at certain price in a restaurant (by eating it), you must pay for it. If you have accepted the offer of a 12-month gym contract for a certain amount each month, you must meet those payments for that period.

Getting out of a contract

There are only a few circumstances that allow you to cancel a contract:

- With door-to-door sales you have seven days to change your mind.
- The Credit Contracts Act gives you three days' cooling off period for things like hire purchase, loans etc.

> **MISTAKES**
>
> When contracting to buy or sell something it's easy to make a mistake. For example, you might agree to buy something for $100. However, when the shop assistant puts this into the cash register, he accidentally makes it $1000 and you sign the credit card slip without really looking. Only when you get home do you realise your mistake.
>
> You have certainly contracted to buy the goods for $1000 – you signed for that amount – but your mistake is covered by the Contractual Mistakes Act. The clear and considerable accidental discrepancy in value shows that a mistake has been made, and you can cancel the contract and pay only the proper price. The same applies if the shop has mistakenly undercharged you, i.e. charged $10 onto the credit card instead of $100. They would be entitled to approach you for the full amount.
>
> A common error is where the price of an item in a shop is incorrect. You might take the pair of shoes marked $15 to the counter thinking that you have scored a bargain. However, the shopkeeper realises the mistake and tells you the shoes are actually $150. You cannot hold the shop to the price on the tag.

- If you have been misled.
- If the other party agrees to the cancellation of the contract.
- If the contract is harsh or oppressive.
- If you are a minor (sometimes!).

Refunds

Many shops have refund policies that mean they will refund goods simply because you have changed your mind, or because the lounge suite does not match the curtains, or you have found one cheaper elsewhere, but they have no legal obligation to do so.

You may be able to get a refund if the goods are faulty (under the Consumer Guarantees Act) or if you have been misled (under the Fair Trading Act).

If you change your mind about a purchase and cannot cancel the contract legally, you may end up losing any deposit you have paid. Further, the seller may pursue you legally to force you to either complete the sale or make up their losses. Obviously this is unlikely to happen with a relatively minor retail sale, but people often sue to force completion of property agreements, car sales and purchases etc.

Contracts and kids

Generally, children under 18 cannot be held to a contract unless a court considers it is fair and reasonable. This means your 12-year-old will have to stick by the purchase of a pair of jeans that she agreed to buy for $80 and then didn't want, but would probably not have to go ahead with the sale of the bike that she had agreed to sell for $15.

The Minors Contract Act covers people under the age of 20, unless they are married. In practice, anyone over 18 can usually be held to a contract, but there is scope for courts to overturn contracts entered into by 18- and 19-year-olds that are harsh or oppressive, or where the consideration is unrealistic.

However, although a young person may be able to escape a contract that he or she has signed, you will not be able to do so if the minor sues you. A minor can enforce a contract with an adult, even though an adult may not be able to enforce a contract against a minor.

AGES OF CONSENT

Some examples of the things children are legally able do at certain ages:

Age 10	Buy life insurance; be held responsible for a criminal act (although they cannot usually be prosecuted).
Age 11	Get a delivery job (between the hours of 6am and 10pm).
Age 14	Become a babysitter; be taken to court.
Age 15	Get a driver's licence.
Age 16	Get a gun licence; get married with parental consent; leave school; leave home; get a full-time job; get a tattoo.
Age 17	Be prosecuted in an adult court.
Age 18	Buy alcohol; vote and stand as a candidate in a public election; bet at the TAB; sign a contract.
Age 20	Get married without parental consent.

QUOTES AND ESTIMATES

When getting major work done, it always a good idea to first get a quote or estimate – preferably in writing. The prices should include GST – if it is not shown they are deemed to be GST inclusive.

An estimate is what the trader thinks the work will cost. It is not a firm price that the contractor can be held to, but is an estimate of costs based on past experience. The trader must use reasonable skill and care so that you can act on good information. Generally, the trader should estimate to within 10 per cent of the final price.

A quote is a fixed price that the trader has to stick to. He must do the work for that price and cannot charge any extra, even when the job turns out to be a lot more difficult than anticipated. A quote should be in writing (especially if it is for a major piece of work) and should show:

- The work that is to be done.
- The price to be charged (or the hourly rate and cost of materials).
- The start and finish dates.
- How long the quote remains open for acceptance by you.

If the final bill is more than the quoted price, you do not have to pay the extra. You should simply write a cheque for the agreed amount, drawing attention to the fact that this was the price that was quoted.

Sometimes you may have to pay for a quote. For example, if you want to have your stereo fixed, the repair shop might charge you $40 to have a look inside and so be able to tell you what needs to be done, what parts are required and what the whole job will cost. This means that you are committed to pay a minimum of $40 and the repairer should not go ahead with any further work until he or she has spoken to you.

If you don't have a quote or an estimate and a bill comes in that seems far too high, you may still be covered by the Consumer Guarantees Act. This says that any price must be 'reasonable' and stops 'price gouging'. You can find out what is 'reasonable' by asking other firms offering the same goods or services what they would charge.

LAYBYS

It is common to purchase something on layby or have an item put aside after paying a deposit. The Layby Sales Act covers both of these situations. Note that a 'layby sale' is in many respects not really a sale – the risk remains the seller's until the goods are paid for in full and collected.

No retailer or business has to offer layby sales – they can refuse to put the goods aside. A business can also decide to allow laybys on some goods but not others.

COMMON CONSUMER MYTHS

There was nothing in writing so there's no contract.

Only some contracts need to be in writing (e.g. sale and purchase of real estate, leasing properties and most money lending). However, though many contracts are oral, they are enforceable. The only obvious problem is, of course, that there are often difficulties proving what was agreed.

I've paid a $40 deposit on a layby purchase – I don't want the goods any more but I will not be able to get the deposit back.

Yes you can. The retailer can only keep an amount equivalent to costs to make the sale and any loss in value. These are likely to be fairly small amounts and so you should get most, if not all, of your $40 back.

I bought some trousers but now I've changed my mind. I can go back to the shop and get a refund.

You might get a refund, but the retailer is not obliged to give you one. In a legal sense, once you have bought the goods, they are yours.

If a shop puts the wrong price on something, they have to sell it at that price.

No they don't. A shop cannot deliberately put the wrong price on something to attract you (that would be a breach of the Fair Trading Act) but if they make a mistake, you cannot hold them to it.

I have been late in paying an account. They have put a late payment penalty on top of the amount owed and I have to pay it.

Not necessarily. You only need to pay this penalty if it was stipulated in the contract that you entered into at the time of purchase. If it was not made clear to you at that time, either verbally or in writing, you should not pay it.

If you put something on layby you should be given a written record, detailing the item and the payments made. Although there is no legal requirement for this to be in writing, most shops do this as a matter of course.

The retailer must continue to hold on to the goods for you, provided that you keep to the terms laid out. If they do not, they must find you replacement goods or give you a full refund. In some circumstances, if the retailer has sold the goods to someone else while you are still within the agreed terms of the layby, the retailer may have to give you the difference between what you were to pay for the goods and what you have to pay to get them elsewhere.

While a *retailer* can cancel a layby sale only if you have failed to keep up payments, the *purchaser* may cancel at any time and ask for a refund. But while many retailers will give you a full refund, they are entitled to withhold an amount that is equivalent to their selling costs (how much staff time was spent on the sale) plus any loss of value over the time they have held the goods, perhaps because the goods are now out of season and so will need to be sold off cheaply. A retailer must be able to justify any amount that it has withheld in these terms.

The refund must be in cash or by cheque – despite any policy of 'no cash refunds'.

HIRE PURCHASE

A hire purchase agreement allows you to buy goods on 'time payment' but take immediate possession. In legal terms, hire purchase is a conditional sale agreement – the sale is finally effected only when all the payments have been made. Until then the goods remain the property of the shop or retail finance company.

Hire purchase is very convenient, which is why it is so popular.

By taking the goods now and arranging

to pay for them in instalments you are, in effect, borrowing money to finance the purchase. Few questions are asked about your financial position (compared with when you take out a bank loan), even when the retailer is acting as agent for a finance company. The retailer may sometimes get a margin for arranging this finance.

Hire purchase protection

Hire purchase is controlled by the Hire Purchase Act 1971 and must also comply with the Credit Contracts Act 1981 and the Credit (Repossession) Act 1997. As well, the consumer has considerable protection under the Fair Trading Act (retailers' advertisements must reasonably represent the hire purchase terms) and the Consumer Guarantees Act.

Hire purchase agreements must be in writing and be signed by both parties. The agreement must include:

- description of the goods
- cash price of the goods
- name of the finance company
- financial details of the contract
- amount of any deposit and instalments
- number of instalments

A copy of this agreement must be given to you within 10 days or the contract has no effect.

There are strict rules regarding cancelling the contract early and what rebate you are due. You should be able to pay off the full amount early without a penalty if you wish to, and should receive back a proportion of the booking fee, administration fee, insurance, service charges etc.

If you have not yet taken delivery of the goods you have three days in which you can change your mind. Notice of cancellation must be given in writing. However, if you have already taken possession of the goods you can only cancel the financing part of the contract. You must still complete the purchase and you have 15 days to pay the cash price in full.

You cannot be forced to take separate insurance for goods if you already have home and contents insurance that would cover them.

When things go bad

When you fail to make hire purchase repayments and fall into arrears, the lender may repossess the item in question, but only if this was agreed to at the time of the initial contract. The law regarding repossession of goods is laid out in the Credit (Repossession) Act 1997:

- A repossession notice must be served, giving you at least 15 days to make up the arrears.
- If the arrears are not brought up to date in that time, the person or business owed the money (the creditor) may repossess the goods. He or his agent can only come to your property between the hours of 6am and 9pm, Monday to Saturday, and not on public holidays. The agent may break into your house but must leave it secure. He must leave a list of goods taken, a statement that he has entered your house, a note showing that he acts for the creditor and a copy of the pre-possession notice. You may stop the repossession by paying the arrears (although you may still have to pay the agent's costs).
- Within 21 days the creditor must give you a notice (post-possession notice) stating the date of the repossession, costs to repossess, what you must do to get the goods back, the value of the goods and what it will do if you do not pay.
- You now have 15 days to make good the default (including possession costs), find a buyer who will pay the value of the goods, or find someone else to take over the agreement. If you do none of these things, the creditor can sell the goods – at auction, by tender or by private sale.
- The creditor must try to get the best price for them.
- If the price obtained is not enough to pay off the debt in full, the lender may try to recover the amount of the shortfall from you.
- The creditor must send you a notice within 10 days of selling the goods showing how much it got for them, any sales commissions (or other costs) incurred and how much you now owe or how much is owed to you. If you still owe money, the creditor will probably pursue you for the shortfall.

Hire purchase is often a very expensive way to buy something. The finance rate, which includes interest, booking fees, administration fees and compulsory insurance, can run to 25 per cent or more. The advertisement promising 'only $10 per week' may sound attractive but the total cost, when calculated fully, can be huge. Generally, you are far better off to fund big purchases through a low-interest credit card or put it on the mortgage.

DEBT COLLECTION

Being unable to repay a debt can be distressing. Creditors are entitled to take action against you, and sometimes in their enthusiasm to get paid they can become quite aggressive in their collection techniques. But you do have rights, and you should not let yourself be pushed around or unduly threatened. Debts fall into two categories:

Debts you dispute

If you do not accept that you owe the money in question, don't just ignore it – that won't make the problem go away. Instead, you should contact the creditor (or purported creditor), or the debt collection agency, if one is being used, and explain why you don't owe the money. This shows that there is a real dispute and the attempts at collection will stop (although legal action will probably start). Do this as soon as possible.

Ultimately the creditor may take the matter to court (or the Disputes Tribunal) to recover the money he believes you owe. You are far better to resolve this by negotiation if you possibly can.

If a part of the debt is not in dispute, offer to pay what you believe is owed, 'as full and final settlement'.

Failing all else, you may have to go to court. In this event the judge (or referee in the Disputes Tribunal) will decide whether there is a debt. Before the hearing, don't be frightened into paying because the creditor tells you that's the only way to avoid costs being added; the judge will probably decide on costs.

Debts that are not disputed

If you do owe the money you have to take steps to pay it. In many cases you'll be able to negotiate a time-payment plan, although the creditor is not obliged to accept this.

The creditor cannot unilaterally apply collection fees or late payment penalties, unless these were agreed at the time you initially contracted for the goods or services, either in writing or verbally.

Disputes Tribunal

The Disputes Tribunal (once called the Small Claims Court) is a very good way to make a claim against someone with whom you have a dispute. The tribunal is attached to the District Court.

The Disputes Tribunal can only hear claims up to $7500 in value, or up to $12,000 in value if both sides agree. A referee will hear both sides of the argument, allow some fairly informal discussion and try to get some agreement between the parties. If no consensus can be reached, the referee will make a ruling, on the basis of the law and fairness. No lawyers can be present at the hearing, although you may bring a support person.

The Disputes Tribunal cannot:

- Be used to simply recover a bad debt – there has to be some genuine dispute that needs to be resolved.

- Be used where there is a specialist tribunal (e.g. matters pertaining to tenancies or employment would be heard by the Tenancy Tribunal or Employment Relations Authority respectively) covering the area.
- Hear matters that are especially complicated (e.g. business goodwill, wills or intellectual property).
- Hear cases concerning matrimonial property, parenting, land ownership or criminal matters.

The most common claims at the Disputes Tribunal concern cars, damage to property (e.g. from a car crash), faulty goods and poor workmanship. The informality makes the tribunal easy for everyone to use and they do not have to follow the fine letter of the law. Sometimes the referee will have legal training, sometimes not. However, in all cases they will be respected members of the community and will have a good deal of common sense.

The kinds of orders that referees can make are:

- That one person pays the other some money.
- That work be done – i.e. repair faulty goods or correct poor workmanship.
- That an agreement is altered or cancelled.
- That the claim is dismissed.

If the order you get from a Disputes Tribunal hearing is not complied with, you can apply to the District Court to have it enforced. Note that it is up to you to initiate this – the court will not automatically check to see that a decision is obeyed.

The costs to take a case to the Disputes Tribunal are:

Claim up to $1000	$30 fee
Claim over $1000 but less than $5000	$50 fee
Claim over $5000 but less than $12,000	$100 fee

THE FINANCIAL SECRETS

- Know your rights and stand up for them – it's your money!
- Consumer law is strong in this country. Use it!
- You are always better to have an agreement in writing.
- Beware buying things simply because there is finance available on it. Hire purchase is easy to get, but it can be very expensive.
- Going to the Disputes Tribunal is a very cheap and easy means of resolving disputes.

CONNECT

- Ministry of Consumer Affairs, phone (04) 474 2750
  www.consumer-ministry.govt.nz
  www.consumerkids.govt.nz
- Commerce Commission
  phone (09) 377 7316, (04) 498 0911, (03) 371 1298
  www.comcom.govt.nz
- Department of Courts
  www.courts.govt.nz
- Consumers' Institute, phone 0800 266 786 (0800 CONSUMER)
  www.consumer.org.nz
- Community Law Centres (see your phone book)
- Citizen Advice Bureau (see your phone book)
- Disputes Tribunal – contact the District Court in your area
- Motor Vehicle Dealers Institute, phone 0800 108 106
  www.mvdi.co.nz
- Autocheck (to see if money is owed on a car), phone 0900 90 977
  (Calls cost $5 plus GST.)

8. TAX
Not a penny more, nor a penny less

Paying some tax is inevitable. The secret is to pay exactly the right amount of tax – not a penny more, nor a penny less.

Not a penny more, because paying too much tax is wasteful. You have no obligation to pay more than your share, and indeed should not do so.

Not a penny less, because to do so puts you at great risk. The Inland Revenue Department (IRD) has considerable power; it can (and does) charge hefty penalties for short payment of tax, which can result in your tax bill being far greater. In any event, you have a responsibility to pay your share.

Nevertheless, everyone should do what they can within the law to minimise the amount of tax they pay. To do this means understanding the tax system and taking good advice when necessary.

Tax is probably the most complicated part of financial planning – it can be very technical. If you are not sure about any aspect, consult a tax accountant. The amount you save in tax will probably far outweigh any fees.

> **THE IRD CHARTER**
>
> The IRD Charter states (among other things) that the department will:
>
> - be prompt and courteous, acknowledge cultural and special needs and follow through what it says it will do.
> - provide reliable information.
> - keep your affairs private and confidential.
> - apply the law consistently, so that everyone pays the right amount of tax.
>
> You have the right to question the IRD and staff will inform you on your options and work to get an outcome simply and quickly.

THE ROLE OF THE IRD

Although the IRD gives advice on tax policy to the government, it doesn't make the rules. The IRD merely administers tax law and ensures compliance. It is bound by the law just as you are, and you can appeal any of its rulings through the courts.

Your IRD number

A key part of the New Zealand system is that any income-producing entity (an individual, company, partnership or trust) becomes a taxpayer and therefore must have an IRD number. You apply for this number from the IRD, and once you have it, you have it for life (unless you go bankrupt). This means that any other new entity which will have income (e.g. a company you set up to trade or own investments) must apply for and have its own IRD number.

PERSONAL TAX IN NEW ZEALAND

New Zealand has a relatively simple graduated tax scale, with the rate increasing for each portion of income that falls within the levels set. Our current personal tax rates are:

Income Earned	*Tax Rate*
Under $38,000	19.5 per cent
$38,001 to $60,000	33 per cent
Over $60,000	39 per cent

While these tax rates apply to all personal income, there are low-earner rebates available. Note that these rebates apply only to income earned through wages and salaries. They do not apply if the income comes from interest, dividends or from a trust.

Tax returns

Most wage and salary earners are no longer required to file an annual personal tax return and the days of filling out an IR5 are gone.

Wage and salary earners pay tax through their employers, deducted as PAYE from their salaries before they are paid. If tax has been deducted at the correct rate – it usually is – and you have no other income or any allowable deductions, then you can relax.

However, the onus is on you to:

- Make sure your employer(s) has the correct tax code.
- Make sure your bank has your IRD number and deducts tax at the correct rate.

Some people, however, may be required to fill in an IR3. This includes those who:

- Are self-employed.
- Receive income from a business (this includes income from rental properties).
- Receive income that was not taxed at source.
- Receive income from overseas.

If you are unsure of your tax position, you can call the IRD and get a Personal Tax Summary (PTS). This is a record of your earnings and the tax you have paid. (In some circumstances it will be sent to you automatically.) Then you can work out whether you are due a tax refund or in fact owe tax. People who need to get a Personal Tax Summary from the IRD include those who:

- Want to claim expenses.
- Are children still at school who have worked part time and have had their income taxed.

- Have total income under $38,000 but who have received dividends taxed at 33 cents.
- Want to claim the under-$9800 rebate and have not used the ML tax code.
- Pay child support and have used the wrong tax code.

In addition, students with an interest write-off due on their student loan will be sent a PTS by the IRD together with an end-of-year repayment calculation form.

Rebates
There are tax rebates available for:
- Those who earned less than $9800 and worked 20 hours a week or more.
- Those who earned under $38,000.
- Those who are under 15 years old (or under 19 and still at school).
- Donations to charities (maximum rebate $500 pa, i.e. $1500 donated).
- Childcare or housekeeper (maximum rebate $310 pa, i.e. $930 spent).

To claim any of these you need to complete an IR526 form, but you don't have to complete a full tax return.

Minimising tax payable

Wage and salary earners
If you earn all your income from wages and salaries you can do virtually nothing to minimise your tax bills. In fact the only expense wage and salary earners can claim is premiums on loss-of-income insurance.

Investors and business owners
Those who receive some of their income from investments or through a business have much more scope to minimise their tax legitimately. These people can:
- Arrange their affairs so that they are tax efficient, being particularly careful about what sort of entity (company, trust or partnership) will own their investments or business.
- Claim any costs they incur to obtain their income.

SALARY SACRIFICE

Those who earn more than $60,000 pa will be taxed at the rate of 39 per cent on every dollar over $60,000. One of the things you can do to reduce the tax you owe is to ask your employer to divert some of your salaried income to a registered superannuation scheme. This will reduce your tax bill because the savings that go to the super fund are taxed at only 33 cents.

For example, if you have income of $70,000 pa, the last $10,000 of your salary will be taxed at 39 cents. If you ask your employor to divert this $10,000 to a super fund, that $10,000 will be taxed at 33 cents instead of 39 cents. This is a tax saving each year of $600.

The downside is that the money is now tied up for a minimum of two years. In addition, because your taxable salary is lower, any ACC payments may be affected, in that any claim will be based on the lower taxable income.

INVESTMENTS AND TAX

In a general sense, all investments are taxed in the same way. Investment income, whether it be interest, dividends, or rentals, is taxed in the hands of the owner. (In New Zealand capital profits are not usually taxed.) But there are some minor variations in application.

In order to avoid the top rate of personal tax (39 cents in the dollar) many investors own their investments through a company, which receives the income and pays taxes at a flat rate of 33 cents. This is only suitable for those with a total income over $60,000 since a company costs money to establish, must file annual returns and involves administrative time and effort.

Interest from deposits

Interest that comes from lending money to others (be it a bank or finance company deposit, family loan etc) is taxed. The Residents Withholding Tax (RWT) is usually applied, which means the interest is taxed at source and paid directly to the IRD. (RWT was brought in because many people were receiving interest from their bank or other sources and not declaring it.)

The financial institution paying the interest deducts tax at the rate of 19.5 per cent if it has your IRD number and 39 per cent if it does not. You can elect to have tax deducted at 33 cents if that is your top marginal rate. At the end of the financial year the institution will give you a certificate showing how much interest you have earned and how much tax has been withheld. If the amount of interest earned is over $200 and you have other income (probably from a wage or salary) you are required to request a Personal Tax Summary from the IRD.

All banks, finance companies and other professional borrowers will withhold tax and give you a certificate automatically.

Family and other less formal loans can be something of a problem. The general rule is that anyone paying more than $5000 in interest for a loan should withhold part of the payment and return it to the IRD.

> **RECORD-KEEPING**
>
> The onus is on you to prove that your tax returns are correct. This means that everyone, particularly someone in business or an active investor, must be able to show that any deductions claimed are accurate. If you cannot prove a claim, the IRD can (and probably will) disallow it. As well, it will charge penalties and use-of-money interest.
>
> You must therefore keep good records, including bank statements, receipts and invoices, records of wages paid to staff, stock lists, lists of debtors and creditors, interest and dividend notes and rent books.
>
> If the IRD assesses your tax it's up to you to show they are wrong, and this will be very difficult without good records.
>
> You are required by law to keep all financial records for a period of seven years.

Bonds

The interest from bonds (government stock etc) is taxed in the same way as any other loan. However, unlike most capital profits from shares and property, any capital profit from bonds is taxable. This could come about when interest rates fall. If you buy a 10-year bond that promises to pay interest of 7 per cent and then market interest rates fall to 6 per cent, someone will pay more for your bond to reflect that lower interest rate and you will be taxed on the profit you have made.

Shares

Dividends from shares are taxable but usually come with imputation credits. This means that tax has already been paid by the company concerned and the dividends are not taxed a second time in the hands of the shareholder. Capital profits from selling shares are generally not taxable provided you are not a share trader and have purchased shares with the intention of selling them at a profit.

See Shares and tax, pp.82-83

Property

The taxation of property investments can be quite complicated and most property investors should hire a good tax accountant to be sure that they are investing in the most tax-efficient way possible.

See Property investment and tax, pp.89-90

Offshore investments

Investments in offshore assets come under quite different rules, which can be complicated. Income from offshore is often treated in total as assessable income – imputation credits do not apply. This can result in double taxation: you invest in an Australian company, it pays a dividend to you from its tax-paid profit, then you have to pay tax again on that investment.

If the investment is in a 'Grey List' country (Australia, the UK, the US, Norway, Canada, Japan or Germany) there is usually no tax to pay on capital gains. These countries are judged to have tax systems sufficiently similar to New Zealand's and a tax treaty operates.

If you invest a sum greater than $50,000 in countries outside of the 'Grey List', the Foreign Investment Fund (FIF) regime will apply. This regime can be quite punitive. Any investment gains that you make will be taxed, and not only on investments that have been sold but also on unrealised gains. In effect, you need to value your investments each year and pay tax on any increase in value. Note that the value change is calculated in New Zealand dollars. That means that even though your investments have not improved in value during the period, if the New Zealand dollar has fallen, thus valuing your investments higher, you must declare and pay tax on that change in value.

BUSINESSES AND TAX

Companies pay income tax at a flat rate of 33 cents; there is no graduation of the rate. Other taxes to be aware of are the Goods and Services Tax and the Fringe Benefit Tax, and the payment of provisional tax.

Goods and Services Tax (GST)

The Goods and Services Tax is applied at the rate of 12.5 per cent on all goods and services sold in New Zealand. There are only a few exceptions. From a tax-efficiency point of view GST is a good tax because it is hard to avoid – there is a complete audit trail that can be followed relatively easily.

See GST exemptions, p.122

GST threshold

If in any one year the goods and services you supply are worth over $40,000 you must register for GST and put in returns at either one-monthly, two-monthly or six-monthly intervals, depending on the level of your annual turnover.

If your turnover is less than $40,000 you may choose to register for GST but you are not obliged to do so. Although doing GST returns is time-consuming, the fact that you can claim the GST on your expenses means it is often advantageous to register. You do so by filling in a form supplied by the IRD. You will then receive a GST number, which will usually be the same as your IRD number.

Charging GST on goods and services

As a GST-registered business you must include the tax in your prices, which should be advertised on a 'GST-inclusive' basis (or at least it should be very clear that your prices exclude GST). If you are not registered you cannot claim the GST you have paid, but nor do you have to charge GST and return it to the IRD. This means that your prices may be cheaper than a bigger competitor's, and you will keep more of the money you receive for your goods and services.

Claiming GST on expenses

You will have to return to the IRD all the GST you have charged to your customers. However, you will deduct from the amount owing any GST you have paid for your supplies. This reduces the amount of GST your business will pay, sometimes even resulting in a refund. To support your claim you must have GST invoices from your supplier showing:

- The name and of the supplier of the goods or services.
- The GST number of the supplier.
- The date of the supply or the tax invoice.
- The price of the goods.
- Whether the price is GST inclusive or exclusive.

GST demands good record-keeping since the whole system rests on those GST invoices. They provide an audit trail that makes the tax hard to avoid. In an audit the IRD may go to your suppliers and check that they have accounted properly for the GST that was charged to you and which you have claimed. Make sure you file all invoices safely so you can produce them when you are audited.

Apportioning GST

Sometimes you can claim only part of the GST from a supplier and have to apportion the GST you have been charged. One of the most common areas is in home-office expenses. If your business keeps an office at home you are able to claim part of the rates, insurance, electricity etc, and the same percentage of the GST on those supplies

GST exemptions

There are two classes of goods that are exempt from GST:

1. *Exempt supplies*

    The main exempt supplies are residential accommodation and financial services (i.e. the charging of interest). Businesses supplying these cannot charge GST on their prices and cannot claim the cost of their supplies. If your business is solely in one of these areas, you will not be able to register it for GST purposes.

2. *Zero-rated supplies*

    The main zero-rated supplies are exports and the sale of a business as a going concern. Exporters can register for GST and claim all the GST costs from their suppliers, but don't have to add the cost of GST to their export prices. If you sell your business or a division of it, you do not have to add GST to the price, even if you are GST registered.

GST returns

At the end of each period the IRD will send you a GST return to fill in and return (by the due date or penalties will apply). When you send back the return you enclose a cheque for the amount of GST payable. If you are eligible for a refund from the IRD you ought to receive this within 15 working days.

The GST return can be completed by most small business owners themselves, provided that they have a good book-keeping system and keep good records. Computer-based book-keeping systems such as MoneyWorks, Quicken and MYOB are fairly inexpensive and help make the return easy. You can also get help from the IRD if you need it. Some small business owners employ an accountant or book-keeper to do their returns for them, which is a good idea if you find book-keeping one of the less stimulating parts of running a business. On the other hand, doing your own book-keeping does give you very good immediate information on how your business is doing.

Fringe Benefit Tax (FBT)

Fringe Benefit Tax was introduced so that people could not take untaxed 'perks' from their employers in lieu of (taxed) salary. FBT taxes benefits received in the course of employment. The most common are:

- Motor vehicles.
- Low-interest loans.
- Free or discounted goods and services (e.g. a clothing manufacturer that allows employers to take some garments).

FBT is paid by the employer, who registers for it and puts in a return. The benefit is given a value and then taxed under a formula provided by the IRD.

Provisional tax

People on wages and salaries have their income tax deducted every pay period through the PAYE system. Companies, trusts and people in business or with investment income pay their tax for the past year in one lump sum (called terminal or residual tax) – or they would, if it weren't for provisional tax. Anyone who has over $2500 to pay in any tax year must pay provisional tax in the following year.

Provisional tax is an estimate of your next year's tax bill, split and paid in three instalments, on 7 July, 7 November and 7 March. Because you don't know for sure what your income or tax will be, your provisional tax is based on either:

1. The tax you paid last year plus 5 per cent.
2. Your best estimate of the year's income and the tax payable. If you underestimate the tax due you will have to pay interest on the shortfall. If you overestimate it the IRD will refund your money with interest, or you may put it towards any terminal tax or the following year's provisional tax.

You must pay terminal tax on 7 February for the previous year (i.e. for the year ended 31 March 2002 you will pay terminal tax on 7 February 2003). This is tax on your final income, less any provisional tax you have paid.

THINK POSITIVELY!

Most of us hate making cheques out to the IRD and the one sent off with the GST return is no exception: the expectation of a refund is much more pleasing. However, think positively. The fact that you owe the IRD money means two things:

1. You have probably received more money in the period than you have spent.
2. You have had the use, interest free, of the government's money during this time.

Frequent GST refunds might feel good, but they could mean that you need to take a closer look at your profitability – you are probably making a loss.

USE-OF-MONEY INTEREST

This is not really a penalty but rather reflects the fact that you have had the use of the IRD's money for a period. Interest applies to any unpaid tax at a rate that is set from time to time by the IRD in line with current interest rates.

Note that if you happen to overpay your tax, the IRD will pay you use-of-money interest.

INCOME SPLITTING

Because New Zealand has a graduated tax scale it is often advantageous to split a family's income among as many family members as possible. This has the effect of lowering the amount of income in the hands of each individual, who then pays tax at a lower rate.

For example, if an individual in a family company is earning $90,000 pa, the income between $60,000 and $90,000 will be taxed at 39 cents. However, if things can be arranged so that $30,000 of this income goes to another family member, the highest rate of tax payable will be 33 cents. The tax saving will be 6 per cent - i.e. $1800.

Income earned as wages and salaries is personal and cannot be assigned to or split with someone else. However, if you are in a business owned through a partnership, company or trust, you may be able to pay part of the profits to your spouse or partner, or in some cases to children.

In the case of partnerships and companies, income split this way must either be earned by way of work done or ownership of the business - i.e. you must be able to justify the income splitting. Trusts can split income to beneficiaries without justification (although any income that goes to beneficiaries under 16 years old will be taxed at the rate of 33 cents, which may be higher than their personal rate of tax).

THE STRUCTURE OF YOUR BUSINESS

There are different tax implications for each type of ownership structure and it is important to choose the one that best suits your purposes. Most people should take proper professional advice before setting up a business.

Broadly speaking, there are five legal entities through which you can trade:

1. Sole trader
2. Partnership
3. Limited liability company
4. Loss-attributing qualifying company (LAQC)
5. Family trust

Sole trader

This is when you own the business in your own name. Many sole traders set up another bank account, perhaps called 'Fred Brown, trading as Acme Cleaners'. This keeps finances separate, making book-keeping easier.

You don't need a new tax number – you use the one you've always had.

For tax purposes, all income goes into your own name and is added to any other income you might have. You are then taxed at the personal rate.

As a sole trader you can employ staff, which might include members of your family. However, the IRD will look hard at any income going to family members to make sure they have earned it through working for the business. Potential for income splitting is therefore limited.

Being a sole trader gives the least amount of flexibility for tax purposes and no asset protection at all. Most advisers regard it as the least advantageous way to trade.

Partnership

A partnership is when two or more people get together to trade as a business. Often this is just a husband and wife, although there are many professional partnerships (e.g. lawyers) with 50 partners or more.

A partnership gives some flexibility to split income because income can be taken from the partnership in proportion to either ownership or effort. This means a spouse can be given some income for tax purposes by virtue of being a partner and owner even though he or she does no work in the business.

Limited liability company

A limited liability company, so called because shareholders have no personal liability beyond the funds put in as share capital, is a completely separate legal and tax entity from its shareholders. As such it has its own IRD number and GST number (if applicable). Any debts are debts of the company, not its shareholders and directors, unless the company has been trading recklessly or they have agreed to guarantee the company's obligations personally.

Accounting costs will generally be higher for companies, because of the need to comply with various forms of legislation, but they do offer some tax benefits.

Shareholders who work in the company or are directors are often paid a salary once the company's profits have been calculated. The shareholders have the flexibility to decide how much profit they will take out personally (to be taxed at their personal rate) and how much will be left in the company (to be taxed at the flat rate of 33 cents in the dollar).

The company can also pay dividends to its shareholders out of tax-paid profit. This would come with imputation credits and would not be taxed a second time.

If, however, your company makes losses, you cannot offset them against your personal income. To do this your company has to be a loss attributing qualifying company.

Loss attributing qualifying company (LAQC)

You can elect to make your company an LAQC by notifying the IRD. To do so your company must have no more than five shareholders, all of whom are 'natural persons'.

In most respects an LAQC is like any other company. The big difference is that if it happens to make losses, those losses can be taken out by the shareholders personally, in direct proportion

---

WHAT IS A BUSINESS?

This may seem like an obvious question, but the issue is more complex than you might suppose. Whether or not you are 'in business' can make a big difference to the amount of tax you pay, so the question is clearly an important one.

There is no doubt that a large and profitable company is a business. But a small part-time consultancy may also be business, even though you still keep your day job. The acid test is whether the activity is *capable of making a profit* and the owners *have an intention* of so doing.

Consider these two examples:

1. You run six sheep on your two-hectare property and intend to make a profit from them. The IRD would argue that there is no realistic prospect of doing so: the operation is a hobby rather than a business.

2. Your hobby is gold prospecting but you never expect to make a profit from it. One day you stumble across a boulder-sized nugget. The profit from the sale of your gold would not be taxable because you never intended to make that profit.

If you are in business:

- You can claim any of the expenses necessary to obtain assessable income.
- The profits will be taxable.
- Any losses may be able to be offset against other income.

If what you are doing is just a hobby:

- The profits will not be taxable.
- You are not able to claim any expenses or deduct any losses.

BEING A SELF-EMPLOYED CONTRACTOR

With a top marginal tax rate of 39 cents on all income over $60,000, many high-salary earners choose to cease being employees in favour of trading through a company in order to pay a flat tax rate of 33 cents. These people often contract back to their previous employer, doing effectively the same job but as an independent contractor instead of as an employee. There are tax advantages:

- You should never have to pay more than the 33 cents in the dollar tax – the maximum companies pay.
- You can split out at least a small amount of income to your partner or other family members (e.g. pay a director's fee to your partner of a few thousand dollars a year), thus attracting an even lower tax rate for that portion of the income.
- You can change the ownership of the shares of a company reasonably easily, allowing you to pay more income to your partner as dividends.

However, there are two difficulties:

1. You will lose your entitlements and rights as an employee. You need to be sure that there is enough payment contracted to cover holiday pay, sick pay etc, which you no longer receive as part of a salary.
2. You will now be bound by the terms of the contract with your former employer and all the protection of employment law (regarding unjustifiable dismissal etc) will no longer apply.

Moreover, you cannot actually make this move purely for tax-saving purposes. The IRD scrutinises such arrangements carefully, looking to see if there is a genuinely independent relationship or whether you have simply entered into this arrangement as a tax-saving device. It will ask such questions as:

- Has there has been a previous employer/employee relationship?
- How integrated is the worker to the business?
- Is the worker responsible for the final product?
- Can the worker delegate or sub-contract out the work?
- Does he/she work or seek work with other clients?

If the IRD believes that the arrangement is a scam entered into for tax purposes, it will tax the income as if it were personal rather than company income.

to the amount of their shareholdings, and offset against any other personal income. This can be very advantageous, especially in the early years of a business when losses are quite common.

The big disadvantage of an LAQC is that if the company becomes insolvent and owes the IRD money for unpaid taxes, the IRD can go straight to the shareholders to recover this money. In this way, an LAQC represents something of a hybrid between a partnership and a company.

Family trust

Family trusts are taxed in much the same way as companies. Any income from a business or investments it owns is taxed at a flat rate of 33 cents.

There is, however, one important difference: the trustees of the trust may choose to pay out income to any of the beneficiaries of the trust. If they do so, that income is taxed at the beneficiary's own rate. This can result in a considerable tax saving if the beneficiary has little or no other income. There is no need for the beneficiaries to have worked for the income from the trust – they receive it because they are beneficiaries, not because they are workers or owners.

There some important points to note:

- The beneficiaries must be over 16.
- The low-income earner's rebate does not apply – therefore all income is taxed at at least 19.5 cents.

- The trustees must elect to distribute income to beneficiaries within six months of balance date. After that the income will be taxed as trust income.

WHAT CAN A BUSINESS CLAIM?
The general principle of the tax system for business owners is that they must pay income tax on the profit the business makes – i.e. after deducting from their income all the costs incurred obtaining that income. Some expenses are obviously not deductible. Private expenses such as food and clothing are not necessary for your business to obtain assessable income. Others are clearly deductible: employees' wages, advertising, stock purchases, rent, interest, accountants' fees etc. Some areas are less clear-cut:

Home-office
Generally the costs of maintaining your home are private expenses and therefore not deductible. However, most people in business work from home to a greater or lesser degree. They probably have an office, they may have clients and staff around and take telephone calls from there.

When you go into business, therefore, what was once solely your home becomes in part your office, and as such some of the costs of running it become deductible. This means you can claim a proportion of your rates, insurance, mortgage interest or rent, power etc. The proportion you claim depends on the proportion of the home you use for work and the amount of time you spend working there. For most business people, a claim of 10-20 per cent of the costs of your house is reasonable.

Motor vehicles
You can claim the cost of business-related expenses of your motor vehicle/s. There are several different ways you can claim and quite strict rules apply. Talk to your accountant to be sure you use the system that suits you best and gives you the greatest tax benefit.

Interest
Interest on money used to fund the operations of the business (to buy plant and equipment, property, working capital) is deductible. Interest on money borrowed for private expenditure (e.g. the home mortgage) is not deductible. However, you should note that it is the *purpose* of the funds that is important, not the security used. This means that you may borrow on the security of the house for business purposes and the cost of the loan will be deductible.

Entertainment

Generally you can claim 50 per cent of the costs of entertaining clients or associates. This is an area the IRD scrutinises quite carefully: it needs to be sure your claim for entertainment costs has a reasonable business purpose and benefit and that you are not simply claiming your costs of going out and having fun with friends.

Repairs and maintenance

The costs of repairing assets (buildings, plant and machinery, motor vehicles) are deductible, but improvement to capital items is not.

This can be a grey area. For example, someone who is in the business of renting out properties may need to put a new roof on one of the flats. If the new roof does not significantly improve the property it will be deemed repairs and maintenance and therefore deductible.

If, however, a brand new tile roof is put on to replace the old rusted iron one, the work will be deemed to be a capital improvement and will not be deductible. The general principle is that if the work done improves the property (or other asset), the cost is not deductible.

Depreciation

This is a non-cash expense that is nevertheless deductible. When you buy a capital item for over $200, the cost of that item is not deductible. However, it is recognised that the asset loses value over the years and you can claim for this depreciation every year.

The IRD sets depreciation rates according to what it deems the useful life of an item and produces a booklet setting out these out (covering everything from buildings to skeletons to electric typewriters).

Note that if you sell the asset for more than the value that you have depreciated it down to, you will have to pay tax on the 'profit', i.e. the difference in value.

TAX AUDITS

The New Zealand tax system is basically run by taxpayers themselves. The taxpayer does a set of accounts, fills in and files a tax return if necessary and pays the tax. However, just to make sure that taxpayers do this properly, the IRD periodically audits businesses and taxpayers to make sure.

Some audits are quite limited. The IRD may write to you asking for invoices for the travel you have claimed or want to look at documents relating to just one GST period. If everything is in order the audit will not go any further.

However, if anything untoward is found the audit may extend much more widely. The IRD has the power to look at all your business records and investigate the entire operation. This can involve inspecting your business premises, your home, all your assets and liabilities, and can extend far beyond the period initially selected. While a full audit is relatively rare, they do happen, and can take months or years. Few people report them as a fun experience.

Why me?
The IRD has a number of ways of selecting taxpayers for audit.

- *Chance*
  Quite simply, sometimes your number just comes up.

- *Inconsistencies*
  The IRD analyses businesses within industries and looks for irregularities – for example a particularly low gross profit compared with sales, or an especially high travel claim.

- *Tip-off*
  This is one of the IRD's richest sources of audit targets – a tip-off from a member of the public, disgruntled spouse or former business partner.

- *Industry audit*
  Sometimes the IRD will do an audit of all of the businesses within a particular industry. Some years ago all the rock bands in one of our cities were audited.

- *Flow-on from another audit*
  If the IRD is auditing one business, it may move on to audit a customer or associate of that business. For example, if a property developer sells a property to another business, the IRD might audit the buyer to check that the sale has been recorded consistently in both sets of books.

- *Your past record*
  If you have been caught out in previous audits you will find you are audited quite regularly.

EVADING, AVOIDING – OR GETTING IT RIGHT

Tax evasion

Tax evasion is about telling lies and hiding income. It is about knowingly failing to keep books or records, withholding information or providing false information. Tax evasion is against the law. Typically, tax evasion is things like taking cash straight from the till, doing contra deals (i.e. bartering your product for someone else's without declaring the profit), claiming personal expenses as business ones, falsifying invoices etc.

Tax evaders feel the full force of the law. The IRD has the ability to charge high financial penalties and publish the names of people caught evading tax in the *New Zealand Gazette*. Moreover, once you have been caught evading tax, the IRD will scrutinise your affairs carefully in the future.

Tax avoidance

Tax avoidance is also against the law. Tax avoidance is about arranging your affairs to directly or indirectly reduce or postpone tax. This means arranging transactions with no commercial basis so that they are really tax devices and shams. People who avoid tax are also subject to penalties.

Tax minimisation

Tax minimisation is legal. Minimising tax means arranging your affairs so that your business or investments are structured in the most tax-efficient way possible. It means knowing what you are allowed to claim and claiming that to the full.

THE FINANCIAL SECRETS

- Pay what you owe but not a penny more. It's *your* money!
- Taxation for wage and salary earners is straightforward. Most do not need to file a tax return.
- Tax is extremely complex. It is worth getting good advice because there is plenty of scope for savings.
- Having to pay a lot of tax is a good problem: it means you are making lots of money.

CONNECT

- Inland Revenue Department, phone 0800 257 777
  www.ird.govt.nz
- Institute of Chartered Accountants
  www.icanz.co.nz

BOOKS

- *Tax in New Zealand (rev. ed.),* Martin Hawes, Shoal Bay Press, 2004.
- The IRD produces a useful series of booklets on nearly all major tax issues.

9. RELATIONSHIPS
Sharing money

Money is one of the biggest causes of discord within relationships. It may be the lack of it, different priorities and attitudes to earning and spending it, arguments over the cost of presents for the children or financial help to one partner's parents or children by a previous relationship, issues of ownership and control – the list is endless.

And yet it is not something people talk much about. Certainly they do when the relationship fails, but not much before the relationship begins, nor during it. Somehow money discussion is just not 'nice', especially at the beginning of a relationship when everyone is convinced it will last for ever. It seems contradictory to discuss the possibility of breaking up just when you are getting together and one partner may see the broaching of the topic by the other as a sign of lack of commitment.

Talking about what will happen if the relationship fails seems to cast doubt on the quality of the relationship itself, and discussions about what is yours and what is mine don't seem right. Nevertheless, this is something you really need to tackle, especially if you have very unequal assets or incomes. Broach the subject as sensitively as you can with your partner, choosing your time and explaining calmly why any issues need to be discussed and agreed.

THE PROPERTY (RELATIONSHIPS) ACT
The Property (Relationships) Act came into effect on 1 February 2002. Its key points are:
- De facto couples are treated as if they were married, for property purposes. This includes same-sex couples.
- A relationship or marriage must have lasted at least three years for the property-sharing provisions to apply.
- The Act defines 'separate property' and 'relationship property'.
- The law works on the 'clean break' principle. One partner does not usually have to make ongoing maintenance payments to the other – on separation each takes a share of the family's assets and the couple go their separate ways.

WHAT IS A RELATIONSHIP?

In the past, courts have sometimes struggled to define whether a marriage is indeed a marriage. With de facto relationships now caught into the same law as marriages, it is likely that this question will arise more often. There may be arguments about the precise date the couple started to live together and therefore whether the relationship falls within the three-year timeframe or not. The following factors are used in assessing whether people are living together as a couple:

- Nature and duration of the relationship
- Nature and extent of a common residence
- Acquisition of property
- Whether or not a sexual relationship exists
- Degree of financial support or independence
- Degree of commitment to a shared life
- Care and support of children
- Performance of household duties
- Public presentation of the relationship, i.e. the way the couple hold themselves out to family and friends

There is nothing precise about these factors – each case will be judged on its merits with regard to the mix as a whole. While one or more factor may not be present, the others may be strong enough for a court to decide that the Act will apply. Given the amount of money that may be involved (and the intense feelings of the partners on separation) there will no doubt be plenty of work for lawyers.

Further points to note:

- If the relationship has not survived for three years, property is divided according to the contribution that each made to it.
- Generally, relationship property will be split 50/50. However, there are provisions within the Act that allow one partner to claim more when the other has greater earning power and that earning power was developed with the help of his or her partner.
- You can both agree to opt out of the Act, but both need to take legal advice.
- Pre-nuptial agreements will be more difficult to set aside, provided that they are properly entered into.
- Agreements that were entered into before 1 August 2001 will stand.

What is relationship property?

Relationship property is property that is intended for common use or benefit. The family home and chattels will thus always be relationship property, but family heirlooms and taonga are not. Investments may be relationship property if the income from them is used for the benefit of the couple. Only the proportion of superannuation schemes and life insurance policies that was contributed during the relationship is deemed to be relationship property.

See also Property sharing agreements, p.134

What is separate property?

Separate property is everything else. It includes assets that are owned by one partner and not intermingled. For example, an inheritance held separately by one partner will remain separate property. However, if it is used to repay a mortgage, pay family bills or to buy an asset that is used by the couple (e.g. a boat), it becomes relationship property.

The passing of the Property (Relationships) Act means that three groups of people in particular must think carefully about how they manage their money:

1. *Those currently living in de facto relationships.*
   There are about 250,000 people living as couples who, while not married, will have their property-sharing rights altered by the Act. These people need to reconsider their position, discuss it and take any necessary steps.

2. *Those who are considering going into a live-in relationship.*
   Very often these relationships do not start with a definite agreement to live together but rather the couple move in together gradually over time. If one partner moves into the other's house, that house could become the family home and therefore be relationship property and available for division if the relationship fails. The same applies to other assets used jointly.

3. *Parents with children who are in relationships or who might go into a relationship.*
   It has always been important for parents to think carefully about making gifts or inheritances to their married children, because these would often be available for division if the marriage failed. Now, however, an inheritance could become relationship property if your child is living with someone and the relationship breaks up.

   Suppose, for example, your son goes off to university and starts living with someone. If he received an inheritance or gift from you, and this money was intermingled and used jointly, or a house was purchased which the couple lived in, this would be considered relationship property and would be divided if they broke up, so long as they survived three years together.

   One option is to establish a trust so that children have the use of assets without ownership. This could be a family trust, formed during your lifetime, or a testamentary trust formed on your death.

   If you are concerned about this, you should at the very least talk to your children and make it known that you don't want to see your assets go to their partners.

PUT MONEY ON THE AGENDA

Everyone needs to think about money issues before they enter into a live-in relationship, whether it is a marriage or not. This is especially so with the advent of the Property (Relationships) Act, with its broad definitions of a relationship.

Younger people usually come into a relationship with a roughly equal amount of assets (often nil!), but older couples may well have quite unequal amounts. Hard though it is, people need to ask themselves the 'what if?' question and arrange their asset ownership with the possibility of eventual separation in mind.

Three groups may be particularly affected:
1. Those who have a relatively large amount of money.
2. Those who may receive a gift or inheritance at some point in the future.
3. Those with children from a previous relationship who want them to benefit from their assets.

There are two main ways to protect your assets so that they are not shared when a relationship fails: property-sharing agreements and family trusts.

Property-sharing agreements (pre-nuptial agreements)

You may opt out of the Property (Relationships) Act and agree between yourselves how your property should be divided. You can draw up a property-sharing agreement before a relationship or during it. However, it needs to be done properly. The agreement must:

- Be in writing.
- Be signed by both partners.
- Be witnessed by a lawyer.
- Have a certificate from the lawyer of each partner declaring that he or she has explained the effect and meaning of the agreement. Each partner must have had independent legal advice.

These safeguards are so that one partner cannot push the other into signing something that would be clearly disadvantageous. While you can agree whatever you want, the lawyers should point out any disadvantageous provisions.

Property-sharing agreements can be overturned only in limited circumstances. There needs to be serious injustice for one partner to be successful in having an agreement that was properly entered into set aside. Without any agreement, on the failure of the relationship, property will be shared according to what you agree at the time or in accordance with the Property (Relationships) Act.

You can agree to change your property-sharing agreement during the relationship.

> There is still some disagreement in legal circles as to whether property that is in trust may be considered to be relationship property. A trust may not completely protect assets when there is no property-sharing agreement. Nevertheless, holding separate property in a trust will certainly make it harder for a former partner to make a successful claim.

Family trusts

Family trusts have been called 'the coward's pre-nuptial agreement'. In effect, assets in a trust may be protected from a new partner or spouse because they are not personal assets (they belong to the trust) and therefore may not be considered relationship property.

Trusts are useful in this instance for people who:

- Have a large amount of assets.
- Have assets they don't want to go out of the family.
- Receive or expect to receive an inheritance or gift. This may mean asking your benefactors to change their wills so that the trust becomes the beneficiary of the will.
- Want to keep assets separate for children from a previous relationship.
- Are worried about their children's relationships. It may be better to have assets that would have gone to your children put into a trust so that the children have use and control over them, but not ownership.

Forming a family trust during a relationship can cause problems. When a trust is formed and jointly-owned assets are sold into it, the couple no longer owns them; they are owned and controlled by the trustees. Very often these trustees may be professionals (lawyer, accountant etc) or wider family members or family friends. Within the terms of the trust (as laid down by the trust deed), these trustees have wide powers and may deal with the assets as they see fit.

Problems have arisen where the trustees are particularly close to one family member. For example, a husband may persuade his wife that a trust is a good idea, set it up, and the couple sell all the family assets into it. The trustees are the husband's brother and an accountant whom the husband deals with on a regular basis. The assets are now controlled by his brother and his accountant and, because of their relationship with the husband, he has most influence over them. On the failure of the marriage the husband has effective control of what were the family's assets (family home, business, investments etc).

The Property (Relationships) Act deals with this problem and trusts formed within a marriage or relationship can be overturned if the trust arrangement has defeated one partner's claim on that property. Nevertheless, in order to overturn a trust and win back the assets, you may have to go to court – an expensive and time-consuming process.

Couples therefore need to be very careful when putting joint property into a trust. In particular:
- Both partners should receive independent legal advice.
- Trustees should not be aligned to just one partner.
- Both partners should have the same powers under the trust.

There is nothing to stop one partner putting separate property into his or her own trust. The best time to do this is before the relationship starts, but as long as it is clear that what is going into

> **BLENDED FAMILIES AND MONEY**
>
> There is great potential for disagreement on money within blended families. This can be for a range of reasons:
>
> - The partners have developed different attitudes towards money during their previous relationships.
> - They may have quite unequal amounts of income and assets.
> - The partners' ex-partners may or may not be contributing to the care of the children.
> - One (or both) of the partners may have spoiled the kids rotten after separation.
> - The children could have been brought up with different expectations about the amount of money available – and the use of it – within the family.
> - The children of one partner may be at a more expensive stage of their lives than the other's, or one may have special needs.
>
> Within a blended family there is often a lingering feeling that each parent will decide about money issues for his or her own children, and such decisions are often taken with little thought for how this may be received by the rest of the family. This can create all sorts of difficult situations, not the least of which is that one of the partners may be seen by the other's children as a new gatekeeper and a 'bad person'.
>
> Usually on separation adults have their children to themselves for a period, which means that they have been able to make financial decisions entirely independently. This changes when a new partner comes along and a family is blended.
>
> Because you are not starting from scratch, these issues need to be discussed. For example: 'My children have always had $5 pocket money a week and yours have had $20. How are we going to handle this?' The time to do it is *before* one of the children is making a ruckus about money. Decisions must be made and policies set at a quiet time devoid of any emotion (and squabbles) so that the parents can present a united front to the children.

the trust is truly separate property, it can be set up during the relationship.

ARRANGING INCOME: ONE POT OR TWO?

The first decision to make at the start of a new relationship is whether income will be shared or kept separate. One pot is the simplest way for a family to manage its money, and is probably still the most common. It requires just one bank account into which all the income is paid and the bills are paid out of this. The simplicity of this arrangement has much to recommend it. However, with the many different configurations of families now (especially blended families) and with many people going into relationships later in life with big differences in both income and assets, two pots need to be considered by many families.

If there are to be two pots, each partner will have to contribute to household expenses and care is needed to make sure that this is done fairly. It can be a good idea to set up a joint bank account (a third pot) for each partner to make regular payments into.

With partners keeping money separate, each will earn and save money at their own rate. This could see one partner become quite a lot better off than the other. Provided this is not intermingled with the relationships finances, it will remain separate property and therefore not be shared if the relationship or marriage fails.

The obvious danger with having only one pot, with both partners' income going into it, is that one partner may feel that the other is not contributing sufficiently, especially if one is not in paid employment. Similarly, one partner may be a bigger spender than the other, possibly because one has children from a previous relationship, or needs to help a parent or other family member, participates in an expensive sport, drinks or gambles or just likes to shop.

A less obvious (but nevertheless very real) danger is that one partner may end up controlling the family's finances and excluding the other. It is critical that both partners know what is happening with the relationship's finances and that both are involved in all major decisions. This is important regardless of who is earning the money. In fairness – and in law – the assets belong to both.

Failure to consult on money decisions is a recipe for disaster on two counts. First, the one who is excluded is likely to feel resentment. Secondly, if the relationship fails, that partner will be severely disadvantaged. He or she may not even know what the relationship owns or how the money has been spent, making it very hard to negotiate a reasonable settlement. This person will also struggle to manage money on becoming single.

Whether you have one pot or two is a decision only you two can make, but as a rule of thumb, the greater the disparity of income or spending, the more likely it is that two pots will work better.

Changing circumstances

Any relationship undergoes financial changes in fortune. For example:

- Incomes rise – or fall.
- One partner receives a gift or inheritance.
- One or both strike financial trouble.
- One develops a gambling addiction.
- One develops a shopping addiction.

Any of these factors will throw strain on the relationship that may or may not prove fatal.

WHEN IT'S OVER

Large numbers of marriages and relationships fail every year. When this happens, all aspects of the couple's life together have to be disentangled – and this includes their financial arrangements.

Dividing relationship or matrimonial property is often difficult, even when there is goodwill between partners. Where there is no goodwill (which is not unusual), the division can see protracted 'negotiations' degenerating into bitter acrimony and ending up in court. At the best of times separation will be stressful and it is during this time that you will need to do some of the most important financial negotiations of your life.

WARNING BELLS

When a relationship fails, people often look back and see that there were warning signs. Sad and strange though it sounds, a lot of people prepare for their separation, planning it to their best advantage.

Sometimes this planning involves hiding money from the other partner through a separate, private bank account or giving money or other assets to a friend to hold in trust.

A clue that this is happening might be when one partner's spending habits change. Previously generous people may become less so as they tuck money away for later.

The only cure is prevention: both partners should be involved in money management and know how all of the relationship finances are spent.

This can be particularly difficult for two reasons:

1. One of the partners may use the family's finances as a weapon in their separation. The separating couple may be arguing about a whole range of issues but one may feel they can hit the other hardest where it will hurt most – in the pocket.
2. Both of you are going to be considerably poorer than you are now – roughly half as wealthy. After a separation many people go from being financially quite comfortable to finding money a struggle. This can be especially difficult for the partner who has lower income-earning capacity.

Get good advice

When you separate your finances you will end up signing a property-sharing agreement. This is the final act in dividing your property and you will need a lawyer to certify that you understand the agreement and have been given proper legal advice.

However, there is much negotiation before this agreement is drafted, let alone signed. The time for good legal advice is not on signing the agreement but right at the beginning.

You need to know your rights and make sure you are not disadvantaged. The best way to be sure of this is to see a good family lawyer who is experienced in relationship property issues. And make it soon – ideally on the day your separation looks certain.

Be wary of depending upon family and friends for advice on this area – these people will probably not be experienced and skilled in relationship property matters, particularly the implications of the new legislation. In any event they may not be unbiased – they may be caught up in the emotional whirl of the separation. A good lawyer will cost you – but not as much as not knowing your rights, negotiating badly and settling softly. If you think a professional is expensive, just wait until you deal with an amateur.

The negotiation process

These negotiations (a benign word that does not really describe what often happens) are difficult and present some great challenges. In a worst-case scenario:

- One partner may be significantly advantaged in the final division.
- Children and other family members may become involved.
- Emotional damage to one or both of the partners results in nervous breakdown, health problems and/or job loss.
- Your negotiations end up in the Family Court.

Common difficulties faced by couples negotiating a separation and division of property are:

- One partner has better financial or business contacts so the negotiations are by no means between equals.
- One can't afford a good lawyer or accountant.
- One partner is far better informed about the family's financial position – and possibly on money matters in a general sense.
- There may be an emotional or sentimental attachment to assets. This may see one partner giving away more than necessary in order to obtain ownership of a desired asset.
- There may be major differences in opinion on what assets are worth. Some assets are easy to value (listed shares, unit trusts, cash etc) while others are much harder (family businesses, heirlooms). If in any doubt at all, get in a valuer.
- Each partner knows the other's strengths and weaknesses very well. One partner may be reluctant to use this knowledge; the other may not hesitate to do so.
- One partner feels guilty about the breakdown of the relationship and to atone for this will settle softly. The other partner may exploit that guilt to advantage.
- There is simply not enough in the way of assets to allow the couple to enjoy the standard of living to which they have become accustomed and to rebuild their lives.

A good lawyer can resolve many of these difficulties. This is obviously going to be expensive, but not as expensive as being manipulated out of things that are rightfully yours.

Going to court

This is not desirable, but sometimes there is simply no choice. Going to court will quite probably cost in the $5-10,000 range and it could be more. Nevertheless, that cost may pale into insignificance if you are dividing assets worth tens or hundreds of thousands of dollars.

In some cases going to court may be the only way to ensure you get your fair share. It is a backstop for people who feel disadvantaged in their negotiations because you know that by going to court you will get a fair outcome.

Relationship property cases are heard in the Family Court, which is less formal than other courts – there are no wigs and gowns and the atmosphere is more welcoming. The cases are not open to the public or media and the names

---

LEGAL AID

If you can't afford a lawyer you may get legal aid for resolving your relationship property division. You apply to the Legal Services Board, which conducts an income and asset test to see whether you are eligible. The form is rather daunting, with several pages of questions about your personal and financial situation.

Legal aid is not easy to get but if it is granted, it can be a huge help. It may pay your full legal costs, or you may be asked for a contribution. Be aware, though, that legal aid is in some cases more of a loan than a grant. If you have assets or end up obtaining assets from the division of your relationship property, you will have to repay most (if not all) of what you have been granted. The Legal Services Board may require some sort of security over your property to make sure that you repay the amount that you do owe.

of the parties are never disclosed. While a few more complicated cases may end up in the High Court, all start off in the Family Court.

However, before you get your day in court, there will be months or even years of filing documents, swearing affidavits, discovery of documents and a settlement conference. This last is a kind of mediation – an attempt to help the partners sort out their differences without a full hearing. This conference is off the record and anything you say cannot be used in the main hearing. Nevertheless, many people find it quite difficult and take their lawyer with them.

Courts can be asked to:
- Divide the property of the relationship.
- Set the value of a particular asset or assets.
- Determine whether particular assets are relationship or separate property.
- Sell property.
- Divide property, taking into account that one of the partners has recklessly run down its value.

The Property (Relationships) Act has a new provision that allows a court to award one of the partners a share of the property greater than 50 per cent where that partner has helped advance the career of the other. In many cases one partner has stayed at home (to the detriment of their own career) while the other has increased their earning capacity. The courts now have the power to make a greater award of the relationship's assets to the one whose career has not been advanced, in view of their reduced earning capacity.

Statistics show that women are often financially disadvantaged following separation – their finances do not recover as well as those of men. They may have let their work skills and employability lapse while they have been looking after the children, and often continue to be the primary caregiver after the separation, which can limit their opportunity to work.

Going to court is time-consuming and expensive, but don't reject the idea out of hand. Those who feel disadvantaged in any way should discuss it with their lawyers; court may be the only way you can get what is rightfully yours.

Adjusting to a new life

As you settle into your newly single state you will need to make a number of financial adjustments to the way you live. For a start:
- *Do a budget*
  There will probably be less income coming into the household and you will have to cut your cloth accordingly. One of the

worst things that you can do financially after separation is live beyond your means – if you do, your finances will go backwards even further. In particular, avoid costly housing – a high mortgage or very high rent will hold you back more than anything.

- *Develop work skills*
  You are on your own now and are going to have to depend on what you can earn. The best way to increase earning power is through the development of work skills. Get them up to speed as quickly as you can.

- *Build a network of contacts within your occupational area.*
  If you have been out of the workforce, you may have to build this network from scratch.

- If you feel financially vulnerable, promise yourself that you will never allow yourself to get into this position again.

CHILD SUPPORT

Parents have an obligation to support their children. Indeed, in separation cases, society and ultimately the courts regard the welfare of children as paramount.

The New Zealand system of dividing property on separation works on the principle of a clean break – the assets are divided and one does not have to pay maintenance to support the other. However, he or she does have to help support the children.

This generally means a non-custodial parent pays money to the custodial parent. This child support is payable if a child is under the age of 19 years and is living with the person claiming it. It is not payable if the child:

- marries
- lives with someone else
- is financially independent
- is on a Student Allowance or benefit
- is employed for more than 30 hours a week.

Calculating the amount payable

The amount of child support varies and will be set in one of three ways:

Voluntary agreement

Provided that the custodial parent is not on a benefit, you two can agree to any amount to be paid. You can, if you wish, register your agreement with the IRD, which will then collect the money and pass it on, or you can pay and collect the money directly yourselves.

> **ADMINISTRATIVE REVIEW**
>
> If you think you have special circumstances and the formula adopted (*see right*) gives an unfair result, you can apply to the IRD for an administrative review. Grounds for such a review may be high travel costs to get to the child, special needs of the child or very high income of one of the partners. There are no grounds based on an inability to pay.
>
> The review is a fairly informal process – no lawyers are allowed to be present. The IRD will take a look at the total situation and make an assessment on what it thinks is fair and just, then give a written decision to both partners, usually within three weeks. If you disagree with the decision you can apply to the Family Court for a departure order, although this will probably involve your lawyer and will therefore be quite expensive.

Court order

You may get a court to stipulate the amount of child support that your partner should pay. This will obviously be expensive and time-consuming and would usually only happen when a court is dividing a couple's relationship property. Any court order can be registered with the IRD, which will then collect the money.

Application to the IRD

You fill in an application form and the IRD does the rest. This is what happens if the custodial parent is on a benefit. The IRD will contact your partner, assess the amount that is payable and collect it. In assessing the amount payable, the IRD follows a three-step process:

1. It ascertains the amount of assessable income the liable parent has.
2. It assesses a 'living allowance' based on the liable parent's circumstances, to a maximum of two and a half times the average wage.
3. It takes into account whether or not the non-custodial parent has other dependants.

The IRD produces a booklet that sets out a living allowance for different circumstances, based on the rate of WINZ benefits.

The balance (taxable income less the living allowance) is then multiplied by a factor determined by the number of children, to calculate the amount of child support payable. The minimum is $12.75 per week.

MONEY AND CHILDREN

Children and money are the two greatest areas of disagreement within families. When you put them together (money and kids) the stage is set!

Perhaps this is most difficult in a blended family. Equity issues can arise if one partner's children requires more support than the other's, or if large amounts of money are going to a former partner to pay for child support. This is a situation where it is often better to keep money separate, having two pots instead of one.

Another common difficulty these days is that children often stay at home longer than they used to or, having left home, return to live with their parents again (the 'boomerang generation'). Children are often trying to save money to reduce or avoid student loans and it is just so much easier (and cheaper) to hang out with Mum and/or Dad. Depending on family circumstances, it is often quite reasonable to ask the 'child' to contribute towards household expenses or to pay board.

In any family, children will cost. There are the usual things of course – food and clothing in particular. However, there are some other things to consider:

Education costs

A good education is so important that many parents resolve to make sure they have the money to fund it. To this end you may want to fund:

- Private school fees
- Special education – e.g. music lessons
- Tertiary fees

These can add up to considerable amounts of money. You may decide to provide for this by:

- *Setting up a dedicated bank account or set of investments.*
  This is relatively cheap and easy and has the added advantage that you could divert the money for other things if you had a financial emergency. But this ability can be a double-edged sword. Be careful you don't end up frittering the money away.

- *Establishing a trust for educational purposes.*
  This will cost around $500 to set up and a bit more to administer. But the advantage of a trust is that there is an imposed discipline – no one can use the funds for anything but education. The other advantage is that the children's grandparents or other family members may be persuaded to contribute.

Children with special needs

Children with special needs generally cost more. Thought also needs to be given to what would happen to that child if you and/or your partner died.

Many people who have children with special needs set up a family trust for their benefit. An alternative is a testamentary trust – a trust formed on your death.

COMING INTO MONEY

You need to think carefully about when your children might receive lump sums such as inheritances or distributions from trusts. Young people are often not able to handle a large lump sum responsibly, and without a clear plan, capital can be frittered away.

It is often a good idea to make it a term of your will that funds are not distributed in full until they have reached the age of, say, 25 or 30. Your will may establish a testamentary trust, which allows for the keep of the children and meets the costs of their education, but permits no major distribution of capital either until they reach a particular age or until some specified occurrence (e.g. marriage or the attainment of a qualification).

Lump sums received by children are not able to be used by the parents for paying everyday expenses (unless this is specified by the donor). The money belongs to the child who can (depending on the terms of the gift or inheritance) use it how he or she wants. The parents, on the other hand, still have an obligation to care for their children – no matter how rich they might be!

If your child does receive a large lump sum, you might try to encourage him or her not to race out and spend it all at once. This may not, of course, be easy. However, if you could get the child to put the money away into a long-term investment (say, for 10 years), they may not miss it and it could be worth a considerable amount on maturity. Alternatively, you might encourage the child to split the money, spending some now while putting the rest away in a long-term investment.

This will mean that the other children get less – or no inheritance at all. Make sure this is discussed within the family so that all members are comfortable with the arrangement.

Pocket money

Most people give their children pocket money. The age at which this starts varies from family to family, but the important thing is that the child is old enough to take responsibility for the money and look after it. One of the positive effects of pocket money is that children learn to budget and to make sure the money lasts until they get some more.

Weekly is best to start off with – it is hard for small children to plan for much longer. As the child gets older you may extend the period so that you give pocket money fortnightly or monthly so they learn to budget and plan for a greater time period.

You need to come to some agreement as to what the child is expected to pay for out of his or her own money, and give a fair and realistic amount to cover these expenses. A small child may get only a small amount, sufficient to buy a couple of little treats during the week, whereas teenagers could be given much more, on the understanding that they will be expected to buy their own clothes (apart from school uniforms), for instance.

Once you have given them their pocket money that should be it until next payday. Children learn a bad lesson if you break the rules – in money matters as in others.

THE FINANCIAL SECRETS

- ❏ You cannot ultimately avoid discussing money within your relationship. Better to do it early, *before* it causes any problems.
- ❏ It is easier to deal with your property at the beginning of a relationship (when you are still in love) than it is at the end.
- ❏ If your relationship fails, get good legal advice regarding your property and your rights.
- ❏ Think about how the Property (Relationships) Act might affect you or other members of your family.
- ❏ Both you and your children need to know how gifts and inheritances may be treated within a relationship.

CONNECT
- Citizens' Advice Bureau (see your local phone book)
- Community Law Centre (see your local phone book)
- Legal Aid/Legal Services Agency (see your local phone book)
- Inland Revenue Department (for Child Support information) www.ird.govt.nz
- Justice Ministry (for Property (Relationships) Act information) www.justice.govt.nz
- Work and Income New Zealand (for information on benefit eligibility) www.winz.govt.nz

BOOKS
Family Trusts (rev. ed.), Martin Hawes, Shoal Bay Press, 2001
For Richer, For Poorer, Maria Konings & Deborah Hollings, CCH NZ, 2001
How Money Comes Between Us, Rhonda Pritchard, Tandem Press, 1999
Relationship Property – A Guide to the Law (Justice Ministry)

10. HOUSING
Your home, your castle

Most Kiwis want to own their own home – we have one of the highest home ownership rates in the world. Coupled with the idea of having our own quarter-acre paradise – even though the quarter acre might have changed to 800 square metres, or become somewhat smaller – is the notion that home ownership is one sure way to get ahead. This has been underlined by the boom in property prices in the last couple of years.

We have all heard the stories: 'I bought this house for $70,000 about 20 years ago and now it is worth $400,000.' Many of us did experience a time when the value of real estate soared, along with inflation. As well, we are practical people, and many of us enjoy knocking out the odd wall, mixing concrete and applying a coat of paint (or removing layers of paint on our way to restoring an old villa). For many of us 'home improvement' is as much a hobby as a necessity. We want the freedom to modify and create our own 'nest', and one day we anticipate a reasonable financial return for our efforts.

House ownership has many benefits:
- It gives a sense of permanence that is important to most families.
- It enforces a saving plan: repaying the mortgage provides a discipline that many people need.
- It provides a natural hedge against any future large increase in housing costs. It may be that inflation does get away again one day, which would be bad news for people who are renting.
- It gives you control over your own environment. You won't have the landlord asking you to move on when he or she has other plans for the property.

Statistics suggest, however, that in recent years there is a trend in New Zealand towards renting rather than buying our houses or apartments. In today's busy world many people no longer have the time or the inclination to potter around the house on DIY projects. In our larger cities, apartment living is gaining in popularity – to some an inner-city 'pad' is more convenient and appealing than the prospect of being tied to perpetual house and garden maintenance somewhere in the suburbs. And at a time of booming house prices young people find it hard to save for a deposit. This is, in part at least, exacerbated by the fact that many people are trying to pay off quite substantial student loans,

TO RENT OR TO BUY?

For practical purposes there are two groups of people who would certainly be better to rent rather than buy their homes. These are people who:
- Are likely to be transferred for work purposes around the county quite often. The costs of buying and selling houses are high (real estate agents' fees, lawyers etc) and if you have to shift often these costs will soon negate any increase in value.
- Like to shift a lot. There are people who simply get sick of living in the same house and who like to move often to greener pastures. They should rent rather than buy for the same reasons.

There is, of course, no reason why people in these categories should not still own property as an investment, but they should consider buying in one of the larger cities, which tend to show more growth than smaller rural centres. While this will not give them some of the advantages of home ownership (e.g. a sense of permanence) it will be a significantly better financial arrangement than forever buying and selling in different markets. It may even give them a base to retire to.

BUYING A HOUSE

Buying a house and taking on a mortgage is likely to be the biggest financial commitment you will ever make (although saving for your retirement may run it close). Big money is involved and there is considerable scope for making costly mistakes. Conversely, there is scope for doing things well and getting ahead financially. If you are planning to buy your first house, don't let the excitement cloud your judgment or push you into acting too quickly. This is something to be taken slowly, so that you don't learn the hard way.

See The monkey on your back, pp.57-66

> **VALUE FOR MONEY?**
>
> There is considerable disparity in the value of housing in New Zealand, depending on where you live. In Invercargill $200,000 will buy you twice, even three times the house that you would get in Auckland. But there's a trap. Many people have moved to a small town, bought a house there and then found it too expensive to move back to the city. If you can, hold on to the house in Auckland, and perhaps rent in the small town. This way you are dealing in only one real estate market and your asset gains or losses are in proportion to others about you.

The house you want

Sometimes you get the house you want easily. It may be that a house in your neighbourhood that you have always admired comes up for sale or shortly after you have started looking, or you walk into a house that is for sale and it just feels right.

More often however, finding the right house comes only after a long search. This can be very time-consuming. To save time and increase the chance of finding the property you want, it pays to list your requirements in priority order. You probably won't get a place that has everything you want so you need to work out what is essential and what is not. Consider these factors:

- location
- number of bedrooms
- section size
- privacy
- sun
- views
- transport
- garage
- state of repair
- maintenance required
- proximity to schools
- proximity to shopping
- noise

Some of these will be non-negotiable for you, while others will only be on your wish-list.

What can you afford?

Two things are important here:

1. *The size of your deposit*
   A few lenders will lend to 95 per cent of the house's value but up to 85 per cent is more common. The amount of house that you can afford will therefore be dictated by how much you have managed to save.

2. *The size of your income*
   Most lenders will want to see no more than 30 per cent of your income going to mortgage repayments. This also limits what you can borrow and therefore how much you can spend.

See Getting a loan, pp.53-56

See How much can you borrow? p.59

If you are a couple and both working you might be tempted to use your combined income to meet high mortgage and principal repayments. If you are thinking of this consider what your position will be if you lose one income for some reason.

> **SELLING YOUR OLD HOUSE AND BUYING A NEW ONE**
>
> Sometimes it's harder to sell your home than you expected. You find the perfect house to buy, but your old house is still sitting unsold. Unless you have enough money simply to buy the new house outright and then take your time selling you have a timing problem. There are choices:
>
> - *Wait until you have sold your existing home before you start looking to buy.*
>
>   This puts you in a strong position as a cash buyer, but the difficulty is that once you have sold you may have only a few weeks to find a new one. If the right house doesn't appear in that time you will be forced to rent in the meantime, or will feel pushed into buying a place you don't really want.
>
> - *Buy a new house conditionally, then put your existing one on the market.*
>
>   You make the purchase conditional on a sale. The problem is that the vendor of the new house will probably limit the time you have to sell and may insist on a cash rollover clause (*see p.153*), possibly forcing you into a rushed sale at a lower price than you wanted.
>
> - *Arrange bridging finance.*
>
>   This is temporary finance that allows you to buy the new house while you still own the existing one. This costs, of course, and the cost continues while your existing house remains unsold. If it does not sell easily this can put you under considerable financial pressure. Bridging finance is only available to those who have a lot of equity in their existing house and sufficient income to meet two lots of mortgage payments. The interest rate charged is likely to be a little higher than for an ordinary home loan.
>
> There is no one correct path. What you do will depend on a range of factors:
> - Whether you have already identified the new house you want to buy
> - The state of the property market
> - Your financial position
> - How much you want or need to move

In any event it's not worth being impatient and trying to buy a house that will limit your lifestyle or other financial plans because of high mortgage repayments. People often get into trouble by being too ambitious; they end up having to sell the house because the repayments are too difficult. You are better to wait a bit and save some more or buy a more modest home.

Real estate agents

When you respond to a real estate agent's ad they will be only too

> **HOW TO FIND YOUR HOUSE**
>
> The obvious place to start is by looking in the newspaper, local property magazine or in real estate agents' windows. You could also try:
> - Putting leaflets in letterboxes in the area you want to buy in.
> - Knocking on the door of a house you especially like and asking if they will sell.
> - Telling your friends and family that you are looking.
> - Using the Internet, which has several sophisticated sites, some of which include the opportunity to take a 'virtual tour' of chosen houses. (See www.realenz.co.nz)

happy to show you that particular house – and will waste no time trying to sell you any number of other properties on their books.

Make sure you brief the agent well or you could end up spending many stressful and depressing hours driving around town viewing houses that are clearly unsuitable. Give the agent your list of 'must haves' and tell them not to show you properties that don't have them. Don't allow them to persuade you that 'you really should see this one. It only has two bedrooms but it has a lovely garden.' If you need three bedrooms then your viewing that house is going to waste everyone's time.

No matter how friendly the agent is, understand that he or she is not working for you. Real estate agents' duty of care is to their client: they almost always work for and are paid by the seller of the house.

Ways to buy

There are three ways to contract for the purchase of a house:

Private treaty

This does not necessarily mean a private purchase where no agent is involved. What it means is that the sale and purchase is negotiated between the parties (buyer and vendor) privately, not at an auction. Most commonly, these negotiations are carried out with an agent involved, who takes offers and counter-offers between the two sides. This process can take days or weeks as the parties finally agree – or not, as the case may be.

All contracts to buy and sell property must be in writing. Typically what happens is that you will put in an offer to purchase, the vendor will change some item on the written contract (usually upping the price you offered, or altering the settlement date), initial those changes and then send the contract back to you via the agent. You in turn may cross out the vendors' change and write your own counter-offer in. The agent is talking to each of you and trying to get agreement. The important thing is that there is no contract until all of the points have been agreed in writing. Until that time, either side can walk away and discontinue negotiations.

Public auction

More houses are now marketed and sold at public auction than ever before. There is nothing to stop you putting in an offer prior to the auction but it will usually have to be an unconditional cash offer. This is because sales at auction are unconditional and few vendors will want to agree ahead of auction to a conditional sale that means withdrawing the property from the market.

The trouble with making an offer before an auction is that you show your hand. The vendor may decline your offer and wait for auction day, thinking that then you will probably bid a bit higher.

Most properties at auction have a reserve price. If the bids do not reach the reserve, the property is passed in and the vendor's agent will hope to negotiate a sale privately. When you start bidding you won't know the reserve, but the auctioneer will usually advise bidders if the reserve has been reached.

If your bid is accepted you have contracted to buy the house unconditionally. That means you must have your finance arranged and have checked out the house thoroughly beforehand. Once the hammer falls, you are committed to the purchase and have to pay a 10 per cent deposit.

Bidding at an auction is hard for a lot of people. The biggest risk is that you'll get carried away in the excitement and bid more than you had ever intended. So before you start, write down the maximum you are prepared to pay, and *don't* go over it. If you are tempted to, perhaps ask the auctioneer to give you a couple of minutes to discuss things with your partner.

Tender

This is the least common form of property sale and purchase. Most tenders have a closing date and you have to have your offer in by then. The difficult thing as a prospective purchaser is that you have no idea what others are likely to offer. You therefore have to tender your best offer – the most you are prepared to pay. Only the vendor sees the other offers, and does not have to accept any of them.

A conditional offer is less likely to be accepted than an unconditional one, even if the price is a bit higher.

If no tenders are received or none is acceptable to the vendor, the property will usually be put on the market by way of private treaty. Many people think this is a better way to buy and so withhold a tender in the hope that the property comes back on the market.

Contracts

All contracts for sale and purchase of real estate must be in writing – you cannot have a verbal agreement. New Zealand is unusual in that real estate agents generally draw up and attend to the signing of contracts. In most countries this is done by lawyers. Although this speeds up the negotiating process and cuts costs, there can be difficulties. Our system means that often neither the purchaser's nor the vendor's lawyers have looked at the contract before it is signed – and of course once it is signed it is binding. You must make sure the contract says and means what you think it does, and if you're in any doubt, call a lawyer and check it out.

The main points in real estate contracts are:

- Price
- Vendor's name
- Purchaser's name
- Legal description of the property (from a rates demand)
- Possession date – the day you pay for the house and are given vacant possession and a set of keys
- Interest rate for late payment
- A list of chattels that are a part of the sale (carpets, dishwasher, drapes etc)
- Any special conditions
- Name of the agent organising the sale (most important to the agents themselves as they want to ensure they get paid)

Most of the other clauses are fairly standard and only usually come into play if something extraordinary happens (e.g. you fail to settle or the house burns down before possession date).

Conditional contracts

Most contracts have special conditions that need to be satisfied before the sale will definitely go ahead. Mostly, these are for the benefit of the purchaser, allowing an out from the sale should certain requirements not be satisfied. The most usual special conditions are:

- *Finance*

    Most conditional contracts are subject to the purchaser arranging 'suitable' finance. Usually you will be given seven days for this although you might ask for longer. This clause will almost always allow you to escape the contract if you need to.

- *Maintenance inspection*

    This gives you a chance to check that the property is structurally sound and in good repair. The cost will depend on how detailed you want the report to be. Talk to a builder or engineer about this, or your agent or lawyer might be able to come up with a name.

- *Land Information Memorandum (LIM)*

    This gives you a period of a week or two to ask your local authority for a LIM. The LIM will tell you things like whether the property has ever been flooded and whether there have been past applications for building permits.

- *Sale of your own property*
  This is a common clause, although for obvious reasons most vendors don't like it. If they think you are unlikely to sell your house within a month or so they will often try to get a 'cash rollover' clause inserted in the contract.

- *Cash rollover clause*
  Unlike most other special clauses, this one is put into contracts for the benefit of the vendor. A cash rollover clause says that if the vendor receives a cash offer before your contract becomes unconditional, which is at the same price or more than yours, he or she can give you a set time (usually only a day or two) to declare your offer unconditional or void the contract. This is tough on buyers but has become a common feature.

- *Lawyer's approval*
  Be aware that if you make the contract conditional upon your lawyer's approval, the only out is if the lawyer finds a problem with the title.

Talk to your lawyer

Once your contract is agreed and signed, make sure your lawyer gets a copy. Usually the real estate agent will organise this. Some people get their lawyer to look at the contract before it is signed, although in most straightforward purchases with an escape clause or two (e.g. a finance clause) this is not usually necessary.

Your lawyer will check the property's title to make sure there are no difficulties with it and then discuss with you the special clauses in the contract and how they are going to be satisfied.

Once you have a suitable offer of finance and have satisfied yourself with the LIM and maintenance report (and any other special conditions), your lawyer will write to the vendor's lawyer declaring the contract unconditional. At this point the contract is binding and you must go ahead with the purchase. When the contract becomes unconditional, you will usually have to pay any deposit that is stipulated in the contract.

Your lawyer will now arrange settlement and the conveyance of the property from the vendor to you on the possession date agreed. He or she will ensure that you become registered on the title as owner, and the lender is registered on the title as mortgagee. He or she

---

Building permits are important because their existence guarantees that any major renovations or additions made to a house are legal. Building permits are issued by the local council, which then checks to ensure that the work is carried out to a proper standard. While it is obviously to your advantage to be assured, for example, that the new deck is strong enough to hold a number of people or that the excavations under the house have been served with adequate drainage, there are other implications. When it comes time for you to sell the house, your purchaser may insist that you get a permit for the unpermitted work done. Then the council might require you to make substantial and costly modifications to bring the work up to standard or, in a worst-case scenario, to remove the deck altogether.

THE COST TO BUY

In addition to the purchase price you will incur other costs for which you should budget. Approximate costs are listed below, but these can vary greatly and you should always ask:

- Lawyer: $500 (perhaps $100 more if there is to be a mortgage)
- Valuer: $300
- LIM: $100
- Maintenance report: $200
- Mortgage application fee

will arrange the transfer of funds, and will apportion rates and any other expenses that the vendor has pre-paid, so that you pay the proportion that applies from possession date.

It is possible do all of this without a lawyer but in the vast majority of cases it is better to have one involved. The New Zealand system of land registration and transfer is very efficient and your lawyer's cost will not be great. Doing it yourself can be very time-consuming and does not give the protection that a lawyer does.

Most lawyers charge a standard fee for a straightforward sale and are happy to give you a quote.

Means of ownership

See Ownership of assets, p.198

Before the property is transferred, you will have to decide how the property will be owned. (The ownership structure may have other quite far-reaching implications.) The property might be owned by:

- You personally
- You and your partner/spouse together (see below)
- Your family trust
- Your company

If the house is to be owned by you and your partner together, there are two main options:

- *Joint ownership (often called joint tenancy)*
  This means you own the property together and if one of you dies that share automatically passes to the other.

- *Tenants in common*
  This means you each own an agreed share of the house and if one of you dies that share passes to the beneficiaries of the estate (who may, of course, be the other part-owner).

SELLING A HOUSE

Selling your house and shifting can be a very stressful time. Selling lacks the excitement of buying, with its prospect of a nice new place to live; it is just a lot of headaches. You seem to be continually tidying up the house, dealing with agents, waiting for a buyer, negotiating, waiting for the contract to go unconditional ... Throughout the process you worry whether you'll get the price you expect, and frequently realise the disappointment that you won't.

Selling the house is a moment of truth. You have always believed that it had a certain value, and now you are putting that to the test. Given that for most of us our house is our most valuable asset, it is a very important test.

There is a great deal of cost involved in selling your house.

1. First is the obvious one of getting the price you are hoping for. Even a small percentage reduction in price can mean a lot of money in absolute terms. For example, if you think your house is worth $200,000 and you get just 2 per cent less than this, that equates to $4000. For most people $4000 is a lot of money and they have to work a fairly long time to earn and save it. Although in relative terms such a reduction may not seem much, you need to keep things in perspective and fight for every dollar.
2. Secondly, there is the expense of such things as tidying the place up, lawyers' fees and especially real estate agents' fees.
3. Thirdly, there is the possibility of being hit with a penalty for repaying your mortgage early.

Do you have to sell?

Perhaps the first thing you should do is think hard about whether you really want and need to sell. Would it be cheaper to fix the things you don't like about the house than to sell it? For example, if you need an extra bedroom it may be cheaper to build one on than go through the stress and expense of a sale. That extra bedroom will also add value that you will eventually recoup if you sell later.

If you do decide you have to sell, you need to make sure you do it as efficiently and as well as you possibly can. That means taking your time and setting a careful plan, which might include:

- Deciding on the season that you will sell: generally spring and summer are best, when the house is bright and sunny and the garden is at its peak.
- Doing any tidying or maintenance work before you even invite real estate agents around to discuss listing. Their first impressions are just as important as your buyer's.
- Getting a valuer in to establish what the house is worth. This will cost but is often a good idea in the long run as you can negotiate (with both real estate agents and prospective buyers) from a position of informed strength.

PROPERTY JARGON

- *Conveyancing.* The process of transferring the property from one owner to another.
- *Leasehold.* Holding land under a lease.
- *Freehold.* Often wrongly used to mean that the property is mortgage free. In fact it means that the property is owned outright – i.e. it is not leasehold.
- *Unit title.* Where you have title to your particular dwelling but you share ownership of part of the property (e.g. stairs, driveways, corridors etc) with others. Most common in blocks of apartments.
- *Easement.* The right for someone to use a part of the land (e.g. to run pipes across, have a right-of-way). The easement is registered on the title.
- *Chattels.* The things that are not fixed to the house, which departing owners can take with them if they are not listed in the contract. Chattels usually left include drapes, carpets, light fittings, oven, dishwasher, nightstore heater, logburner etc.

THE COST TO SELL

Real estate agent. A percentage of the price you receive for your house.

Lawyer. Generally around $500, depending on the extent to which you involve him or her, whether the property has a mortgage and how smoothly the sale process goes.

Valuer. About $300.

Penalty for early mortgage repayment if on a fixed rate loan.

- Choosing which form of sale to use – private sale, auction, sole agency etc. If you make a firm plan you are less likely to be talked into something else by an agent.
- Choosing which real estate agent to use.

Ways of selling

You have a number of choices about how you are going to sell.

Private sale

This means selling the property yourself, without using a real estate agent. The main advantage of this is, of course, cost – real estate agents take a good slice of the sale proceeds. Some people find that dealing with agents is stressful anyway: conflict between vendors and agents is quite common. However, agents can help the sale process along considerably. If you want to go it alone, there is a number of things you'll have to do:

- Get a copy of a sale and purchase agreement (ask your lawyer) and familiarise yourself with it.
- Get a copy of the house's title.
- Consider getting a valuer's report to give you a good idea of a reasonable price.
- Plan a marketing campaign – signs, newspaper advertising, flyers to give to people who view your home etc.
- Arrange open days and times to view. Make sure you stay near a phone and that people can contact you easily.
- Be prepared to negotiate.
- Involve your lawyer in this process, especially if you want help on drawing up the sale and purchase agreement.

Most people find all this too hard and too time-consuming, and choose to use an agent. However, if you think you can handle it, there is certainly money to be saved.

Sole agency

Real estate agents love to have a sole agency, which means they will get a fee no matter who the property is sold to or who arranges the sale. Even if you sell the property to your neighbour or a friend and the agent had nothing to do with the sale, if you have signed a sole agency agreement they still get their fee. However, you can exclude certain potential purchasers from the sole agency agreement. For example, if any friends have expressed interest in your house before it went on the market you might have the sole agency specifically exclude them. Then if they do buy the house you don't have to pay the agent.

Agents say that sole agencies work because they do more and work harder to sell your house. There is a fair bit of truth in this. They can control the process better and have a vested interest in selling the property. It also works quite well for you if the agent is a good one. You won't have to deal with a whole host of agents, some of whom may bring clients through the house before they have even seen it themselves.

Sole agencies are for a limited period of time. Agents will try for as long as possible but you should give them 30–60 days at most. This is especially important if you do not know the agent, have not dealt with them before and do not know how they will perform.

General agency
This is where you appoint a number of agents to sell your property. This has the advantages of spreading the word more widely, and of course leaves it open for you to sell the property yourself.

Agents claim they won't work as hard for a good price if others are also out there trying. An agent in competition with others is more interested in a sure sale than gaining a few thousand dollars more in price and risking the loss of the deal. You also don't get a co-ordinated effort to sell. Agents won't spend as much money on advertising your property because it's wasted (for them) if another agent sells the house.

Most people will use a general agency only if the property fails to sell through a sole agency.

Auction
Many agents will try to talk their clients into going to auction. The argument runs along the lines that an auction generates some excitement and gives a definite date by which buyers have to make up their minds. There is also the dream that you just might get two people bidding against each other at the auction, running the price up and up. While this does happen, it is fairly rare, except when the market is particularly bouyant. An auction can, however, be a good option if your house is special in any way and difficult to price.

Agents say a large percentage of the properties they list for auction sell either before the auction, at auction or fairly soon thereafter. There is little doubt that

---

PREPARATION FOR SALE

Two things you need to think about in preparing your house for sale:

Tidiness and maintenance
Untidy and badly maintained houses do not attract buyers and the price is affected accordingly. Get any repairs done well before the house goes on the market and give the house a good clean. The garden should also be given a good tidy-up. First impressions count.

Security
You are going to have a lot of strangers through your home, often while you are not there. Make sure nothing valuable is left lying around to tempt someone, or to encourage anyone to make a return visit after dark.

AGENTS LIKE TO SELL AT AUCTION ...

... because they get a sole agency that will usually extend for a couple of months after the auction. They also like it because it is usual for the vendor to pay for part or all of the advertising. Most auctions are advertised with large block advertisements in the newspaper (often with a colour photo) as well as with printed flyers. While it might be reasonable for you to contribute to this advertising, you should negotiate with the agent to ensure that you don't pay the lot.

the auction system, with its greater advertising and sense of urgency, does sell property, but there is clearly a cost attached.

Dealing with real estate agents

Agents get paid by commission. There is no standard fee: different agencies offer different fees and you can (and should) negotiate. The usual fee works on a percentage basis, with 3.75 per cent of the final price being the higher end of the scale (for less valuable properties) and 2 per cent being the lower end (for more expensive properties). The agent who sells the property usually get about half the commission, and the company for which they work gets the rest. Sometimes the selling agent must share part of it with the person who listed the property.

The commission is paid for achieving an unconditional contract – nothing is payable before then. This means that if the agent gets an unconditional contract but the property is not settled (perhaps because the buyer can't find the money), the agent is entitled to take the commission from any deposit received.

Finding a good agent is like finding any good professional – difficult. The sale of your house is too important to give the listing to someone on the basis of friendship –you should do it on the basis of ability. Judging agents' ability will often come down to reputation and referrals from friends and family. It is often a good idea to select an agency with offices in your area. If there is an agency that dominates your locality, most buyers will eventually find their way to its doors. The agent you choose should be:

- personable
- competent
- honest

Ultimately it comes down to judgment. Don't appoint an agent if you have any doubts whatever. There are lots of them out there and it's worth spending some time finding a good one.

Once you have appointed an agent you have to manage them.

- *Get their estimate of the likely price bracket in writing.*
  There is always the suspicion that agents give their vendors a high estimate of price in order to get the listing, and then as the sale process goes on spend their time conditioning you for a lower price. You need to be able to point to what they estimated in the beginning.
- *Remember that the agent is working for you.*
  At times they can seem to be on the purchaser's side as they start to point out everything that is wrong with your property. You may have to remind them who is paying them.

- *Don't put up with undue pressure to sell.*
  The agent is on a commission and gets paid only if a sale is made. As such, they are not a disinterested party and have a vested interest in you selling. Don't be pushed around.

- *Listen to your agent.*
  What they are saying may be self-serving, but it may also be true. If you have had a lot of people through your house and no offers – or only low offers – the agent might be right in telling you that you have unreasonable expectations.

- *Complain if necessary.*
  You can complain in the first instance to the agent's manager and, if you get no satisfaction there, to the Real Estate Institute of New Zealand.

See CONNECT, p.162

RENTING A HOME

Although this does not carry the financial commitment of owning a home, there are traps for the unwary – traps that can cost you a lot of money and cause difficulties in your life.

The relationship between landlord and tenant is often categorised as an antagonistic one and it certainly is an area where there is a great deal of conflict and dispute. The best thing you can do before renting a house or unit is to understand the rules surrounding renting, and in particular understand your rights.

Tenancy Services (a division of the Ministry of Housing) has produced a series of excellent booklets and pamphlets and you should get copies of these. Tenancy Services is there to help both landlords and tenants and most people report that their service is very good indeed.

Finding a house to rent

Most people find houses to rent through their local newspaper or through a real estate agent. Many real estate agents have divisions specialising in rental accommodation and will advertise in the newspaper and in the windows of their office.

Most rental agents are not as energetic as sales agents. The fees they receive are not as high and many people say they find difficulty getting agents to take them to properties. Usually an agent will suggest that you drive past properties they have for lease and if you are interested come back to the office and they will show you through.

The generally low standard of service from rental

WHO IS RESPONSIBLE FOR THE LEASE?

Groups of young people frequently share rental accommodation and quite often there is a lot of coming and going as flatmates move in and out. If you are the person who has signed the lease agreement, you are responsible whether you continue to live in the house or not. If you are moving on and other flatmates are taking over, you must notify the landlord to end your responsibility. If you are moving in with a group of people, it is a good idea for you to have all your flatmates sign the agreement so the responsibility is shared.

agents is frustrating, but a great deal of leasing is done through them, so if you want to find the right property to rent you will probably have to use one.

Agents charge for their service and the person who pays is you, the tenant (although this is likely to change so that it is the landlord who will pay the commission). Typically the cost of this is one week's rent plus GST.

Once you have identified the property you want, you will have to negotiate for it in much the same way as negotiating for the purchase of a house. This will mean putting in an offer to rent and agreeing terms with the landlord.

Tenancy agreements

All tenancy agreements must be in writing and both landlord and tenant must retain a copy. If your tenancy is arranged through an agency they will have agreement forms. If not, you can obtain standard agreement forms through Tenancy Services.

The tenancy agreement covers such things as:

- Length of the lease
- Rent and how often it is to be paid
- Bond (if any)
- Maximum number of people who can live at the premises
- List of chattels (e.g. dishwasher, fridge, drapes etc)
- Notes of any damage to the premises
- Letting fee (if an agent is involved)

Term of the tenancy

1. *A periodic tenancy*

   This has no set term and will therefore continue until either you or the landlord gives notice to end it. You must give 21 days' notice to end a tenancy, and the landlord must give 90 days' notice, unless the property is to be sold or used by the landlord or family. This and other aspects of the tenancy are governed by the Residential Tenancies Act 1986.

2. *A fixed-term tenancy*

   This runs until a pre-determined date, perhaps for six months or a year, and neither party can give notice to quit during that time. If you want to leave the premises you will need to find another tenant as a substitute and so sub-let. Most landlords like a long fixed-term tenancy because this gives them security of income.

Rent

The rent payable will be set as a weekly amount. The landlord can charge a maximum of two weeks' rent in advance.

The rent cannot be increased during a fixed-term tenancy. It can be increased during a periodic tenancy only on giving 60 days' notice, and then not within six months of the start of a tenancy or within six months of the last increase. You can go to the Tenancy Tribunal if you think a rent increase is significantly higher than the market rate.

Bond

The landlord can require a bond to be paid as security, but it can be no more than four weeks' rent. Tenancy Services must hold this bond, not the landlord. You will receive the money back at the end of the lease, although the landlord may get some of it if there is damage, unpaid rent or some other claim against you.

Inspection and repair

Landlords must give you 48 hours' notice if they want to inspect the property and 24 hours' notice if they need to do repairs. You do not have to give the landlord access to the house outside these times.

Repairs and maintenance

The landlord is responsible for any maintenance required unless you (or your guests) are responsible for damage. Notify the landlord of any repairs that are necessary and, if you cannot get the landlord to get the work done, contact Tenancy Services. The landlord is not allowed to make any alterations or renovations without your permission.

THE COST OF GETTING INTO A FLAT

Many people get an unpleasant surprise at how much it costs at the outset to rent a property. The bond, a letting fee and two weeks' rent can add up to quite a lot of money to be paid out before you move in. For example, if you rent a flat for $200 per week the costs could be:

Two weeks' rent in advance	$400
Bond (four weeks)	$800
Letting fee (one week's rent plus GST)	$225
TOTAL	$1425

Clearly, these costs need to be budgeted for.

Gardens

You are responsible for keeping the garden tidy unless you have agreement with the landlord stating otherwise.

Inventories

At the start of the tenancy you should make a record of any chattels and their state of repair, and any damage to the house. These lists should go in the tenancy agreement so that there is no argument at the end of the tenancy.

THE FINANCIAL SECRETS

- Taking on home ownership and a mortgage are the biggest financial decisions most of us make. Study the options and proceed with care.
- Buying and selling houses and shifting are expensive. Don't do it more often than you have to.
- Renting is full of traps. Know the law and take advice from Tenancy Services if necessary.

CONNECT

- Real Estate Institute, phone (09) 356 1755
  www.reinz.org.nz
- New Zealand Property Institute (formerly Institute of Valuers)
  phone (04) 384 7094
  www.property.org.nz
- Tenancy Services, phone 0800 836 262 (0800 TENANCY)
  www.tenancy.govt.nz
- District Law Societies (see your local phone book)
- Other useful web sites:
  www.realenz.co.nz
  www.privatesale.co.nz
  www.open2view.com

BOOK

- *How to Get the House You Want*, Consumers' Institute, 1996

11. EDUCATION
What's it worth?

Education has a cost, to society and to individuals, and it also has a value. And no, the two are not the same. A society that values education will increase social equity, tolerance and prosperity. For individuals, there are many pay-offs: self-esteem, employability and the ability to choose one's own path in life.

New Zealand has an unfortunate history of putting a low value on education and permitting very early departure from the compulsory school system. This is changing amid a great deal of political hype about the so-called 'knowledge economy', but statistics still show certain groups to be poorly educated and greatly disadvantaged in a world that requires better skills for employment.

The money spent on education should be seen as an investment: the returns will more than justify the expenditure.

THE LAW
The Education Act 1989 states that it is compulsory for children to attend school between the ages of six and 16 (although home schooling is an option for some). They have a statutory right to education between the ages of five and 19 but they can lose this right for gross misconduct, continual disobedience or behaviour that is harmful or dangerous to others. If a child is suspended or expelled, the school has an obligation to ensure that the student's learning process is continued.

The Act also provides for children with special educational needs arising from a disability or for other reasons. They have the same rights to enrol at a state school and to receive appropriate education.

> **WHAT DOES YEAR 8 MEAN?**
>
> The primary school system caters for children between the ages of 5 and 12, referred to now as Years 1 to 8. Many primary schools go only as high as Year 6, with separate intermediate schools catering for Years 7 and 8. The secondary school system caters for Years 9 to 13, which usually corresponds to students between the ages of 13 and 17.

THE COST OF COMPULSORY EDUCATION
School fees
Under the Education Act students are entitled to a free education at state schools. These are administered by boards of trustees elected from within the school's community.

Ministry of Education guidelines make it clear that boards of trustees cannot demand fees to cover the cost of tuition, books or materials used in the provision of the curriculum at a state school, but in practice the funding that schools receive from the government is barely sufficient to cover their costs. Most schools not only engage in fundraising activities but also charge parents a school fee.

School 'fees' are, by law, voluntary – in a legal sense they are really a donation. Therefore no state school has the right to withhold reports, portfolios of work or such items as student ID cards to students if fees have not been paid. Certainly schools need the money, and most people make their donation happily, but it is not compulsory.

Parents may be asked for contributions to specific activities (e.g. school camps). These are not compulsory either. Your child may not be able to go to the camp, and have to stay at school while the others go into the bush for a few days, but the school cannot force you to pay for an activity. Many schools charge a fee for courses that have a 'take-home component' (photography or food technology, for example) to cover the costs of equipment and materials. If the cost has been made clear before your child enrols in such a course, the school is within its rights to insist on payment of such a fee.

School uniforms

Individual schools, primary and secondary, may choose to have a uniform, and may also require students to wear it. Although, in the long run, a school uniform may well be the cheapest form of clothing for children, the initial outlay can nevertheless be difficult for some people. Parents who receive a benefit from WINZ may be entitled to some assistance with school uniform costs.

Some schools and communities organise a market for second-hand school uniforms – a reasonable option for many, given the robust nature of the clothing and the fact that many children outgrow their uniform before they wear it out.

PRIVATE SCHOOLING

Some parents choose to enrol their children in a private or independent school. Costs vary considerably, depending on the character and location of the school, and can range up to $2500 per term ($10,000 per annum). Boarding at the school may cost $1700 per term (roughly $7000 per annum) and there are likely to be considerable other costs for classes and other activities.

For more information on private schools see:

www.privateschools.org.nz

WHAT PRICE A 'GAP' YEAR?

There has been a trend in recent years for people to take a year off after they finish school and before they begin tertiary study. This allows people to have a look at the world outside academia, to grow up a bit and to come to their tertiary studies with renewed energy and purpose.

However, some do it for financial purposes, believing that if they spend a year working and saving they can avoid taking out a student loan (or at least take a smaller one).

This makes no sense financially. The problem is that during that year off you will be paid at the rate of an unqualified 18-year-old and therefore not save much at all - if anything. However, if you get on with getting a qualification, when you finish you ought to be paid at a higher rate, which should make up for the interest you pay on a student loan.

By all means take a year off for personal reasons, but financially you are better off to plunge into your education and reap the benefits sooner rather than later.

TERTIARY EDUCATION

No longer does tertiary education simply mean attending a university or a polytechnic. There are hundreds of institutions offering training and education in just about every topic and discipline you can imagine. In fact the term 'post-compulsory' is coming to replace 'tertiary' to encompass the wide range of education available to school-leavers, because there is considerable overlap in some of these courses with the senior levels of secondary school.

Perhaps the biggest thing to watch is that you choose a course that will be recognised by employers both in this country and overseas. If you are going to spend the time and money studying, you should be sure it will count. In this respect it is best to choose an establishment that is recognised by the New Zealand Qualifications Authority. NZQA recognition means that the course is well designed, and providers are monitored to ensure they offer the course they have promised.

> **NEW ZEALAND QUALIFICATIONS AUTHORITY (NZQA)**
>
> The New Zealand Qualifications Authority is a crown entity established under the Education Act 1989. It co-ordinates qualifications in secondary schools and in post-school education and training, maintains national standards, ensures recognition of overseas qualifications and administers national secondary and tertiary examinations. Its aim is 'to ensure that national qualifications have a high credibility both throughout New Zealand and overseas, and are related to each other in ways that assist people to upgrade their qualifications without having to repeat unnecessarily previous study and assessment'.
>
> Contact NZQA at: www.nzqa.govt.nz

Funding tertiary education

The cost of the various forms of post-compulsory education depends on what you choose to study, where you study and whether you are full time or part time. For example, it will cost nearly $10,000 a year for a medical degree – and considerably more for overseas students.

It can be difficult for students to find the money to pay course fees and make ends meet while they study. Courses are expensive, as are living costs, and most students can no longer find the well-paid holiday jobs that their parents did a decade or two ago. But there are a number of forms of assistance to fund your education.

Student Allowance

The Student Allowance is designed to assist with students' living expenses. It is available only to full-time students on an approved course at a recognised tertiary institution. The NZQA and the Ministry of Education determine which institutions and which courses are approved (though most courses at universities and polytechnics are on the approved list). To qualify, you must be a New Zealand citizen, permanent resident or refugee. You must be over 18, although there are some exceptions made.

The amount payable depends on your circumstances, including your age, domestic situation and whether you have to live away from home while studying.

TAKE YOUR ENTITLEMENT

The fees for tertiary education may seem very high, but they are, in fact, heavily subsidised by the government. For example, a year of study for an arts degree might cost you around $3500, but the government is likely to be subsidising your university by at least that amount in order to pay for your education. For some courses the cost is very much higher.

If you don't go into tertiary education, then there is a government grant going begging ...

OTHER FUNDING SUPPORT

There are other forms of support potentially available to you as a tertiary student. These include:

- Community Services Card
- Accommodation Supplement
- Away-from-home Allowance
- Childcare Subsidy
- Training Incentive Allowance
- Disability Allowance
- Special Benefit
- Special Needs grant
- Recoverable Assistance Programme grant

Contact WINZ to discuss your eligibility for a Student Allowance and any of the above at : www.winz.govt.nz/student

---

Student Allowances are income-tested. If you are single and earn over $135.13 per week (before tax) you will not qualify for one.

If you are under 25 and not living with a partner, your parents' income will also be tested. The combined taxable income of both parents must be under $50,752 if you live away from home, or $45,760 if you live at home. An extra $2200 of income is allowable for every additional student under 25. It doesn't matter if your parents are living separately – their income is still combined and the same limits apply. There are a few exceptions to this, particularly if one parent has died.

Some parents use family trusts to 'shelter' income so their children can get Student Allowances. This is done by putting the family business or farm into a trust so that the income is the trust's, not their own.

Your parents will not be income-tested, however, if you are married or live with a partner. (Some students have even married so they can get a Student Allowance without their parents being income-tested.) There are various rules regarding how much you will get if you are with a partner: for example, someone living with a partner who is earning will get a student allowance of $55.83 per week, a student with a dependent partner is entitled to $257.58 per week, and a couple who are both eligible students will receive $128.79 per week each.

Students under 25 can also get a Student Allowance if they have children. Other conditions (e.g. income-testing) still apply.

There are some other conditions for Student Allowances that you should be aware of:

• If you have had Student Allowance you must pass at least 50 per cent of your course.

• You can usually only get the Student Allowance for 200 weeks in total.

Unemployment Benefit Student Hardship

This is a benefit for students who cannot find work in the holidays. It is not designed to provide you with income during the holidays, but rather as a subsistance benefit to keep you going while you look for work. You must, therefore, have signed a Student Job Seeker Contract (through Student Job Search), and have registered for work.

You must generally be able to qualify for a Student Allowance (although there are exceptions if you are in hardship), plan to return to full-time study after the holidays and be over 18. If you are claiming for a partner (and have no dependent children under six) he or she must also be actively looking for work.

You will also be asset-tested. If you are single, you must have assets of less than $4300 to qualify; if you have a partner (or a child) your assets must be less than $7464. The amount you get depends on your age, marital status, whether you live at home and whether you have a partner or children. It ranges from $107.76 per week for a single person aged 18-19 years who is living at home, to $286.28 per week for a couple with two children.

As with all benefits, you must tell WINZ if your circumstances change.

THE STUDENT LOAN SCHEME

The Student Loan Scheme is one of the most controversial (and hated) policies in this country. While the scheme has some good points, many students resent leaving education with a large debt to repay, particularly when they discover how easy it was for their parents to fund their way through tertiary education.

Society will have to grapple with the funding of post-compulsory education (particularly the Student Loan Scheme) over the next few years, and this is an ongoing political issue.

The economy cannot afford to make all tertiary education free and support students to the degree they would like, and the Student Loan Scheme is the best compromise we have been able to come up with to date. It does, after all, allow some students to receive education and training who would otherwise not be able to do so. It also seeks to balance the public good with private good. Although there is a public benefit to having a well-educated population, there is also a private benefit to those who get the education and subsequently earn higher incomes. There appears to be a consensus that the public, through the government, should pay for some post-compulsory education, but the individual should pay for some too.

Society needs to encourage people into education, and yet the Student Loan Scheme has

---

SHOULD YOU GET A LOAN?

This is really the wrong question. A better question to ask yourself is: should I get an education? The answer to this is a resounding 'yes'. The question, then, is how to fund this education.

If the only way is to take a loan, the loan should be seen as borrowing to purchase an investment asset. If education is seen as an asset (and it should be), borrowing to get it makes sense.

In this respect it is much like borrowing to buy an investment property. Thousands of people do this. They purchase an investment property for its income and borrow to do so. When you get an education you are also purchasing an income-producing property ('intellectual property', if you like), which is no less valuable than a block of flats.

Borrowing for an education is not like putting a holiday on a credit card. In that case, after the holiday you still have the debt but nothing to show for it. A student loan means you will have a debt – but the liability is more than matched on the other side of the balance sheet with the asset of your increased knowledge, skills and marketability. An education adds to both your net worth (providing that you see education as an asset) and your long-term income.

been a major disincentive. People have gone to great lengths to avoid the scheme: contemplating marriage and bankruptcy, going overseas and, worst of all, forgoing education completely.

How it works

The Student Loan Scheme is also run by WINZ, although at the end of the year(s) of study your file is passed on to the IRD. To get a student loan you need to be studying an approved course at an approved institution. Special conditions apply if you are under 18. Student loans are not income-tested but you can't get one if you get a student allowance of over $150 per week or if you or your partner are on a benefit.

The loan is a debt and you should take it seriously. You will have to sign a loan agreement, which is a legal document. If you are under 18 it must be signed by your parents. You can cancel the loan, but you will have to pay any monies owing immediately.

There are three things you can borrow for:

- *Course fees.* These are paid directly to the educational institute – you never handle the money (but you are responsible for its repayment).
- *Course-related costs.* This is to a maximum of $1000 per year and is to cover things such as books and materials.
- *Living costs.* You can borrow up to $150 per week if you are a full-time student.

Loan costs

You have to take out a new loan and open a new loan account for each year of your studies. Each loan attracts an administration fee of $50.

The government reviews the interest rate you will pay (currently 7 per cent) each year on 1 April. You may qualify to have the interest written off while you are studying. To be eligible for this, your annual income must be below $25,073. Apply to the IRD for this.

SHARP PRACTICE?

Most students don't have to pay loan interest while they are studying. Some people take advantage of this by borrowing as much of this interest-free money as they can – even when they don't need it – and investing it. This means they earn some interest at no cost. Financially this is quite straightforward, but there are two things to watch:

1. The money needs to be invested safely. Don't use it to try to play the sharemarket or chase higher returns through risky investments.
2. As soon as you stop studying and start paying interest, stop the investment and pay off the loan.

Before you get a student loan

Do a detailed budget. Students have always been hard up, but one of the things that people with little money need to do is make sure every dollar is well spent. The key to that is to do a budget, and stick to it.

It is important that you don't take on any more debt than you have to. The rules for borrowing for education are the same as borrowing for any other purpose. Even if you don't have to pay interest while you are studying you will eventually pay interest on every dollar you have borrowed, so you want to borrow as little as possible. For example, you are able to borrow $150 per week for living costs. If you can do a budget that shows that you only need $120 for living costs, that is what you should borrow.

Crunch time: paying it back

You should aim to pay back your student loan as quickly as possible, applying any spare money you have to reducing it. The interest rate is quite high (currently 7 per cent) and student loans are not tax deductible. You may be tempted to put some spare cash into an investment instead, but to make that worthwhile you would need to get a return of 7 per cent *after* tax and all fees, which is not easy to get.

You can pay off the loan in whole or in part at any time, even when you are still studying.

When you have stopped studying, you will deal with the IRD in repayment. If you are earning less than $15,132 pa you are not obliged to repay anything (although don't forget that interest will be accumulating). As soon as you earn over $15,132 pa ($291 per week) you have to start paying 10 per cent of your income to the IRD as loan repayments. Note that that income includes wages and salary, dividends, income from trusts and interest received. The IRD looks only at your income, not your partner's as well.

Assuming that all your income comes from wages or salary, you should tell your employer to use the student loan tax code (SL). Your employer will deduct your student loan repayment from your wages and pass it on to the IRD. If you have other income (from a business, or investments or from a trust) you are required to make interim payments to the IRD during the year.

The IRD can impose penalties if you breach the terms of the loan. If you don't make payments on time you are charged a penalty of 2 per cent per month on the outstanding amount. Note that the penalty compounds – if you fail to pay the penalty it, too, is

> **A CONTRIBUTION FROM PARENTS**
>
> Remember, it is very expensive for your children *not* to have an education. Ideally, you should start as early as possible to make some provision towards ensuring they get the best opportunity possible.
>
> Some parents (or grandparents) set up a trust to save towards their children's education costs. A simple trust for this purpose is usually quite inexpensive to set up and manage, and has the advantage of keeping such funds separate and untouchable. Alternatively, you can save through a dedicated bank fund or spread of investments.
>
> Either way, it is good to start early. For example, $1000 put on the birth of a child into an investment returning 6 per cent, plus $50 per month, will see $13,200 in the account when the child turns 18. That's a good start for any tertiary student.

added to the amount owing; if this continues the total owed can spiral out of control. If you make no payments for two years in a row, the loan may be repayable in full immediately.

The payments and most other terms continue while you are overseas. If you are going overseas for more than three months you must contact the IRD and give them your address. The IRD will calculate what payments are due, and you must make the payments each quarter.

Many people repay only the minimum but this is false economy. You can and should make the payments as high as you can to get rid of the loan as soon as possible.

THE FINANCIAL SECRETS

- Education costs money – but it is worth it.
- Treat education as an investment. You are acquiring an asset on which you will get a return for the rest of your life.
- In the end a student loan makes sense. Treat it like any other borrowing:
  - Buy the right asset.
  - Manage it.
  - Pay it back as soon as possible.

CONNECT

- Inland Revenue Department (IRD), phone 0800 377 778.
  A student loan calculator is available from the web site:
  www.ird.govt.nz
- New Zealand Qualifications Authority (NZQA), phone 0800 802 3000
  www.nzqa.govt.nz
- Student Services Centre (part of WINZ), phone 0800 88 99 00
  student.services@winz.govt.nz
  www.winz.govt.nz/student
- Education Review Office (ERO) (see your local phone book)
  www.ero.govt.nz
- Other useful sites:
  www.geocities.com/kevin_summersby/education
  www.privateschools.org.nz

12. EMPLOYMENT
Finding, keeping and leaving your job

Most of this book is about managing your money but this chapter is about where you get it from. It makes sense to be an efficient money manager and to cut your outgoings, but you should also try to increase what you have coming in.

It always seems remarkable that two 18-year-olds who leave school with similar abilities and qualifications can be in quite different career positions as 30-year-olds and even further apart at 40. The choices that you make in finding a job, growing it and leaving it are vitally important over the course of your life.

Most people get most of their income from a job. Knowing how to approach employment matters will have a huge impact on the income you receive over your lifetime.

Flexibility and ongoing, continuous training are the keys. You cannot expect any longer to have just one job, in one industry, with one employer for a lifetime. Not only is it unlikely, it is probably undesirable. To advance a career you need a portfolio of skills, probably acquired with a variety of employers. Those setting out to advance their careers keep moving quite deliberately from job to job and quite often from employer to employer as they build their range of skills and network of contacts.

> **SMALL GAINS, BIG EFFECT**
>
> If you earned an average of $35,000 pa for 40 years, your total income would add up to $1.4 million. If you can increase that amount by just 2.5 per cent, you will add an additional $35,000 to that amount – an extra year's worth of income.

Many people fail to put enough emphasis on the development of their careers. They go to work, turning up punctually and reliably, and do a good enough job without ever putting in that little bit of extra effort or energy that could see them break through to another level. It might be some training at night school, a willingness to leave one employer for something more challenging, a committed self-development programme or building up skills outside work (e.g. becoming the treasurer of the golf club).

These relatively small things can make a big difference to your employability – and your pay packet. Remember that developing a new skill is not likely to be a short-term one-off. The benefits will be with you for life. If you think about the lifetime value of the extra salary from this little bit of extra effort, it is well worth it. This is an area where you can get great leverage.

This chapter is in three parts:
1. Getting a job
2. Developing your job and career
3. Leaving your job

GETTING A JOB

It can be hard to get started. It can be hard to front up and ask for a job. It can be hard to put your CV (and yourself) up for scrutiny. It can be hard to be rejected. It can be hard to pick yourself up and try again. However, these are all things that you are going to have to do. Time and time again you will find yourself in that Catch-22 situation: you can't get a job because you don't have any experience – and you can't get experience until you have a job.

Be proactive

Look for vacancies in the obvious places: your daily newspaper, the Internet, the noticeboard at your local supermarket. And don't forget word of mouth: tell your friends and family you're looking for a job. Many good jobs are never advertised, and those that are usually attract a lot of applicants – you will have competition. So don't rely on the Situations Vacant column. Put out the word that you want a job, telephone places you would like to work and ask if they have any vacancies, or even call in to see them. Be proactive: don't sit at home waiting for the paper.

The job interview

This can be a harrowing experience. The most important thing is to act naturally – be yourself!

Prepare for the interview by finding out as much as you can about the company and the position you are applying for. Their

---

SEVEN STEPS TO GETTING A JOB

1. Treat it like a project. Open a file (or get a folder) and organise for it.
2. Set your goals and put them in writing. Describe what you want in your job (e.g. pay rates, potential opportunities, etc).
3. Update your CV.
4. Start looking.
5. Fill in any gaps in your skill sets (i.e. you may need to learn how to make a spreadsheet).
6. Prepare for interviews. Get a friend to question you in a mock interview.
7. Ask for what you want – a bigger role, some training, more money etc.

web site might be a good place to start. Dress well but don't overdo it. Know the name of the person you are seeing, and don't be late (some people hate even 30 seconds of lateness!).

You will be asked about yourself, your past employment and your qualifications for the position. Make sure you are positive and maintain eye contact. Tell the employer you are the right person for the job – and say it as though you mean it. You will be asked if you have any questions: ask about the job, opportunities for training, self-development and promotion, who will supervise you, dress standards etc.

Employment agreements

If you get the job you will need an employment agreement with the employer. It may be a collective agreement (negotiated by a union) or it may be an individual agreement. You are entitled to negotiate the points of the contract; you and the employer must both negotiate in 'good faith'.

All employment agreements must be in writing. By law they must include a job description, the hours of work and the wages or salary. There are also minimum legal requirements for leave and holidays.

You may be offered a fixed-term position, stipulating that your employment will cease on a particular date. However, an employer can only offer a contract like this if the nature of the work genuinely requires it. Similarly, you may be given a trial period, but at the end of that period the employer cannot simply dismiss you without explanation and cause.

Pay

You can negotiate any rate of pay you like, provided it is not below the legal minimum:

- Minimum wage for those aged 16-17 years: $6.80 per hour, $54.40 for an eight-hour day, $272 for a 40-hour week.
- Minimum wage for adults: $8.50 per hour, $68 for an eight-hour day, $340 for a 40-hour week.

CURRICULUM VITAE

Curriculum vitae (CV) is Latin for 'course of life'. A CV spells out the course your life has taken: the things you have done, your qualifications and skills, previous employment, experience, interests and hobbies.

A good way to think of your CV is as your sales brochure – the sales literature you give prospective employers to sell yourself. As in all sales, you should accentuate the positive and eliminate the negative. That does not mean exaggerating or lying (you will almost certainly get found out). It means drawing attention to the good things you have done – your achievements and experiences to date.

Keep it short and precise: a CV doesn't need to be elaborate and most certainly shouldn't be too wordy.

All prospective employers will ask for a CV, so producing one should be the first thing you do. If you have trouble writing it, (lots of people find it hard to write about themselves) or getting it to look professional, there are firms that will do it for you – for a fee.

Your CV needs to have three things:

- Personal details (name, address, contact numbers etc). You do not need to give marital status, age, informmation on children etc.
- Employment history and skills, listed chronologically – beginning with your most recent job and working back.
- Education and training (courses attended, certificates, diplomas, degrees etc).

Attach copies of any references, certificates or qualifications, then photocopy the whole thing. (Don't give out the originals – you may never get them back.)

Neither you nor your employer can legally negotiate below these rates.

Employers may not pay different rates to men and women for substantially the same work. Nor can an employer discriminate against anyone in terms of pay, hiring, firing or promotion on the basis of gender, race, pregnancy, marital or family status, religion, ethnicity, political opinion or sexual orientation.

You should have nothing deducted from your wages unless you have agreed in writing (e.g. superannuation) or it is required by law (e.g. PAYE, child support). If you are ever overpaid, an employer may recover the overpayment by deduction from your wages, but only under strict conditions.

Holidays

The Holidays Act sets out the minimum holidays and how they should be taken. All employees are covered by the Act – full-time, part-time, casual and fixed-term. You may not opt out of the Act – i.e. you and your employer cannot agree that you should have fewer holidays, although you can agree to more.

There are two types of holiday leave:

1. *Public holidays*

    There are 11 public or statutory days each year. If a public holiday falls on a day you would usually work, you are entitled to the day off on pay. These days are: Christmas Day, Boxing Day, New Year's Day, 2 January, Waitangi Day, Easter Friday, Easter Monday, Anzac Day, Queen's Birthday, Labour Day and your provincial Anniversary Day. You do not have to work on any of these days unless you have agreed to do so in your employment agreement. If you do work, you will usually be paid for the day's work and, in addition, get a day off in lieu. Waitangi Day and Anzac Day have slightly different rules.

2. *Annual holidays*

    You are entitled to a minimum of three weeks' paid holiday each year after you have completed 12 months' continuous service with the same employer. You will be paid in lieu of holidays if you leave the employer before you have taken your holiday entitlement. Normally your holiday pay will be 6 per cent of your total gross earnings.

Other leave

After you have been with the same employer for more than 12 months you are entitled by law to five days' 'special' leave. (Some employment agreements allow more than five days.) This can be used for:

- Sick leave
- Domestic leave to care for a sick spouse or dependent parent or child
- Bereavement leave upon the death of a close family member

Special leave cannot be accumulated if it is not taken in any one year, unless your employer agrees.

DEVELOPING YOUR JOB AND CAREER

Whether your aim is to become a CEO, earn a higher hourly rate or simply remain employable, you need to think about how you will grow in your job. You must take responsibility for your own career planning and development – no one else will do this for you. While it is never too late, the sooner you begin to develop your career the more leverage you will have. There are four things you need to think about:

1. *The essentials of your current job*

    Are you getting the job done? Ask yourself why they have you doing what you do. What is your job description? Think laterally about the way you work. For example, your job may be to sweep the floor, but what the company really wants is for the floor to be clean. You may be able to find a better and more efficient way of achieving this. Satisfying the company's need – knowing why they pay you – is the first thing to think about. And if you are not performing the role to everyone's satisfaction you might be lucky to hold on to your job, let alone advance.

2. *The discretionary things.*

    How could you go that extra mile and transform yourself from a valuable employee into an invaluable one? What is it that would get people saying they couldn't do without you? It may be something small, like being utterly reliable and punctual. It could be your attitude, your cheerfulness and willingness to get on with things, or a flexibility and ability to work across a range of tasks. These extras, whatever they might be, form the base for advancement. They can get you noticed and marked for higher jobs.

3. *The stepping-stones*

    Show your employer that you expect training and development – that you're

---

SIX STEPS TO GETTING A RAISE

1. Treat it like a project. Open a file (or get a folder) and organise for it.
2. Set your goals (more money, promotion) and put them in writing.
3. Prepare your case. List what you have achieved, skills acquired, value you have added to the business, etc.
4. Investigate what the market pays for your level of skills and experience.
5. Ask your manager for a time to meet to discuss your job and conditions.
6. Make your case. Use logic and facts (e.g. what you would be paid elsewhere).

Remember: you cannot be fired for asking for a raise!

not planning to spend the rest of your life in the same job. If you take up outside training and education, let your employer know you're doing it.

4. *Reaching a dead end?*
Sometimes an employer cannot envisage a worker in any other position and will not consider him or her for promotion. If you were hired as a receptionist it may be impossible for your boss to see you as a marketing assistant, in spite of your eagerness and new qualification. You may be doing too good a job and he or she is reluctant to promote you away from it! Or you may be in the wrong company or the wrong industry, or working for someone who will never be capable of recognising talent and ability. The answer is to leave for something better and make a fresh start.

LEAVING YOUR JOB
There are several ways your employment may come to an end.

Resignation
You may opt to leave by resigning, which is probably the way most of us go. You can resign from your job at any time, whether you are on a fixed-term agreement or not, but you have to give notice. The length of notice depends on the circumstances and the position you hold, and will usuallly be spelt out in your employment agreement. If you are a shop assistant, a week's notice is probably adequate; if you are a CEO, a month might not be enough.

If you resign, your employer has a choice. He may require you to work out your notice, or he may send you home for the notice period (but he must keep paying you). If your pay is stopped before the end of the notice period, you can make a claim for the wages you have missed.

If you do not give notice you only have to be paid up until the time you stopped working. The employer cannot make any deduction in lieu of notice unless you agree to this in writing or your employment agreement specifically provides for it.

Dismissal
You may not be dismissed from your job without good cause and the dismissal must not only be fair, it must be procedurally fair.

It should be made clear to you from the start what your job requires, what behaviour is expected, and what could lead to dismissal. If your employer is unhappy with your work, you should be given clear standards to aim for and a genuine opportunity to improve. Unless you are being dismissed instantly for serious misconduct you should be given every chance to put a problem right. This means that if there is an ongoing problem the employer should warn you, in writing, of disciplinary action if the problem continues. You should take any such warning seriously. If the standards required are clearly and reasonably laid out, you can be dismissed if you do not meet them.

In all cases, the employer must give the reasons for the chosen course of action and you must be given a genuine opportunity to express your side of the story before the employer takes matters any further. Any investigations should be carried out fairly and in an even-handed way.

You are entitled to ask your employer for a written explanation of your dismissal within 90 days. At this point it may be possible for the you and your employer to resolve the grievance. If not, and you feel you have been unjustifiably dismissed you may be able to take a personal grievance claim to the Employment Relations Authority.

> See Taking a personal grievance claim, p.178

Constructive dismissal

If you are forced out of your job by being pressured to resign it is effectively a 'constructive dismissal'. It happens where an employer:

- Sets out to force you to leave.
- Gives you a choice of resigning or being dismissed.
- Gives you no choice but to resign because of a breach of your employment agreement or other unfair treatment.

You are entitled to pursue a personal grievance claim in the event of a constructive dismissal.

Redundancy

A lot of people lose their jobs through redundancy. In a genuine redundancy:

- Your position is no longer needed.
- The employer has decided on redundancy for genuine commercial concerns.

Sometimes it is obvious that redundancies are genuine – for example if a company is in serious financial trouble. It is clear in such a case that it is not *you* who is being made redundant but your *position*. However, sometimes employers will use the excuse of redundancy to get rid of an individual. This is likely to be an unjustifiable dismissal and you can bring a claim.

The employer should consult with you before making any decision on redundancy. This is to give you a chance to suggest other positions that you could fill or other ways of organising the business. If the employer does not act reasonably and fairly in this regard you may again be able to bring a claim.

Redundancy payments

There is no law in New Zealand requiring employers to make redundancy payments. However, redundancy payments may be covered in your employment agreement. If not, or if the agreement stipulates that no redundancy shall be payable, you or your union will have to negotiate, with no guarantee of success. In any event, the employer should give you reasonable notice, and most employers will off re-employment assistance and counselling.

Retirement

The law provides that there is no set retirement age and you cannot be forced to retire simply because of your age. The only exception to this is if you have an employment agreement which is dated before 1 April 1992 and specifies a retirement age.

TAKING A PERSONAL GRIEVANCE CLAIM

The Employment Relations Act allows you to bring a personal grievance claim against your employer if you have been unfairly dismissed, harassed, disadvantaged in your employment or discriminated against. An employer cannot discriminate against you on the basis of race, age, gender, religious or political beliefs, disability or involvement in union activities. Nor can the employer or your supervisor sexually or racially harass you. If you are harassed by a co-worker or customer you can complain to your employer and your employer should then take steps to see that it does not happen again.

You have 90 days from the time of the 'offence' to either raise the matter with your employer or take your case to a mediation service, the Employment Relations Authority or the Employment Court. Clearly it is better, if you can, to discuss the matter with your employer and try to resolve the issue in house, but often this is not possible (for example, in the case of an unfair dismissal). You may have to go to the Department of Labour's mediation service for assistance, and if a solution cannot be found there, to the Employment Relations Authority or the Employment Court.

THE 'GOLDEN HANDSHAKE'

If your position is made redundant, you may receive a lump-sum redundancy payment. This is taxable (your employer will deduct the appropriate amount of tax) but is not subject to ACC levies.

This lump sum can provide a considerable opportunity to improve your financial position, but some people squander it.

The best use of this money for many people is to repay the mortgage, or at least part of it. However, in so doing you need to make sure you keep enough to meet everyday expenses for a while, until you have a cash income again.

If you have no mortgage you will probably choose to invest the money. It is fairly common for employers to help you in this regard by bringing in a financial adviser.

Many people have used their severance pay to buy a business. This is much more difficult than it sounds and there are many traps for the unwary. The most important thing is not to be hurried into it just because you feel a need to get back into the workforce. In this situation it is easy to pay far too much for a small business – effectively investing your capital to buy yourself a job.

Losing a job is a difficult time. You are under great stress at a time when you are faced with big decisions that can have long-lasting implications. You should get good advice before you do anything major.

Employment Relations Authority

The ERA is a relatively informal body that will look at your case and make a determination on the basis of fairness rather than strict legal technicalities. Run by the Department of Labour, it is based in Auckland, Wellington and Christchurch, though it does travel to other places to hear cases. You can choose whether or not to be represented at any hearing. The authority will try to resolve issues by consensus, and at any time may direct you and your employer to mediation.

You apply to the Employment Relations Authority by filling out a simple form obtainable from the Department of Labour's Employment Relations Service. In this you state the problem and what remedy you are seeking: reinstatement, reimbursement and/or compensation.

- *Reinstatement*
  This means getting your job back. In some cases this is impracticable, where the relationship between the employer and employee has completely broken down.

- *Reimbursement*
  You may seek reimbursement of wages you believe you are due, e.g. if you think you have been underpaid holiday pay. In this case you would ask the authority (or court) to have the employer make up your loss.

- *Compensation*
  You may be compensated for such things as humiliation, loss of dignity or injury to feelings. This is quite common in cases of unjustified dismissal. You can also claim for loss of any benefit that you might have expected had the grievance not arisen.

Employment Court

This is more formal than the Employment Relations Authority. You go to the Employment Court only if you are unhappy with a decision from the Employment Relations Authority. Most people choose to be represented in court by a lawyer, union official or employment relations consultant.

The Employment Court may again direct you to mediation. However, it also has the power to overturn ERA decisions and make binding rulings.

The ERA and the Employment Court may also make rulings in cases of sexual or racial harassment. This may include transfer, disciplinary action or making recommendations for workplace changes to ensure the harassment does not happen again.

THE FINANCIAL SECRETS

- ❏ You cannot expect any longer to have just one job, in one industry, with one employer for a lifetime.
- ❏ You will earn a lot of money over the course of your life. Just a small percentage increase in your wages or salary can make a big difference to your finances.
- ❏ Do what you can to raise your pay by taking every available opportunity to improve your skills.
- ❏ Being in continuous employment (and upgrading that employment) is probably the most important thing you can do to ensure your financial security.
- ❏ Employment law in New Zealand gives you considerable protection: know your rights and exercise them.

CONNECT

- ❏ Council of Trade Unions, phone (04) 385 1334
  www.union.org.nz
- ❏ Citizens Advice Bureau (see your local phone book)
- ❏ Employment Relations Service, phone 0800 800 863
  www.ers.dol.govt.nz
- ❏ Human Rights Commission, phone 0800 496 877
  www.hrc.govt.nz
- ❏ Other useful web sites:
  www.monster.co.nz
  www.jobhuntersbible.com

BOOKS

- ❏ *Buying and Selling a Business*, Keith McIlroy, Shoal Bay Press, 1999
- ❏ *A Guide to the Employment Relations Act*, Tom Gilbert, Andrew Scott-Howman & Karen Smith, Butterworths, 2000
- ❏ *New Zealand Employment Law Guide*, Richard Rudman, CCH, 2000
- ❏ *What Color is Your Parachute?*, Ten Speed Press, 2002

13. GOVERNMENT ASSISTANCE
Getting help

New Zealand is a civilised and affluent country, a country where there is a general belief that no one should go without the necessities of life. We have long organised things so that those who are not in a position to care for themselves (either temporarily or permanently) are cared for and have the means to afford at least the basics. It is reassuring to live in a country where you know that no matter what happens you, your children or grandchildren will not be put in the gutter and left to starve.

This is not charity. Our welfare system is a kind of insurance – we never know who may fall on hard times and need some assistance, whether financial or other.

This is our entitlement – we have all paid taxes to sustain the system. Those taxes are a kind of insurance premium (in our case the insurer is the government) and having made the payments you are entitled to the benefits if you need them.

WORK AND INCOME NEW ZEALAND

Work and Income New Zealand (WINZ) is the government department charged with ensuring that we can all meet our basic needs. WINZ has six main roles:

- Income support for those who need help.
- Provision of assistance to help people get back to work.
- Administration of the Student Loans Scheme and Student Allowances.
- Provision of Community Services Cards.
- Assistance (financial and other) to encourage employers to employ staff.
- Administration of the New Zealand Superannuation scheme.

When you become a WINZ 'client' you will be assigned a case manager who will keep your records and handle all your dealings with the department.

INCOME SUPPORT

Much of WINZ's massive budget (over $13 billion) goes on benefits, grants, allowances and superannuation payments.

> **RIPPING OFF THE SYSTEM**
>
> WINZ has wide powers, and will check all the information you give them regarding income, employment and expenditure against the records of other government agencies (Inland Revenue, Customs etc). They also have the power to talk to your bank, previous employers and education providers.
>
> WINZ may also look to see if you have deprived yourself of an asset so you can get a benefit. For example, if you had made gifts or shifted assets out of your name and into someone else's, WINZ would have the power to decline you a benefit.
>
> You must tell WINZ of any major or material change of circumstances in your life (for example if you marry or start to live with someone, get a job, receive an inheritance etc).
>
> The penalties for benefit fraud include fines and imprisonment.

As will be seen by the figures that follow, none of the benefits paid is particularly generous nor they would afford a lavish lifestyle. Public policy for the last decade or more has been to keep benefit levels low and try to encourage people into work.

Moreover, WINZ staff do not give out public funds unless they are deserved. There are strict criteria for eligibility to any benefit and WINZ has the power to ensure that the public is not defrauded of government money.

The following are the main benefits and the rates paid as at December 2003.

Unemployment Benefit

To be eligible for the dole you must be 18 or over (or 16-17 and living with a partner), have little or no income and be available for and actively seeking full-time work. Working with your case manager, you will be expected to come to an agreement (called a Job Seeker's Agreement), which spells out your obligations in receiving this benefit. This agreement will cover such things as being available to look for work, taking a job that is offered, training and up-skilling etc. If you do not meet these obligations your benefit may be stopped.

The current weekly rates for the Unemployment Benefit (after tax) are:

Single, no children, under 20 years, living at home	$107.76
Single, no children, under 20 years, not living at home	$134.70
Single, no children, 20-24 years	$134.70
Single, no children, 25 years or over	$161.65
Couple, no children	$269.40
Sole parent, 1 child	$231.53
Sole parent, 2 or more children	$252.60
Couple, 1 or more child	$286.28

Domestic Purposes Benefit

This is a benefit paid to people without partners who are caring for children or an adult who needs constant care. In some cases an older woman living alone may also be eligible.

There are obligations when you receive this benefit: if your youngest child is over 14, or you have no one at home during the day, you must look for full-time work. If your youngest child is between six and 13 you must look for part-time work (15 hours a week or more). Your case manager will give you guidance and support to get you ready for work and in some cases you may get financial support and training if you want to start a business. The benefit rates (after tax) are:

Woman alone, or single adult	$168.38
Sole parent, 1 child	$231.53
Sole parent, 2 or more children	$252.60

Sickness Benefit
This is to provide for people who cannot work or look for work due to sickness, injury, disability or pregnancy. You must be 18 or over (although in a few cases you may be eligible at age 16-17). The rates are the same as for the Unemployment Benefit.

Invalid's Benefit
This is a benefit for those who, because of a medical condition, are unlikely to be able to work or look for work for at least two years. The rates are:

Single, 16-17 years	$163.51
Single, 18 years or over	$202.05
Sole parent, 1 child	$265.43
Sole parent, 2 or more children	$285.03
Couple	$336.76

Transitional Retirement Benefit
This is for people who have retired and/or have a low income, but have not yet reached the age to receive superannuation. The rates are the same as for the Invalid's Benefit.

WINZ can provide additional support through other allowances:

Accommodation Supplement
This is to help with housing costs, whether you own your own house, rent or board. You do not need to be on a benefit to get this, but you no longer get it if you rent from Housing New Zealand. The tenants of Housing New Zealand now qualify for income-related rent.

Eligibility for an Accommodation Supplement depends on a range of factors:
- Your accommodation costs.
- Your income.
- Whether you have income-earning assets.
- Where you live (some locations are more expensive than others).

Childcare Subsidy

This gives a subsidy for childcare for children under the age of five years for up to nine hours per week. You can get a subsidy for up to 37 hours a week if you are working, on an approved training course or are ill. This subsidy is income-tested – the amount of the subsidy you receive is based on your weekly income.

In addition there is the OSCAR subsidy, which provides for out-of-school care for older children (between five and 13). It is only for those who are working, on an approved training course or are ill. Again, this is income-tested.

Disability Allowances

There are three allowances available for people with disabilities:

- A Disability Allowance is available for those who have a disability that is likely to last six months or more. This allowance is income-tested: a single person may get the allowance if his or her annual before-tax income is $20,592 or less; a couple with children may get the allowance if their income is under $34,320.
- The Child Disability Allowance is not income-tested and does not depend on your costs. It is for those with children under 18 years who need constant care and attention for at least 12 months because of the disability. You may be able to get both the Disability Allowance and the Child Disability Allowance.
- A Modification Grant, which covers special equipment or modifications to the workplace, is available is to make things easier for those with disabilities at work.

Training Incentive Allowance

This is available for those on Domestic Purposes, Widow's or Invalid's Benefits, or an Emergency Maintenance Allowance. It is to help with things like textbooks, fees or childcare when people take a training course in order to increase their chances of getting a job. The training course must be recognised by the New Zealand Qualifications Authority. You can get up to $75.38 per week, or a maximum of $3015.20 a year.

If you have dependent children aged 16-17 years who must live away from home to attend a training course, you may be eligible for an Away-from-home Allowance for them. To qualify you must be on income support or have a low income. The amount you receive depends on your costs and income.

Community Services Card
The Community Services Card gives you subsidised health care. It provides a subsidy for doctors' visits and for prescription costs. The current subsidy for doctors' visits are:

Adult	$15
Child 6 years or over	$20
Child under 6 years	$32.50 (available to non-card-holders also)

The Community Services Card is income-tested. Your income includes wages and salaries, benefits, investments, Student Allowances, rent from boarders, ACC payments and Family Assistance. The allowable annual income level rises according to the number of people in your family:

Single, sharing accommodation	$19,439
Single, living alone	$20,593
2-person family	$30,748
3-person family	$35,815
4-person family	$40,883
5-person family	$45,952
6-person family	$51,022

You cannot get a Community Services Card if your income exceeds these levels.

High-use Health Card
This is for people who have visited the doctor at least 12 times in the last year and provides additional subsidies for both doctors' visits and prescriptions. It is not income-tested.

Special needs and emergency grants
A range of grants, benefits and allowances is available to those facing particular hardship. There are one-off grants for emergency situations, and ongoing allowances to cover a major deficiency of income over expenditure. Some of these are recoverable (i.e. must be repaid) and some are not. All require strict income and asset tests.

FINDING WORK
Another of WINZ's major roles is to get people into work. To this end it:
- Encourages clients to go on training courses to increase job skills.
- Offers clients work experience. Employers who take people on work experience do not pay the worker's wages, making this a win-win situation.

> **WORKING WHILE ON A BENEFIT**
>
> You can work while on most benefits. Generally, you will be able to keep some of the money you earn, but as your income rises your benefit will be reduced. While different benefits have different rules, typically you can earn about $80 a week before the benefit starts to abate.

- Encourages clients to get involved in 'Activity in the Community' projects, allowing certain community projects to be completed at no cost.
- Runs recruitment services and a 'talent bank' free of charge.
- Gives employers subsidies to take on workers in certain circumstances.

The Taskforce Green project also offers subsidies to groups doing projects that will benefit the environment and/or communities.

FAMILY ASSISTANCE

Family Assistance is an umbrella programme designed to help low- and middle-income families. It is organised through the IRD for most people, although those who are on benefits receive theirs through WINZ.

Family Assistance is for those with children under 18 who are living at home and financially dependent. It takes four forms:

- Family Support
- Child Tax Credit
- Family Tax Credit
- Parental Tax Credit

You may qualify for more than one form of assistance. The amount you receive will depend upon:

- How many children you have.
- Your total family income.
- Where the income comes from (i.e. whether it is from wages, salaries or benefits).

You apply for Family Assistance by filing out a FS1 form, which is available from any WINZ office. If you qualify, the amount due will be credited directly into your bank account (and to your partner's bank account as well, in some cases). You do not need to keep applying for Family Assistance – it rolls over from year to year – but you must remember to advise WINZ if your personal circumstances change.

Family Support

Family Support is paid to families according to their income and the number of dependent children. Just over $200 a week will be paid to a family with six children on an annual income of $9500, and the payment abates as income rises and the number of children falls. You may qualify for Family Support if you have an annual income of:

1 child, and income less than	$30,946
2 children, and income less than	$36,493
3 children, and income less than	$42,040
4 children, and income less than	$47,586
5 children, and income less than	$53,133
6 children, and income less than	$58,680

Recipients of Family Support may also receive money from other Family Assistance programmes.

Child Tax Credit

An income-tested Child Tax Credit is available to those who do not receive a benefit, New Zealand Superannuation, a Student Allowance or weekly ACC payment. The maximum rate is $15 per week for each dependent child. It is paid directly into your bank account each fortnight. You may qualify for a Child Tax Credit if you have:

1 child, and income less than	$33,546
2 children, and income less than	$41,693
3 children, and income less than	$49,840
4 children, and income less than	$57,986
5 children, and income less than	$66,133
6 children, and income less than	$74,280

Family Tax Credit

A Family Tax Credit is designed to ensure that all families have an annual income of at least $18,368. It is a top-up payment for families with at least one parent working for wages or salary. It can be paid as an annual lump sum or fortnightly. In two-parent families half is paid to each parent.

WINZ APPEALS AND REVIEWS

If you disagree with a decision made by your WINZ case manager you are entitled to appeal and ask for a review. In the first instance you should state your reasons to your case manager, and listen carefully to the reply. If you still disagree, you can appeal either by writing a letter, or by filling in an appeal form (available from all WINZ offices).

Your appeal will be reviewed in the first instance by a senior WINZ official, who will write a report and give you a copy. If this report agrees with you, things will be put right. However, if you disagree with the report in whole or in part, you can proceed with your appeal, which will be heard by the Benefit Review Committee. This is made up of three people, one of whom is a member of the community. None of the the committee will have had anything to do with your case.

The committee will hear your case – you don't have to attend if you don't want to – and will report its findings, usually within five weeks.

If you still do not agree, it is possible to appeal further to the Social Security Appeals Authority. This is an independent judicial authority and none of its members work for WINZ.

Parental Tax Credit

A Parental Tax Credit is worth up to $1200 a year to the principal childcarer during the first eight weeks of a baby's life. Again, the payment amount depends on your income and the number of days the baby is in your care. If you have one child and an annual income of $59,617 or less you may qualify for a Parental Tax Credit. The allowable income level rises as the number of children increases.

ACCIDENT COMPENSATION CORPORATION

The Accident Compensation Corporation (ACC) is a crown-owned entity. Its main roles are:

- The payment of compensation to people who have been injured.
- The rehabilitation of injured people.
- The prevention of accidents.

In New Zealand, people who have been injured cannot generally sue for damages (other than exemplary or punitive damages, and these are rare). In adopting the ACC scheme, we gave up the right to sue. Although this was controversial, it has to be said that there are considerable advantages in being able to be compensated for an accident without having to sue some liable party. It avoids the time-consuming, costly and risky business of going to court – and some of the bizarre cases that happen in other countries.

Compensation can be paid to anyone who has had an accident, regardless of how it was caused – ACC is a 'no fault' scheme. Your medical practioner will help you make a claim if you are injured in an accident.

What ACC covers

ACC covers you for personal injury, both physical and mental (where the mental injury was caused by a physical one). This includes:

- Accidents at work, at home or on the road.
- Work-related accidents and infections, including gradual ones.
- Medical misadventure.
- Sexual assault or abuse.

All New Zealanders are covered, whether or not they are earning income, and will generally be covered if the accident happens while overseas, provided that you are normally resident in this country. Overseas visitors are also usually covered.

Compensation

If you are injured in an accident and your claim is accepted by the ACC you are covered for compensation for lost earnings, medical costs, rehabilitation costs and death.

Compensation for lost earnings

There is a one-week stand-down period, during which time your employer will pay your wages. After that, the ACC will pay you 80 per cent of your taxable weekly earnings. If you are off work for up to five weeks your weekly earnings are calculated from your last four weeks' wages. If you are off work for longer than this they will be based on your last 52 weeks' earnings. You must have been earning immediately before the accident and you will need a certificate from a doctor stating that you cannot work because of your injury.

Medical costs

This includes compensation for the cost of most forms of medical and dental treatment, including visits to your GP, prescriptions, x-rays, physiotherapy, artificial limbs, optometrists, counselling etc. You may also be entitled to compensation for transport costs for treatment. You may have to pay part of the cost if it exceeds the ACC's ceiling.

Rehabilitation

The ACC will work with you to develop a rehabilitation plan to get you back to work and independence. This could include vocational assessment, help to look after the children, equipment (e.g. a wheelchair), and modifications to your home or workplace.

Death by accident

The spouse or partner and children of those who have died because of an accident may receive compensation:

- *A funeral grant*, to a maximum of $3284.
- *Survivor's grants*. A bereaved partner may receive $4702; a child under 18 may receive $2351.
- *Weekly compensation*. This is to compensate for the deceased's lost wages. It can be up to 60 per cent of the weekly wage and is paid to the bereaved partner for five years, or longer if the deceased's children are still be cared for and under 18. Remarriage does not affect the compensation paid.
- *Childcare payments*. The ACC may pay $105 a week if there is one child, $126 a week for two children and $147 for three or more children. This money is paid for five years or until the child turns 14 (whichever comes first). It is paid to the partner or a trustee until the child turns 16.

WHAT DEFINES AN ACCIDENT?

The definition of an accident is by no means black and white. For example, a heart attack would not normally be classified as an accident, but if it was caused at work through excessive exertion you would probably be covered by ACC.

An injury can be considered to be the result of normal 'wear and tear' rather than an accident.

ACC DISPUTES

Such questions as whether a particular injury constitutes an accident, and when someone is fit to return to work, are open to argument and a great number of disputes arise between the ACC and its clients. There is a disputes procedure to follow if you think you are being treated unfairly.

The first thing you can do is to ask the ACC for a review of any decision you are unhappy with. This will be conducted by someone who was not involved with the original decision. If you are not satisfied with the result of the review, you may appeal. Further information on ACC appeals is available from district court offices.

BENEFITS ARE A BACK-UP

The benefits and allowances we are entitled to from the government are a source of back-up finance but they do not provide enough to live the life most people want. Planning for today and tomorrow – with insurance, savings and investments – is critical to ensure there is enough money available in case of emergency or when things simply don't go to plan.

THE FINANCIAL SECRETS

- Your entitlements are just that. You have contributed to them: they are not charity.
- Benefits provide a safety net; they will not make you well off.
- You need to know what you are entitled to. You cannot rely on WINZ to tell you. Always ask questions of your case manager.
- Most benefits require strict income and asset tests.

CONNECT

- Work and Income New Zealand (WINZ) (see your local phone book) www.winz.govt.nz
- Accident Compensation Corporation, phone 0508 222993 www.acc.org.nz

14. RETIREMENT
You've earned it

Moving into retirement is a time for planning. A change of life and a change in circumstances mean you must rethink your life strategies and adopt new ones.

The plan you set may need to carry you through for a long time: if you retire at 65 you could easily be retired for a couple of decades or more. Conversely, at any time something could happen to disable you and means that you need care. You need to arrange your affairs and set your plans so that you will be comfortable whatever happens. You need, therefore to plan:

- *The amount of money you will want or need to live on*
  The time to plan and arrange these things is now – whatever age you are.

  See Superannuation, Chapter 6

- *Where you want to live*
  Will your present house continue to be suitable for retirement? Do you want to move closer to family, or think about a smaller house or possibly a retirement village?

- *Succession planning*
  The terms of your will need to be reviewed, and some people will want to consider a family trust.

- *Who will take care of you when and if you need it*
  Consideration also needs to be given to making out an Enduring Power of Attorney, which allows someone to deal with your affairs if you become incapacitated.

There is no escaping the fact that old age is a time when some functions and abilities diminish. This may not happen to you to a significant degree for decades but it could happen at any time quite suddenly. A good financial plan – one that could be followed easily by anyone who ends up looking after you – is therefore essential.

PLANNING YOUR INCOME

This is probably the most important thing to get right – you don't want run out of money! By the time you reach retirement you'll know how much you have saved. and also what you will receive

> **CONTINUING TO WORK**
>
> You may continue to work to some degree after you have reached retirement age. This trend is likely to increase as work becomes less manual and more knowledge-based. Older people often make good, knowledge workers as they have decades of experience. In any event, recent changes to the law mean that you can no longer be forced to retire simply because you have turn 65.
>
> Those who do continue to work, on a full-time or part-time basis, report that they stay fitter and more alert, and have better social lives. And of course the extra money helps!

from the government. It should then be a fairly simple exercise to do something of a budget: planning your expenditure and therefore your lifestyle.

In retirement you will be on a fixed income, so your budget is likely to be tighter than it was. You can't simply do a bit of extra overtime to make up for some unexpected bill. If you spend money on something for which you had not planned, it is likely to have to come out of your savings – which might adversely affect your future income.

The other thing people struggle with in retirement is being asset rich and cash poor. Many retirees have a lot of their wealth tied up in the family home, a holiday home or investment property. Although they are quite wealthy on paper, they have trouble paying for the groceries. A bit of planning should ensure that you have good income (or at least ready cash). This may involve selling the family home and buying a more modest one, or selling an investment property so that there is both good income and readily available cash.

Government help

New Zealand Superannuation

This a pension paid by the state until death. To qualify you need to be over the age of 65 years and have lived in New Zealand for 10 years since you turned age 20 years, including at least five of the last 10 years.

Currently, if you have no other taxable income, the after-tax rates for New Zealand Super are:

Single (living alone)	$245 per week
Single (sharing)	$226 per week
Couple (both qualify)	$377 per week
Couple (only one qualifies)	$189 per week

Although New Zealand Super is taxed, it is not means tested. For a couple who both qualify it is set at between 65 and 72.5 per cent of the average ordinary-time wage and is adjusted for inflation.

Other state assistance

You may be eligible for one or some of the following:

- *Community Services Card.* This reduces the costs of visits to the doctor and for prescriptions, providing your income is below a certain level.

- *High-use Health Card.* Even if you are not eligible for a Community Services Card, you may qualify for assistance if you have high health-care needs for ongoing conditions.
- *Pharmaceutical Subsidy Card.* This will reduce the cost of drugs if you need a lot of prescriptions.
- *Disability Allowance.* The government will help towards extra costs if you have a disability that is likely to last for at least six months. This can help with things like hospital or doctors' visits, prescriptions, extra clothing, special foods and travel.
- *Accommodation Supplement.* Help is available for housing, depending on your costs and income.
- *Funeral Grant.* If you are the partner, parent or guardian of someone who has died you may be eligible for an asset-tested grant to help with funeral costs.
- *Special benefits and grants.* If you have a financial emergency you may receive a special benefit or grant to help with things like food, clothing, dental care or bedding. Sometimes you can receive a grant for things like car repairs but these have to be repaid.

For more details on whether or not you qualify for any of these, call Work and Income on 0800 552 002 or go to www.winz.govt.nz

Rearranging your investments

At retirement, you should review your investments. Typically at retirement people sell out of growth investments (shares and property) and go into income investments (bonds and bank deposits). However, you may be retired for a long time and inflation can whittle away at cash savings. Certainly your portfolio may become more weighted towards income investments but you should retain some growth investments as well. The idea of balance remains important.

Many wise investors in retirement buy into things that pay a high dividend (perhaps as much as 10 per cent) but will still grow in value to some (smaller) extent, for example:

- Commercial property syndicates.
- Listed property shares.
- High-dividend shares.
- Ungeared property investments.

Annuities

You can add to your regular income by the purchase of an annuity. This is an investment purchased with a lump sum from your savings, which then pays you an agreed monthly amount for the rest

HOME EQUITY ANNUITY MORTGAGE

This is a type of annuity but instead of providing a lump sum to purchase it, you provide the deeds to your house. The life insurance company takes a mortgage over the property and makes payments to you. It may be by way of regular monthly payments or it might involve an arrangement for you to draw cash on the facility as you need it.

When the house is sold, or when you die, the life insurance company is repaid its outlay, with interest. Clearly this will decrease any inheritance you were planning to leave your children.

These facilities, common overseas, are offered here by only two companies: Invincible Life and Taranaki Savings Bank.

of your life. An annuity is something of a gamble, because you may live and receive payments for a long time – or you may not.

It is useful to think of annuities as the opposite of a mortgage: with a mortgage you receive a lump sum (which you use to buy a house) and then dripfeed this back with interest over a long period of time. With an annuity you give a lump sum and receive it back by a dripfeed over a long time.

The size of the monthly payments you receive depends on a number of factors:

- How much you outlaid (the more you put in the greater the payments)
- Whether or not it automatically increases periodically. Some annuities contain a clause stipulating that the monthly payment will increase by, say, 2 per cent each year.
- Whether or not there is a guaranteed minimum payment. Annuity payments usually continue until death, but they can be purchased so that if you die within 10 years your estate will receive payments.
- Whether you are male or female. Women live longer so their monthly payments are smaller.
- Whether the annuity is payable to two people or one. An annuity for a couple would generally reduce when the first partner dies but continue until the death of the second partner.

Annuities are offered only by life insurance companies. Their minimum capital requirement is regulated so they are deemed unlikely to take your cash and then go broke before they have made your monthly payments.

Annuities are more common overseas, particularly in Europe, where pension regulations often require retirement savings to be taken as an annuity. However, most major New Zealand life insurance companies offer them, and they are an ideal retirement investment for those who want a regular income but don't want to have to manage their own money. On the downside, you have no control over payments, which can leave you high and dry if you have an unexpected large expense.

EXPENDITURE

As well as planning your retirement income you also have to plan your expenditure. As a rule of thumb, your expenditure in retirement is likely to be around 70 per cent of what it was before retirement. Some of your costs will probably rise (health care, leisure activities) while others will fall (clothing, transport).

Obviously this figure will vary enormously between individuals, depending on their lifestyle and circumstances but it is a reasonable starting point.

RETIREMENT BUDGET

When you have planned both your income and expenditure, you can finalise your budget. If it doesn't balance you'll need to either increase income or reduce expenditure.

While reducing expenditure is people's natural response to a shortfall, make sure first that you have tapped all possible sources of income. Look at spending some of your savings, rather than just the income from your savings. People always seem to try to keep their capital intact, which is strange, really, given that they have worked to save it for retirement. Well, when retirement arrives, it is okay to spend your savings – although you have to be careful that they don't run out before you do!

If you cannot achieve enough income, you'll have to work on the expenditure side of the equation, cutting your lifestyle to fit your circumstances.

SUCCESSION PLANNING

Succession planning is about passing on your assets after you die. This is important for everyone, but especially those in retirement.

There are some people who don't especially want to leave any legacy or inheritance – they are quite happy to see the cheque to the undertaker bounce. These people believe they have built up their assets and intend to enjoy them to fullest. However, most of us want to leave something behind to help our offspring get on.

The aim of succession planning is to be sure your assets go where you want them to. This is not necessarily as easy as it sounds – there are plenty of examples where assets have gone to someone who was not contemplated by the deceased.

New Zealand now has no estate duties (death duties were abolished in 1992), nor any form of inheritance tax. However, it is still important to take care in working out how you want to dispose of your assets – and get it right.

Wills

Everyone should have a will. Dying without one (called dying intestate) means that your assets will be distributed according to the Family Protection Act. It is quite possible this will see your assets distributed in ways you would not have chosen (see p.197).

Having a will means that you can:

- Ensure that your assets go to the people you want to have them.
- Have your will administered by someone you know and trust.
- Appoint guardians for your children.

Making a will

A will must be in writing and witnessed. A person who is a beneficiary cannot be a witness to the will.

It is possible to make your own, either by writing it yourself or by using one of the 'wills kits' that are available. However, for the vast majority of people, and certainly those who have significant assets, it is far better to have one drawn up by a solicitor or trust company. Many lawyers will not charge for drawing up a will (but ask first!), especially if it is fairly simple and they are to be appointed executor. The Public Trust does not charge for drawing up a will, providing it is appointed executor.

Having a professional draw up your will means it gets done properly, and the document, or a copy of it, is well looked after.

Overturning a will

Wills can be overturned on four grounds:

1. That you were not of sound mind.
2. Testamentary promise. If someone feels that they have been deprived of an asset that was promised (perhaps because they did something for you) he or she can challenge the will.
3. Under the Family Protection Act you have a duty to care for a spouse or children and such family members may be able to overturn your will if they are excluded from it.
4. The Property (Relationships) Act, previously known as the Matrimonial Property Act, now applies to de facto couples. In some circumstances the Act can override the provisions of a will.

Taking professional advice on drawing up a will should prevent problems such as challenges. However, where large amounts of money are involved in estates, old family difficulties can cause bitter legal disputes. Even though your will may clearly state your wishes, there is no guarantee that someone will not use legal methods to try to overturn it.

The executor

The executor is the person or organisation that administers your will and makes sure your wishes are carried out. Interestingly, many people appoint an executor who is likely to die before they do – i.e. someone older than they are.

Most people choose two executors, not only to avoid this sort of difficulty but because it shares the load. While there is no legal requirement to do so, it is nevertheless a good idea to ask people first if they are willing. This reduces the chance that they will decline to act after you have died, meaning the court must have someone else appointed.

It is probably wise to have an executor who is a professional – generally either a lawyer or a trust company. This person will be able to handle the more formal part of executing a will (e.g. getting probate). The second person appointed as executor will often be a friend or family member, who may do less of the work but will oversee things to make sure everything is handled according to your wishes.

Executors may charge for their services (provided this is allowed for in the will). Lawyers will usually charge an estate on a time basis, while trust companies will probably charge a percentage of the value of the estate or a set fee.

The first job for the executors is to help with the funeral arrangements, ensuring that the funeral is according to your wishes. They will also get a copy of the death certificate and start to assemble a list of the deceased's assets and liabilities. This task will be made considerably easier for them if you have kept good records and file copies of any financial documents (insurance policies, mortgage documents etc).

Probate
The executor will then have to go to court to get probate. This simply means that a court has 'proved' the will. The Grant of Probate is important because share registries and fund managers will

---

DYING INTESTATE

Dying without a will can create big problems. For one thing it means the estate will incur increased costs. A court will have to appoint executors (which might be costly in itself), and there is a far greater chance that someone will make a claim on your estate and advance that claim through the courts. The Family Protection Act lays down how assets are to be divided in the absence of a will. The rules are:

If you have a spouse, but no children or parents:
- The whole estate goes to your spouse.

If you have children but no spouse:
- The whole estate goes to the children, divided equally.

If you have a spouse and children:
- Your spouse receives all personal chattels, the first $121,500 and then one-third of the remainder of the estate.
- Your children receive two-thirds of the remainder of your estate, divided equally.

If you have parents but no children or spouse:
- Everything goes to your parents.

If you have a spouse and parents but no children:
- Your spouse receives all personal chattels, the first $121,500 and then two-thirds of the remainder of the estate.
- Your parents receive one-third of the remainder.

If you have no spouse, children or parents:
- The whole estate may go to blood relations, but if they are too remote it goes to the Crown.

GUARDIANSHIP

While you have children under 18 your will should appoint a guardian to care for them in the event of the death of both parents. Be sure to ask this person's permission (and think carefully about all the implications before you agree to become the guardian of someone else's children).

> **KEEP YOUR WILL UP TO DATE**
>
> Your will is the primary document dictating what you want to happen when you die, but it needs to be kept up to date. Circumstances in life change and you should make a new will when something major happens in your life, like marriage or the birth of children or grandchildren. A previous will is automatically revoked when you marry, unless it was made in contemplation of marriage.

not allow assets to be dealt with until it has been sighted. When probate has been granted by a court and recorded with all registries, the executors will then justify any liabilities and debts.

Trustees

At this point the role of executor becomes that of trustee (executors and trustees are nearly always the same person in a will). The trustees distribute the assets to the beneficiaries as laid out in the will. Sometimes the trustees have to hold on to the assets because beneficiaries are only to benefit when they have reached a certain age. This can mean that the trustees have to manage and administer the estate for months, years or occasionally even decades.

Ownership of assets

The way that assets are owned (particularly the house) can affect the surviving partner's circumstances after the other dies.

- Ownership as 'joint tenants' means that on the death of one, the entire asset passes to the other partner, regardless of what a will might say or whether the deceased died intestate.
- Ownership as 'tenants in common' means the share of the asset owned by the deceased can be dealt with under the will.

Enduring Power of Attorney

This is another document that everyone should have, but especially those in retirement. An Enduring Power of Attorney appoints someone to look after your affairs in the event of your becoming incapacitated. Usually it gives someone the power both to take care of the person who has become incapacitated (ensuring that you are in a good, safe environment) and also the power to deal with property and make decisions regarding financial matters.

If you become mentally unsound and have not given power of attorney, it can be a difficult and expensive legal process going to court to have someone appointed to look after your affairs.

An Enduring Power of Attorney must be properly drawn up and executed by a lawyer or trust company. Usually this will be done at the same time as you draw up your will. On your death, the power of attorney is automatically revoked and the executors and trustees of your will look after your estate.

FAMILY TRUSTS

A family trust is another way to manage the succession of your assets. Family trusts have been called 'living wills' because your assets are put into trust for beneficiaries while you are still alive. You no longer own your assets – they are owned by the trustees, who hold them for the beneficiaries.

It is possible for you to be a trustee of your own trust, increasing the amount of control you have over what happens to your assets.

People set up family trusts for all sorts of reasons, including tax minimisation and asset protection. From a succession planning point of view, there are six main reasons:

1. *Ensuring that your will cannot be overturned.*
   A will can be attacked and possibly overturned through testamentary promise or the Family Protection Act. However, with a family trust, beneficiaries or family members and others generally have no rights to a benefit – no member of your family nor anyone else can attack your trust and demand a benefit. This makes a family trust ideal for people who want to ensure that someone in particular does not benefit from their assets. For example, if you have already provided a great deal of financial support for one of your children and don't want to see that child getting more, a family trust can get around the problem.

2. *Making benefits contingent upon something happening.*
   It may be that you wish your children to receive a benefit only upon the occurrence of some particular event, e.g. when they have attained a certain age, married or gained an academic qualification. A family trust can achieve this by making it a term of the trust. (This can also be achieved through a testamentary trust formed through your will upon your death, but many people feel more confident if they can see the trust operating properly while they are still alive.)

3. *Being eligible for rest-home care subsidy.*

4. *Ensuring that your assets are not lost to your family through a marriage or relationship break-up.*

   See Family trusts, p.134-35

5. *Ensuring that your assets do not pass to a new partner of your spouse.*
   It is quite possible that after you die your partner may re-marry. If in turn he or she dies, without a family trust what were once your assets could go to your partner's new spouse or partner.

6. *Estate duties.*
   New Zealand no longer has estate duties (death duties), but in the past family trusts were widely and effectively used to avoid them. Of course, should a future government reintroduce some

sort of estate duty, there is no guarantee that a family trust will provide the same sort of protection.

Wills and trusts

It could be argued that once you have placed all your assets into a family trust you no longer need a will, as you no longer own anything to bequeath. However, this is seldom the case in reality:

- You will need a will to nominate the trustees of your family trust after you are gone.
- You may need to decide how young children will be cared for.
- You may want to give instructions regarding your funeral.
- You are unlikely to be in a position where you own nothing at all – things like your car, clothing and other personal effects are unlikely to be in the trust.
- The trust may still owe you money that has not yet been gifted to the family trust. This is still an asset to be dealt with under your will.

See Guardianship, p.197

Most lawyers and trust companies make the writing of a new will standard practice when they help you form a family trust. Often that new will says all of your remaining assets are to go into the trust – i.e. the family trust is the sole beneficiary of your will. This makes the administration of your estate much simpler.

ASSET TESTING FOR RESIDENTIAL CARE SUBSIDIES

When (or if) you go into residential care, you may receive a government subsidy for the cost. Rest-home care is expensive (around $30,000 per annum) and if you have to pay this yourself it will quickly eat into your assets.

Not everyone receives a subsidy – most people are too 'wealthy' by the standards of the government. The government, through WINZ, tests your assets and income and if there is too much of either will not subsidise your care.

To apply for a subsidy from WINZ:

- You must be 65 or older (there are some exceptions to this).
- You must have had a needs assessment done, confirming that you need care in a licensed rest-home or hospital.
- You must need this care for an indefinite period.

To qualify for a subsidy, your assets must be less than:

- $15,000 for a single or widowed person.
- $30,000 in joint assets if you are both in care.
- $45,000 in joint assets if one of you is in care.

The Government has introduced legislation to increase these asset threshholds, but any changes made will not come into effect until the 2005 year.

The asset test
Assets include investments of all types (including loans to other people) and your house, chattels and car (if you live alone). If you don't live alone, your house, chattels and car don't count. Personal clothing and jewellery and pre-paid funeral expenses up to $10,000 are not counted.

If your house is counted as an asset (i.e. if you live alone) you will not get a subsidy. However, WINZ will effectively lend you the money for care, to be repaid when your house is sold or when you die. This loan is supported by a caveat on the title of the house.

WINZ will also ask you if you have made any gifts in the previous five years. If any gifts total over $5000 in any one year, you will be declined a subsidy. (This includes assets gifted to your family trust.) This asset test for residential care has caused much resentment. Few other government benefits are asset tested in this way.

The income test
Any income you earn has to go towards your care, up to an amount of $636 per week. This is the maximum contribution you can be asked to make, regardless of your income. Income includes New Zealand Super, pensions, annuities (although only half of annuity payments are usually counted), contributions from relatives, ACC payments and investment income. If you have to contribute all of your income you will receive a personal allowance of $27 per week and a clothing allowance of $200 per annum.

If your partner works, he or she can earn $27,000 per annum before tax before being asked to contribute (although the earnings figure may be higher if you have dependent children).

Avoiding the asset-testing regime
The asset-testing regime means your assets must be used for your residential care. This, of course, reduces any inheritance you can leave to your children. This has upset many older people and encouraged them to look for ways around the regime.

There are some things you can do which will reduce the size of your estate without affecting your children's inheritance:

1. *Pre-paid funeral trust*
   Usually funeral expenses will come out of your estate. However, you can pre-pay your funeral expenses up to a maximum of $10,000. This pre-payment is not regarded as an asset by WINZ

in testing for a residential-care subsidy. Be sure that your pre-paid funeral expenses do not go to a funeral company directly but are paid into a trust so they remain secure. The Public Trust offers funeral trusts.

2. *Gifts to your children (or others)*
You can gift money to your children, or others. However, you need to start doing this early. WINZ will look back five years to see what gifting has been done and if you have made gifts in any one year totalling $5000 or more WINZ will decline a subsidy.

3. *Establish a family trust*
If your assets are owned by a family trust they are not your assets – they are the trust's – and so are not caught by the asset-testing regime. But there's a catch: when you form a trust you sell it your assets so the trust owes you money. This debt the trust owes is an asset and so must be gifted to the trust. This is usually done at the rate of $27,000 a year (the maximum allowable before gift duty) and you must have finished your gifting to the trust five years before you apply for a subsidy. Many people leave the forming of a trust too late to be able to gift everything to it.

4. *Own your house with you and your partner as tenants in common*
This means that you and your partner each own a share of the house, which you can deal with as you wish under your will – in other words, you do not own the entire house. This reduces the total assets you own.

RETIREMENT VILLAGES

At present, only a small number of New Zealanders opt to live in retirement villages, but this is growing trend. The term 'retirement village' puts many people off, but it has to be said that the concept offers considerable advantages for older people.

Retirement villages are owned by a range of organisations: religious or charitable organisations, friendly societies or private enterprises. They range from the luxurious (and expensive) to the quite basic.

The first thing to think about is whether you can or should carry on living independently in your own home. The thought of giving up that independence (along with the habits of a lifetime) makes most people reluctant to consider anything else. However, there is a lot of independence in retirement villages too – people come and go as they please, take part in activities as and when they want (but not if they don't) and maintain their freedom in many ways.

Other advantages include:

- Security and safety – emergency call button, medical care etc.
- Being surrounded by people of the same age (a disadvantage to some!).
- Access to increasing levels of care if required.
- Amenities on site – sports groups, hairdresser, transport, classes, activities, entertainment etc.
- Freedom from housework and home maintenance.

Means of ownership

The means of owning a unit in a retirement village varies: there are strata titles, registered leases, licences to occupy and cross-leases. There is no 'right' or 'wrong' way – in all cases you should have security of tenure. Just make sure you talk to your lawyer before you sign anything.

Picking the right place for you

In some parts of the country (e.g. Auckland, Tauranga) you will have considerable choice; in other areas there may be few retirement villages to choose from.

The first factor for many people will be cost (see below). The second will probably be the location of the village: most people want to be close to the area they have always lived in, close to family, or perhaps somewhere offering a desirable climate.

If you have a choice, some other factors are:

- The level of security offered.
- The level of independence and privacy.
- The recreational activities offered.
- The quality of management.
- The stability of management.
- The availability of and increasing levels of care.
- The amount of say you will have in how the village is run.

The cost

If ever there was an area that required good research and shopping around, this is it. Retirement villages have all sorts of different ways of charging and, just as important perhaps, different rules regarding how you can sell your unit.

With a house you decide where you want to live and what amenities you want, and then simply write a cheque when you have found something that suits. With retirement villages there is a confusing matrix of charges and costs that mean there's no quick and simple way to compare costs.

There are five main things to find out, consider and compare:

1. *Up-front cost*

    This is likely to be many thousands of dollars. You need to decide whether you can afford it and whether you think it represents good value for money. You also need to work out how much of this capital you will get back when you sell the unit (see below).

2. *Ongoing costs*

    This can cover everything from the wages of managers, rates and insurance to maintenance, which you will pay for on a weekly/fortnightly/monthly basis. You are reimbursing the manager for these costs, which will vary from village to village.

3. *Internal costs*

    These are the ongoing costs for your own unit: power, phone, insurance etc. In addition, there may be a requirement that you redecorate periodically and keep the unit in good repair.

4. *Deferred management fee*

    This is the big one for many people – the area where the village's developers and managers expect to make their profits. The deferred management fee is taken when you sell the unit. When you buy into a retirement village, you agree that on sale you will give to the developer a percentage of the value of the unit. This percentage varies greatly, sometimes being calculated on the price you paid, sometimes on the price at which it is sold. This fee puts many people off retirement villages – the deduction of, say, 20 per cent of the value of a unit can be quite a lot of money, although if it is spread over 10 years of residency it may be relatively small on an annual basis.

5. *Selling rules*

    Most retirement villages have rules as to whom you can sell to. Generally there is an age restriction (55 or 60 years) and a rule barring investors from buying units – i.e. they must be owner-occupied. Moreover, some villages insist that they resell your unit. This is often not a good idea, as they may hold out for top dollar (or be building more units and concentrating on the sale of these) and in the meantime you still have to pay ongoing fees. Some villages offer a guaranteed repurchase scheme – i.e. if your unit has not sold within a certain time-frame, the developers will buy it back after an independent valuation.

Don't sign up in a hurry!

Going into a retirement village is a big decision, and choosing the right one is almost as big. Don't sign anything until:

- You fully understand the pros and cons of the particular village.

- You fully understand all its costs.
- You have compared the costs with those of other villages.
- You fully understand all the various rules.
- You have taken advice from a lawyer.

THE FINANCIAL SECRETS

- ❏ You may be in retirement for a very long time and should plan carefully and early.
- ❏ Make a will and keep it up to date.
- ❏ Have an Enduring Power of Attorney and keep it up to date.
- ❏ You can beat the asset-testing regime, but you must act early.
- ❏ A family trust gives considerable protection from an attack on your will.

CONNECT

- ❏ Consumers' Institute, phone 0800 266 786 (0800 CONSUMER)
  www.consumer.org.nz
- ❏ Work and Income, phone 0800 552 002
  www.winz.govt.nz
- ❏ Retirement Villages Association
  www.retirementvillages.org.nz
- ❏ Age Concern (see local phone book)
- ❏ Citizens' Advice Bureau (see local phone book)
- ❏ Budget Advisory Service (see local phone book)
- ❏ Public Trust, phone 0800 371 471
  www.publictrust.co.nz
- ❏ www.sorted.org.nz

BOOKS

- ❏ *Family Trusts, A New Zealand Guide (rev. ed.)*, Martin Hawes, Shoal Bay Press, 2001
- ❏ *Keep Your Money Working,* Consumers' Institute, 1997
- ❏ *Lifestyle Retirement, A New Zealand Guide to the Retirement Village Option*, Barrie Flint, Random House, 2001
- ❏ *A New Zealand Guide to Living Well in Retirement*, Noel Whittaker & Roger Moses, Hodder Moa Beckett, 1995
- ❏ *The Realities of Retirement,* Bill Jamieson, Shoal Bay Press, 1998
- ❏ *Successful Super,* Martin Hawes, Penguin, 1997
- ❏ *Your Retirement Action Planner* (a booklet produced by the Office of the Retirement Commissioner)

15. FINANCIAL FAILURE
When things go wrong

Bad things happen: people go bankrupt, companies go into receivership or liquidation. No one wants it to happen, but insolvency is common enough. In some cases one financial failure can result in a chain of insolvencies as one failure leads to another. And yet, when it does happen, people behave as if it is a most unexpected event and has never happened before.

You need to think about this issue for two reasons:

1. You (or a family member) may become insolvent. If you do, you need to know your rights and obligations.
2. Someone who owes you money may become insolvent. If that happens, you need to know how you can recover as much as possible.

INSOLVENCY: THE BASICS

People (and companies) are said to be insolvent either when they can no longer pay their bills as they fall due, or when their liabilities (debts) are greater than their assets. People are insolvent when they owe more than they own.

Generally, insolvency happens to people and companies that take on debts, but this is not always the case: a person or a company may be sued and not be able to make the payment; they may be assessed for additional taxes they can't afford; they may be prosecuted and fined and not have the money to pay. A workplace accident might result in a costly action under Occupational Safety and Health (OSH) regulations. Usually, however, people fail financially because they have excessive debts.

Creditors

Broadly, there are three types of creditor:

- *Secured creditors*
  These are creditors who have some security over the debtor's assets. They may hold a mortgage over a property, a debenture over a company's assets, or security over a car or other plant and machinery. Secured creditors get paid first from the sale of assets over which they have security.

- *Preferential creditors*

    These are creditors who get paid in preference to other creditors (although they usually do not get paid before creditors who have some security). Preferential creditors include the IRD for unpaid taxes and staff for unpaid wages, holiday pay etc.

- *Unsecured creditors*

    These are the people who are last to get paid – they have no assets as security. As such they often miss out on receiving anything at all from an insolvency.

Bankruptcy

Only people can become bankrupt. This may come about because a creditor has applied to court to have a person declared bankrupt, or the person may declare him or herself bankrupt.

Receivership

Companies go into receivership. Receivers are appointed by a debenture-holder (usually a bank). The receivers manage the company, usually selling off assets – although sometimes they keep the company trading – until the debenture-holder receives what is owed. The company is then given back to the directors to manage. If the financial situation is very poor (as is frequently the case) the company may bypass receivership and go straight into liquidation.

Liquidation

Liquidation is the company's equivalent of bankruptcy. A liquidator is appointed by the directors/shareholders – or perhaps at the instigation of a creditor – and it is the liquidator's role to sell all assets and pay as many of the creditors as possible. When the liquidation is finished, the company will cease to exist.

BECOMING A GUARANTOR

Guaranteeing someone else's obligations is another way many people get into financial difficulty. People sometimes give guarantees to the bank for their own family company, for their children to buy a house or to go into business, or for other family or friends to borrow money. If the loan goes bad, and you or the person you have guaranteed cannot make up the shortfall, you are in trouble.

The lender can pursue you, as guarantor, for any unpaid amounts, right to bankrupting you if necessary. You can try to get reimbursement from the borrower for any money you paid the lender, but that is unlikely to be of much comfort – the borrower is unlikely to have any money.

Guarantees are to be avoided where possible. If you do feel it necessary to guarantee a loan, be sure that you are confident that you could meet it if it was called on. This means not offering as security anything which you cannot afford to lose, such as your family home.

If you are asked to be a guarantor take legal advice and think very carefully before signing. Be sure you have all the necessary information you need about the financial standing of the borrower and the terms of the loan. Think also about how reliable and responsible the borrower is. Do not forget that if the guarantee is to a bank, it will be for all the obligations that the borrower has to the bank – and the borrower could increase his or her borrowings at any time without your knowing. As well, there may be unpaid interest added to the loan, as well as other costs and charges (all of which will be your responsibility).

See also Guaranteeing a loan, p.56

FINANCIAL FAILURE

> **THE OSTRICH APPROACH**
>
> When some people hit financial problems they bury their heads in the sand, hoping the problem will go away. At the risk of mixing metaphors, this is like a possum being caught in the headlights of a car – the lights are so dazzling, the terror so great, that the possum (you) does nothing and duly becomes road-kill.
>
> Own up to the financial trouble – call it what it is. There is no point trying to fudge the situation or wish it away: you can't. The sooner you take some action the better.
>
> This includes getting good advice. You might even go to the offices of the Official Assignee to get more information regarding your options. If the situation is truly hopeless, own up to it and file for bankruptcy. Nobody likes the idea, but people report that once they have taken the step, they feel that the worst has happened – they have reached the bottom and things can only get better.

GOING BANKRUPT

When you have financial difficulties and cannot pay your bills, bankruptcy is one of your options. However, declaring formal bankruptcy is not a step to be taken lightly – there are major implications for your financial and personal future. Henceforth, for three years at least, you may not manage a company, go overseas or take on any borrowings without the approval of the Official Assignee.

So, if things look bleak, take some advice and consider some other options:

- Sell some assets.
- Budget to reduce your outgoings or increase your income. In particular look at getting rid of high-interest debts such as hire purchase (this may mean selling some assets).
- Enter into arrangements with creditors so that you pay off debts by instalment (either weekly or monthly).
- Offer your creditors a percentage of the amount owing as full and final settlement of their debts.
- Ask the District Court for a Summary Instalment Order. This means that you repay creditors over time by weekly instalment. This is supervised by a court appointee and creditors cannot take any further legal action while the order is in place.

What happens

Bankruptcy can happen in either of two ways:

1. *You can be pushed*

   One or more of your creditors can ask the High Court to declare you bankrupt. The court will look at the evidence from you and from your creditor(s) and decide whether to declare you bankrupt. This can take months and some people use it to delay their bankruptcy, usually in the hope of a reversal in their fortune.

2. *You can jump*

   You can file a voluntary petition for bankruptcy at the nearest High Court. If your financial position is hopeless, this is a good idea as it lets you get on with your life as quickly as possible. You might as well bow to the inevitable. In one of the most ironic twists imaginable, you have to pay a fee to file for bankruptcy!

When you go bankrupt the Official Assignee will take over your financial affairs. The OA is an officer of the High Court and it is his or her job to administer fairly the assets and liabilities of bankrupt people. The OA will set to and sell your assets, using the proceeds to pay off your debts in their proper priority.

Usually there is a shortfall between what the assets will realise and the value of debts, meaning some creditors will be paid in part or be paid nothing at all.

The OA will also investigate your affairs and may take action if there have been any serious breaches of insolvency law. For example, if you have paid a creditor in preference to others just before your bankruptcy, the OA may void that payment and ask the creditor for the money back so it can be shared among all the creditors.

What happens to *you*

All your assets and liabilities go into the hands of the OA. The only things you are allowed to keep are:

- Personal effects and furniture to the value of $2000.
- Money to the value of $400.
- The tools of your trade (if you have one) to a combined value of $500.

However, going bankrupt gives you immediate relief from all your debts – they are now in the hands of the OA. You no longer deal with any of your creditors, including the IRD. The only liabilities that you are left with are:

- Court fines.
- Child support or maintenance payments.
- Orders for reparation made by a court.
- Any debts you incurred after the date of your bankruptcy.

At an initial interview with the OA you will be asked a lot of questions and asked to fill in some forms. You will be given a notice that proves you are bankrupt – you can show this to creditors so they no longer pursue you for money. You make a fresh financial start in that nearly all your debts are wiped. You will even get a new IRD number.

However, your bankruptcy will be advertised in the local newspaper. The OA may make an inspection of your house to see if you have any saleable items and sometimes you will be asked to go to a meeting with your creditors.

Being 'in bankruptcy'

Bankruptcy usually lasts for three years, after which you will be 'discharged'. In some extreme cases the OA or a creditor may seek to extend that time. The OA is your supervisor while you are an 'undischarged bankrupt' and may seek information from you, which you are required to disclose. You must advise the OA if you change your address.

There are other requirements too:

- You cannot be self-employed or employed by a member of your family or manage any business without the approval of the OA.
- You cannot be a director of a company. Sometimes this ban may be extended beyond the period of bankruptcy.
- You cannot leave New Zealand without the OA's consent.
- You cannot take on any credit (i.e. take a loan) of more than $100 without telling the lender that you are an undischarged bankrupt.

Discharge

When you are discharged from your bankruptcy, usually after three years, you will be free from all of your debts. However, secured creditors (such as the bank with the mortgage over your house) will still have the same rights they had – i.e. they can sell up the house to repay the amount that they are owed under the mortgage. (Usually the house will have been sold during your bankruptcy and your equity used to repay creditors, but where there is little or no equity and the bank is happy to keep its mortgage in place you may be able to keep the house.)

On discharge you will not receive back any assets that the OA took control over. Usually these will have been sold, but some assets prove hard to sell or take a long time to realise. The OA will keep these and use any eventual proceeds to pay creditors.

On discharge you may again go into business and manage a company. You can also borrow money, although for a while you may find this hard to do. The credit rating agencies will have recorded your bankruptcy and any prospective lender is likely to check up and see your previous failure and so be wary of lending to you. Over time it will become easier, but your bankruptcy will stay on credit agencies' records for some years.

BEING A CREDITOR

When someone who owes you money goes broke, you stand to lose money.

People are rightly angry and frustrated when someone can no longer pay them because they have become insolvent. There is often very little that can be done except wait for the liquidator/receiver/Official Assignee to do his or her work and hope there might be something left over for a payment.

You have good cause to get emotional about this. However, this is not a time to get mad – it is a time to get smart, which means making sure you have no other bad debts.

The best time to think about how to avoid losing money through bad debts is *before* you give someone credit. This is the case whether you are in business or making a loan to family or friends.

> **DEBTORS AND CREDITORS**
>
> These two terms are often confused. Debtors are people who owe money; creditors are people who are owed money. Usually, it is good to be a creditor, bad to be a debtor.

Ways to avoid having bad debts

- Document your loans properly. Make sure your customers know and agree to your terms of trade – and put them in writing. It also means properly documenting any loans to family and friends. You may end up dealing with someone else – it is possible that the person to whom you made the loan will die and you'll end up dealing with the executor of his her estate.
- If you supply goods as part of your business, include a Romalpa clause in your terms of trade. This says that the goods do not belong to the debtor until all obligations have been met. If the debtor goes broke before you have been paid, the goods are still yours and you can go and pick them up.
- Take security if you can. This may be a personal guarantee from the directors if you are dealing with a company, or a guarantee from another party, or security over the debtor's property (house, car etc).
- Be sure there is a clear date when you should be paid. It's a good idea to have a penalty interest rate applying from that date too. This gives the debtor every incentive to pay.
- If the debt is not paid on due date, get in touch with the debtor immediately and ask for payment. Don't be bashful about this – it's your money: ring up and ask for it. The squeakiest wheel gets the oil – be a squeaky wheel!

THE FINANCIAL SECRETS

- ❑ Bad stuff does happen.
- ❑ Confront financial problems early.
- ❑ Avoid giving credit if possible. Businesses need to be especially careful with credit to customers.
- ❑ Consider carefully before giving anyone a loan and document it well.
- ❑ Insolvency law is very complex: seek good advice.

CONNECT

- New Zealand Insolvency and Trustee Services (Official Assignee)
  www.insolvency.govt.nz
- Companies Office
  www.companies.govt.nz

BOOK

Banks, Banking and Bankruptcy, Keith McIlroy, Shoal Bay Press, 1997

Glossary

active funds. Unit trusts where the manager goes out and trades shares actively.

actuary. A statistician who works out the risk that a particular event will happen (e.g. a car crash or an accidental death) and then calculates what it should cost to insure against that event.

annuity. An investment which, when purchased, yields a regular agreed amount for a specified period (typically life). Each payment comprises partly a return of capital and partly income from the investment.

application fee. A fee payable at the time of applying for a loan. Usually refundable if your lender declines your application, but not if you decide not to go ahead with the loan.

assessable income. Income after any deductible expenses. on which you are assessed for income tax.

asset testing. The regime that allows a benefit or not according to the amount of assets that you have.

bankruptcy. Individuals go into bankruptcy when they are insolvent, either because a court declares them bankrupt or because they declare themselves bankrupt.

beneficiary. The person who will benefit under a will or a trust.

bequest. A legacy or inheritance.

bond. An investment paying a fixed rate of interest for a fixed period of time, often known as 'stock' in this country (although in many other countries 'stocks' are what we call 'shares').

capped rate. A loan where the interest rate can move down but not up above a predetermined cap.

Catch-22. A situation that, by its nature, is impossible to escape from. From the title of a novel by Joseph Heller.

chattels. The things that are not fixed to the house, which departing owners can take with them if they are not listed in the contract. Chattels usually left include drapes, carpets, light fittings, oven, dishwasher, nightstore heater, logburner etc.

churning. An unscrupulous practice whereby an adviser shifts customers from one product to another, largely so he or she can charge additional fees or receive commission on the 'sale'.

collateral. The security that is put up for a loan.

company tax. Tax paid by a company – at a flat rate of 33 cents in the dollar.

contributory mortgage. A fund raised from investors then lent on to someone on mortgage security. Usually offers high interest rates and high risks.

conveyancing. The process of transferring the property from one owner to another.

creditor. Someone who is owed money.

CV. Curriculum Vitae - literally 'the course of life'.

debenture. A security over a company's assets, allowing the holder to get priority in payment over other creditors.

debtor. Someone who owes money.

deductible expense. Any expenses allowed to be deducted from taxable income.

default. When a borrower misses a repayment or in some other way breaks the terms of a loan or loan agreement.

deferred management fee. A charge paid out of the proceeds of the resale of your retirement village unit.

depreciation. This is a non-cash, tax-deductible expense which recognises that assets lose value over the years.

direct bank. A lender without branches that goes direct to the public via the telephone or Internet.

discretion. A banker might have discretion to $500,000, which means he or she can approve a loan to that amount without reference to someone higher up.

dividends. A distribution from the net profits of a company to its shareholders.

easement. The right for someone to use a part of the land (e.g. to run pipes across, have a right-of-way). The easement is registered on the title.

equity. The interest of ordinary shareholders in a company.

establishment fee. A fee charged at the beginning of a loan.

executor. The person who executes or administers a will.

facility mix. The proportion of different loan types under one loan agreement. For example, you might have total borrowings of $100,000 from one lender and you split that between a fixed-rate facility of $70,000 and a revolving-credit facility of $30,000.

FASTER: The Stock Exchange's system for storing the registered ownership of shares electronically.

FBT. Fringe Benefit Tax which companies must pay on employees' 'perks'.

FIN: Your FASTER Identification Number (used like a PIN on an eftpos card).

fine print. Conditions of a contract, for instance, set in very small print. Easy to skip over, but important to read!

fixed-rate loan. A loan where the interest rate is fixed and cannot be varied during the term by either the lender or the borrower.

floating-rate loan. A loan where the interest rate fluctuates according to prevailing market rates.

freehold. A means of owning property, the other main one being leasehold. The word 'freehold' is often incorrectly used to mean mortgage free.

freehold. Often wrongly used to mean that the property is mortgage free. In fact it means that the property is owned outright – i.e. it is not leasehold.

gearing. Borrowing to buy a larger asset than you could otherwise afford. Usually that asset is for investment purposes (e.g. a rental property). Often gearing is called leverage.

'golden handshake'. A lump sum given to an employee who has been made redundant.

guarantor. Someone who guarantees the financial obligations of someone else.

hedge funds. Protection against loss through future price fluctuations, eg investing in futures.

imputation system. The system that avoids dividends being taxed twice. Most dividends come with imputation credits, meaning that tax has already been paid.

indemnity insurance. An insurance that pays out the depreciated value of your property.

index funds. Funds that passively track a share index (sometimes called 'tracker funds' or 'passive funds').

Index. An artificial portfolio of shares, weighted according to each company's size.

inertia selling. ending you something you have not requested and implying it is yours unless you expressly reject it.

insolvency. The state of being unable to pay your bills as they fall due, or having more liabilities than assets.

interest only. A loan where the borrower pays only interest and does not have to repay the principal until the end of the loan.

intestate. Dying without having made a will.

joint ownership. A form of property ownership whereby on the death of one partner, his or her share goes to the other.

leasehold. Holding land under a lease.

LIM. Land Information Memorandum, which advises on any special conditions, building permits etc applying to your land.

line-of-credit loan. A loan that you can draw on and pay back at will. Sometimes called a revolving-credit facility.

liquidation. The end of a company. A liquidator is appointed, who sells all assets and uses the proceeds to pay off creditors.

loan offer. An offer of finance from a lender to a borrower, giving the terms of the finance that is being offered. When it signed it becomes the loan agreement.

loan sharks. Fringe lenders who lend at very high interest rates – 50 per cent is not uncommon.

loan-to-security ratio (LSR). The percentage of a loan compared with the value of the security being offered. Also known as a loan-to-value ratio (LVR).

margin. A lender's profit. The difference between the rate at which a lender borrows money and the rate at which it is lent out. Sometimes called a spread.

mortgage indemnity insurance. Insurance taken out to cover the lender if the borrower defaults on a loan. It covers the lender but is often paid for by the borrower.

mortgage protection insurance. Insurance offered by lenders which insure the borrower against disability or death.

mortgagee. The lender who is taking a mortgage over a property for security for a loan.

mortgagor. The person borrowing money, allowing a mortgage to be placed over his or her property.

negative gearing. Borrowing for investment purposes so that the interest cost is higher than the rental income. The loss is offset against other income for tax purposes, often meaning the investor gets a tax refund each year.

NZSE 50. The New Zealand Stock Exchange's index of the top 50 companies.

Official Assignee. The person who administers the affairs of bankrupts and sometimes acts as the liquidator of companies.

personal tax summary. A PTS is provided by the IRD on request (and sent automatically to some people). It shows the amount of income you have earned and the tax you have paid, so you can work out whether you need to pay more tax or are due a refund. Once a PTS has been requested any tax owing to the IRD becomes payable.

personal tax. The tax paid by individuals. There is a scale of rates so that the more you earn, the higher the tax rate.

power of attorney. Legal authority to act for another person.

preferential creditors. Creditors who get paid before unsecured creditors, eg staff and the IRD.

premium. The annual amount you pay for insurance.

principal and interest loan (P&I). Loans where part of each payment reduces the principal owing.

principal. The amount that is borrowed, or is left outstanding.

probate. The proving of the will. When probate is granted by a court, the will is valid and can be executed.

property developer. A person who buys property for the purposes of selling it again.

property sharing agreement. An agreement by a couple as to how they will share their assets (including money, houses, inheritance and debts). This may be entered into before a relationship (commonly called a pre-nuptial agreement), during a relationship or when it is over.

provisional tax. Tax paid by people and companies in business during the year that they are earning the income. Provisional tax is usually paid in three instalments – 7 July, 7 November and 7 February.

receivership. A debenture-holder may place a company into receivership to recover a debt by appointing a manager to sort out the company's affairs. It often, although not always, means the end of the company's trading.

replacement insurance. An insurance that pays out sufficient to replace your property.

Residents' Withholding Tax (RWT). A tax deducted by a borrower before it pays you interest. The tax witheld is credited in your tax return.

revolving-credit facility. Another term for a line-of-credit loan.

rollover. The renewal of a loan on substantially the same terms.

Romalpa clause. A clause in a sales agreement which states that the goods in question remain the property of the seller until they are paid for in full.

secured creditors. Those who have some security over assets – e.g. a mortgage or debenture. They get paid out first in the event of a bankruptcy or liquidation.

secured guarantee. A guarantee where the guarantor provides some security.

service fee. The fee charged by a bank for holding a line of credit or for operating an account.

speculation. Buying something in the hope of making a profit.

stagging. Buying new shares before they list in anticipation of a quick profit on their resale.

table loan see *principal and interest loan*

taxable income. See assessable income.

tenants in common. A form of property ownership whereby two people each own a defined share of the property and on the death of one that share can be sold or transferred to someone else.

terminal tax. The final tax to be paid for the previous year (the total due, less any provisional tax paid). Terminal tax is usually paid a year after the end of the year that is being assessed – e.g. terminal tax for the year ended 31 March 2002 would be due on 7 April 2003.

trail fee. A fee paid to an adviser after an investment, mortgage or insurance policy is sold. The adviser will receive small but regular amounts from the company provided that you stay with what you have purchased.

transaction fee. The fee charged by banks for operating accounts –usually charged per transaction.

trustee. A person who owns and holds assets for the benefit of others.

unit title. Where you have title to your particular dwelling but you share ownership of part of the property (e.g. stairs, driveways, corridors etc) with others. Most common in blocks of apartments.

Unsecured creditors. Creditors who have no security and rank last in getting any payment.

variable-rate loan. See floating-rate loan.

Index

Numbers in **bold** refer to information in boxes.

AA (Automobile Association) 104
abatement, benefit **186**
ACC *see* Accident Compensation Corporation
Accident Compensation Corporation 42, 118, 188-89
accident, definition of **189**
accidental risk insurance policy 39
Accommodation Supplement 183, 193
accountant 25; seek advice from 90, 116, 120, 122, 127
active funds 80
Activity in the Community projects 186
actuaries 37
administrative review (child support) **142**
advisers: accountant 25; choosing 23-24; financial 29-32; insurance 27-29; mortgage 25-27; lawyer 25-26
AGC 75
agents, definition of **26**
ages of consent **108**
agreed value cover (car insurance) 40
'all obligations' guarantee 57, **207**
American Express 47
annuities 97, 193-94
annuity mortgage 194
antiques 69
application fees (loan) 50
arithmetic of home loans 63-64
art 69
assessable income (re child support) 142
asset rich, cash poor 192
asset-testing: for beneficiaries 185; for funeral grant 193; for legal aid **139**; for residential care subsidies 200-02; for Student Allowance 167; for superannuation 94
'associated persons' 90
assurance, life 41
'at call' deposits 74, 75
auction: buying at 106; buying house at 150-51; selling house at 157-58
audit, tax 128-29
availability of goods 101
Away-from-home Allowance 184

baby boomers 94
bad debts, avoiding 211
balloon payment 62
bank 11, 34-37; adverse publicity for 53; base fees 35; bills 75; deposits 74, 75; direct 53; loyalty to 35; overdrafts 49; profit margins on loans 50; promotion of good practices 37; relationship with 58; and Residents' Withholding Tax 74, 119; sensitivity about reputations 27; as sources of finance 51

bank fees 35-36, 50; saving on 47; negotiating 50, 64-65
Banking Ombudsman 33, 36-37
banking services 34-35; complaints about 36-37
bankruptcy 54, 168, 207, 208-10
Baycorp 54, 54, 105
beneficiaries (of estate) 197, 198, 199
beneficiaries (trust) and tax 126
Benefit Review Committee **187**
benefit fraud **182**
benefits, government 18, 55, 166, 181-190, 193
bereavement leave 175
bills, bank 75
blended families **136**, 142
BNZ Finance 75
board, paying 143
boards of trustees 163, 164
bond (rental) 161
bonds 76-77; tax on 119-20
book-keeping 119,122-23
'boomerang generation' 142
borrower, rights of 50
borrowing 46-66; to buy shares 83-84
bridging finance 149
brokers, definition of **26**
BT Registries **79**
Budget Advice Services 21, 22
budget 18-22, 140-41, 169, 192, 195
building permits **153**
burglar alarms **38**
business accounts for self-employed 54
business, definition of **125**
businesses and tax 120-28

calculating your net worth **17**
capital gains, tax on 72, 77, 82, 120
capital index 82
capital items: improvement to 128; replacement of 19
car insurance *see* insurance
car: buying 104-06; more expensive than necessary **20**; sale of 105; and tax 127; with warranties 105-06
career, development of 18, 171, 175-76
case manager 181
cash management trusts 75
cash rollover clause **149**, 153
cash withdrawals on credit card 48
cashflow 59; assessment by lender 54-55, 89; deficit 88
cashing in life insurance policies 41
Catch-22 **54**, 172
Certified Financial Planner 32
Certified Life Underwriter 28

217

INDEX

CFP *see* Certified Financial Planner
character, assessment by lender 53-54, 59
charge cards 47
chattels, definition of **154**
cheques: dishonouring 36; fees 36
Child Disability Allowance 184
Child Tax Credit 187
child custody 141
child support 55, 118, 141-42,174, 209
Childcare Subsidy 184, 189
childcare tax rebate 118
children: ages of consent **108**; and contracts 108; educational trusts for 143, 169; and family trusts 135; guardians for **196**; and inheritances **143**; and money **136**, 142-44; and pocket money **136**; and relationships 135; and tax 117, **124**; with special needs 143-44, 163
'churning' 27
CIBA *see* Corporation of Insurance Brokers
client confidentiality 32
clothing allowance 201
CLU *see* Certified Life Underwriter
Code of Banking Practice, The 37
collateral 55-56, 59
collectibles 69
Commerce Commission 103
commercial property investment, pros and cons of 86
commission, payment to: advisers 24; financial advisers 30; insurance advisers 27; mortgage brokers 26; real estate agents 158, 160
Community Services Card 185, 192
Companies Office 105
company tax 120
comparative pricing 101
compensation 106, 179, 188-89
complaining 100, 102-03, 104, 159
compound interest 96, **97**
comprehensive cover: car insurance 40; health insurance 43
Computershare **79**
conditional contracts 152
conditional offer 151
constructive dismissal 177
Consumer Guarantees Act 100, 103-04, 105, 106, 107, 108, 109, 111
consumer law 100-14
consumer myths 110
consumption, borrowing to pay for 46, **48**
contents insurance *see* insurance
contract note (shares) 79
contracting out of: Consumer Goods Act 104; Property (Relationships) Act 134
contractor, self-employed **126**
contracts: and children 57, 108; consumer 106, 107-08, **110**; employment 173-75; real estate 150, 151-154; share 79; Student Job Seeker 166
Contractual Mistakes Act **107**
Contractual Remedies Act 107
contributory mortgages 76
conveyancing, definition of **154**; fixed price for 24
Corporation of Insurance Brokers 28
court order (re child support) 142

Credit (Repossession) Act 1997 111
Credit Contracts Act **50**; 107, 111
credit cards 20, **36**, 46, 47-48, 49, 68, 112; lenders' profit margins on 50
credit check 53-54; making your own 54
credit note **102**
credit rating agencies 54, 210
credit unions 76
credit, free 47
creditors 76, 206-07, 210-11; definition of 211
creditworthiness, proving **35**
'Cullen Fund', The 94
currency, New Zealand dollar 91, 92, 120
Curriculum Vitae (CV) **173**
custody of children 141
CV *see* Curriculum Vitae

de facto couples 131, **132** 133
death by accident 189
death duties 195, 199-200
debenture-holder 75, 207
debt collection 102, 112-13, 211
debt consolidation 48, 65-66
debt, elimination of 68
debtor, definition of 211
debts, avoiding bad 211
declining net worth 17
deferred management fee (retirement villages) 204
defined-risk insurance policy 39
defined-benefit contribution schemes 97, 98
Department of Labour 178, 179
deposit on house 148
deposits 69, 73-77
depreciation 89, 128
description of goods 101
Diners Club 47
direct banks 53
direct investment 72
Disability Allowance 184, 193
disability insurance *see* insurance
discharged bankruptcy 210
disclosure statements, financial advisers' 31, 32
discounts, insurance premium **38**
discrimination 174, 178
dismissal 176
dispute resolution procedures: ACC **189**; accountants 25; banks 36-37; employment 178-79; debts 113; insurance companies 44; motor vehicles 106; WINZ **187**
Disputes Tribunal 100, 102, 104, 106, 113
diversification 71-72, 79, 98
dividend imputation system *see* imputation credits
dividends: from shares 78, 125, 126; tax on 82-83, 91, 118, 120
documentation fees (loan) 50
Domestic Purposes Benefit 182-83, 184
donations 118
door-to-door sales 107
double taxation 82-83, 91, 120
dying intestate 195, **197**

early repayment penalty (home loan) *see* penalties

218

Earthquake Commission 40
earthquakes, insurance against *see* Earthquake Commission
easement, definition of **154**
Education Act 1989 163
education 163-70
educational trust 143, 169
Emergency Maintenance Allowance 184
emergency grants 185
emerging markets 73
employee share plans 81
employees, definition of **26**
employer-subsidised superannuation schemes 97-98
Employment Court 178, 179
Employment Relations Act 178
Employment Relations Authority 114, 177, 178, 179
Employment Relations Service 179
employment 171-79
employment agreements 173-75, 178
endowment policies 41 *See also* insurance, life
endowment warrants 84
Enduring Power of Attorney 191, 198
entertainment (and tax) 128
EQC *see* Earthquake Commission
equity in house 95
establishment fees (loan) 50
estate duties 195, 199-200
estimates 102, 109, 158
evasion, tax **129**
executor (of will) 196-97
exemplary damages 188
exempt supplies (GST) 122
expenditure 19-22; in retirement 194-95
expensive habits 95
exporters, and GST 122

Fair Trading Act 57, 100-03, 104, 106, 107, 108, 111
false representations 101
Family Assistance 186-88
Family Court 138, 139, 140, **142**
Family Protection Act 195, 196, **197**, 199
Family Support 186-87
Family Tax Credit 187
family loans 52
family trusts 11, 133, 134-35, 166, 199-200, 202; and tax 126-27
FASTER 79
faulty goods 108, 114
FBT *see* Fringe Benefit Tax
fees, up-front 30, **49**, 50, 52, 53, 72, 75
fidelity fund (MVDI) 105
FIF *see* Foreign Investment Fund
FIN **79**
finance companies: as sources of loans 51; and deposits 75; profit margins on loans 49, 50; and Residents' Witholding Tax 74, 119; and risk 74
finance companies, retailers' 52, 111
finance rate **49**; 112
finance, sources of 50-52
Financial Planners and Insurance Advisers Association 28, 29, 32; ethical and professional standards 28, 32; six-step process 29

financial advisers 29-32
financial difficulty 46, 47, 48, **62**, **207**, **208**
financial failure 206-11
financial planners *see* financial advisers
financial secrets 12, 22, 33, 45, 66, 92, 99, 114, 130, 144, 162, 170, 180
finding work 185
fine print, the 102
fire insurance *see* insurance
fixed-interest investments 76, 77
fixed-rate loans 60, 61
fixed-term tenancy 160-61
floating-rate loans 60, 61, **63**, 64
Foreign Investment Fund regime 91-92
foreign investments *see* offshore investments
fortnightly mortgage payments **64**
FPIA *see* Financial Planners and Insurance Advisers Association
franking credits 83
freehold, definition of **154**
friendly societies 76
Fringe Benefit Tax (FBT) 123
Fund Source 30, 73
fund manager 29, 30, 31, 72, 73, 75, 79, 80, **87**, 197
fund, choosing 73
funeral arrangements 197
funeral expenses, pre-paid 201
funeral grant 189, 193

'gap year' 164
gearing 84, 85; negative 88-89
gender, and insurance costs 43
general agency (real estate) 157
gift duty 202
gift horses **70**
gifting **182**, 201, 202
gifts 133, 135, **143**, 201, 202
goals 16, 19, **22**, 30, 31, 69, 77, **172**, **175**
'golden handshake' 178
Goods and Services Tax (GST) 101, 109, 121-23
government assistance 165-67, 181-190, 192-93
government stock 74
government valuation *see* rating valuation
Grant of Probate 197-98
'Grey List' 120
gross index 81
gross yield 87
GST *see* Goods and Services Tax
guaranteed repurchase scheme 204
guaranteeing a loan 56-57, **64**, **207**
guarantees, consumer 103-04
guarantor, protection for 57; putting up security 57, **207**
guardian 196, **197**

harrassment 178, 179
hazardous activities, and insurance costs 42, 43
health insurance *see* insurance
health, and insurance costs 42, 43
hedge funds 11
heirlooms 132,139
High-use Health Card 185, 193

Hire Purchase Act 1971 111
hire purchase **20**, 47, 50, 51, 52, 55, 65, 68, 105, 107, 110-12
hobbies, and tax 125
holiday pay 174
Holidays Act 174
home equity annuity mortgage **194**
home loans 52, 53, 54, 57-66. *See also* loans
home office 90, 122, 127
home ownership, benefits 146
home schooling 163
hospital waiting lists 43
hospital-only cover (health insurance) 38, 43
house as security 58
house insurance *see* insurance
house, additional costs to buy **153**; additional costs to sell **155**; buying 147-54; private sale 156; registered valuation of 59; renting 159-62; as security 127, **207**; selling **149**, 155-59; too expensive **20**
Housing New Zealand tenants 183

ICANZ *see* Institute of Chartered Accountants
IIBA *see* Independent Insurance Brokers Association
impulse buying **16**
imputation credits 82, 83, 91, 120
income support 181-85
income testing 166, 184, 185, 201
income-related rent 183
income-replacement insurance *see* insurance
income: increasing, 18, 22, 171; disparity of 133, **136**,137; loss of **43**; 18, 22, 136, 148, 171; splitting 124
Independent Insurance Brokers Association 28
independent product comparisons 30
index funds 80-82
index trackers 80
index, the 81-82
industrial property investment, pros and cons of 86
industry audit 129
inertia selling 102
inflation 95, 146, 193
inheritance 68, 95, 132, 133, 134, 135, **143** 144, 195, 201
Inland Revenue Department (IRD) 116-29 *passim*, 141, 142, 168, 169, 170, 186, 209
insolvency 206-07
insolvency law 209
insolvent investments 73
instant gratification 46
Institute of Chartered Accountants 25
Insurance and Savings Ombudsman 33, 44
insurance 27, 28, 34, 37-44; car 38, 39, 40-41; contents 38, 40; disability 42, 97; fire 39, 40; health 38, 43-44; house 38, 39-40; income-replacement 38, 42-43; life 38, 41-42, **41**, 98; mortgage 59; natural disasters **40**; trauma 43
insurance advisers 27-29, 34
insurance companies 11, 27, 28, 34, 37; disputes with 44; financial soundness of 38-39; paying on claims 39; payment to 28; sensitivity about reputations 29
insurance industry bodies 28-29
insurance premiums 28, **38**, 40-44

insurance research houses 24
insurance specialists *see* insurance advisers
'interest free' offers 102
interest-only loans 62
interest rates, home loan 60-64
interest, compound 96, 97
interest, tax on 119, 127
Internet banking 35, **36**; 53
interview for a job 172-73
intestate 195, **197**
Invalid's Benefit 183, 184
inventory 162
Investment Advisers (Disclosure) Act 1996 31, 32
investment 68-92
investment advisers *see* financial advisers
investment research houses 24, 30, 73
investments, and Property (Relationships) Act 132
investments, reviewing 18 193
Invincible Life 194
IRD *see* Inland Revenue Department

jargon, property **155**
jewellery, insurance for 40
Job Seeker's Agreement 182
job: finding 172-73, 185-86; leaving 176-78
joint bank accounts 136
joint ownership 154
joint tenancy 154, 198
junk fees 50

knowledge economy 163

Land Information Memorandum (LIM) 152
Land Transfer Office 58
land registration 57-58
landslips, insurance against *see* Earthquake Commission
LAQC *see* loss attributing qualifying company
late payment penalty **110**
lawyer 24-25; costs 53, 58, 153, 154, 155, 196, 197; seek advice from 134, 135, 138, 139, 142, 152, 153, 156, 196, 198, 203, 207
Layby Sales Act 109
laybys 109-10
LBA *see* Life Brokers Association
lease, responsibility for **159**
leasehold, definition of **154**
leave, special 174-75
Legal Services Board **139**
legal aid **139**
lender's costs, liability for **56**
lenders 49-53
Licensed Motor Vehicle Dealers (LMVD) 104-05
Life Brokers Association 29
life assurance **41**
life insurance policy, surrender value of 41, cashing in 41
life insurance *see* insurance
lifestyle 20, 21, **38**, 94, 95, 96; 149, 192
LIM *see* Land Information Memorandum
limited liability company 125
line of credit 47, 49, 62-63, 64, 68

220

liquidation 207
listed funds 72
living allowance (re child support) 142
LMVD *see* Licensed Motor Vehicle Dealers
loan agreement (student loan) 168
loan sharks **56**
loan, non-recourse 84
loan-to-security ratio 56, 59
loan-to-value ratio 56
loans 46, 49-57. *See also* home loans, student loans
local authority stock 74
loss attributing qualifying company (LAQC) 125-26
loss of income **43**; compensation for 189
loss of income insurance 42-43; stand-down period 38
lotto **22**
low-income earner's rebate 126
LSR *see* loan-to-security ratio

Macquarie Bank 84
maintenance: inspection 152; rental property 161-62; and tax 128
making a complaint 100, 102-03, 104, 159
managed funds 72-73, 86, 97
margin 83
margin call 83, 84
margin trading 83-84
marriage *see* relationships
Matrimonial Property Act 196
mediation 140, 178, 179
medical history, and insurance costs 42
medical insurance *see* insurance, health
Million Dollar Round Table 29
minimum wage 173
minimum warranties, car 106
Minors Contract Act 108
mistakes (consumer) **107**, 110
Modification Grant 184
money, family: borrowing 52-53; control by one partner 135, 137; discussing with partner **21**, 131, 133, **136**, 137
MoneyWorks 122
monkey on your back 57
Morningstar 30, 73
mortgage annuity 194
mortgage brokers 25-27
mortgage income trusts 75
mortgage insurance 59
mortgage payments 148, 149; as percentage of income 54; fortnightly **64**
mortgage *see* home loans
Motor Vehicle Dealers Act 104, 105
Motor Vehicle Dealers Institute 104, 105
Motor Vehicles Disputes Tribunal 106
motor vehicles *see* cars
MVDI *see* Motor Vehicle Dealers Institute
MYOB 122

natural disasters, insurance against: *see* Earthquake Commission
needs assessment (for residential care) 200
negative gearing 88-89
negotiating: application fees 50, 64; bank fees 36, 50, 64-65; to buy house 150; credit card fees 65; debts 113-14; employment agreements 173; establishment fees 50; home loans 64, 65: insurance premiums 64; interest rates 64; redundancy payments 178; relationship settlement 137, 138; with your bank 65; with real estate agents 158
net worth 17
net yield 87
New Zealand dollar 91, 92, 120
New Zealand Gazette **129**
New Zealand Law Society 25
New Zealand Mortgage Brokers Association, 27
New Zealand Qualifications Authority (NZQA) **165**
New Zealand Stock Exchange **78**, **79**
New Zealand Superannuation 94, 192
no-claims bonus: car insurance **38**; health insurance 44
non-recourse loan 84
'now' society **16**
NZMBA *see* New Zealand Mortgage Brokers Association
NZQA *see* New Zealand Qualifications Authority
NZSE 50 index 81

Occupational Safety and Health regulations, breach of 206
Office of the Retirement Commissioner 95, 96; web site 96
Official Assignee 208, 209, 210
offshore investments 90-92; tax on 120
options 84
origin of goods 101
OSCAR subsidy *see* out-of-school subsidy
OSH *see* Occupational Safety and Health
out-of-school subsidy 184
over-insurance 37, 38
overdraft 49, 62
overtime 18, 55
ownership investments 73
ownership of assets 198
ownership structure (business) 154

packaging, misleading 101
Parental Tax Credit 188
partnership (business) 124-25
passive funds 80, 81, 90, 91
PAYE 117, 174
penalties: early repayment of home loan 60, 64, 155; late payment **110**; student loan 169-70; tax **119**
penalty interest 211
performance risk 70, 71, 79
'perks' 123
periodic tenancy 160
Personal Properties Securities Act **105**
Personal Tax Summary 117-18, 119
personal grievance claim 178-79
Pharmaceutical Subsidy Card 193
planning 15-22, 29; for retirement 191-92; superannuation 95-96
pocket money **136**, 144
portfolio, diversified 96, 97; reviewing 193; risk/return mix 70-72

possession date 152
power of attorney 191. *See also* Enduring Power of Attorney
pre-nuptial agreements 132, 134. *See also* property-sharing agreement
pre-paid funeral expenses 201
preferential creditors 207
premiums *see* insurance premiums
'price gouging' 109
primary school system **163**
principal and interest loans 61, **62**. *See also* table loans
privacy laws 54
private sale 103: house 156
private schools **164**
private treaty (real estate) 150, 151
probate 197-98
problems with budgeting 20-21
product supplier liability **26**
promotion, seeking 18, 175-76
Property (Relationships) Act 12, 131-32, 133, 134, 135, 140, 196
property developers 76, 90
property investment 69, 84-90
property investment, tax on 120, 128, 147
property jargon **155**
property values, increase in 89
property-sharing agreement 134, 138
provisional tax 123
Public Trust 196, 201
public health waiting lists 43
public holidays 174
punitive damages 188
purchase price, house 59

quality, buying 19
Quicken 122
quotes 102, 109
raise, asking for 18; 175

rating valuation (RV) 59
Real Estate Institute of New Zealand 159
real estate agents 149-50, 153, 155, 156, 157, 158-59; 159-60
receivership 207
record-keeping **119**, 197
recovered depreciation 89
reducing loans 62
redundancy 177-78
refunds (consumer) **103**, 108, 110
refunds (tax) 83, 88, 117, 121, 122, 123
registered valuation 59
registration of shares 79
rehabilitation 189
reimbursement 179
reinstatement 179
relationship property 131, 132, 133, 134, 139, 140
relationships 131-40; definition of **132**; failure of 131, 132, 133, 134, 135, **137**, 138
remedies **102**
remortgaging, fixed price for 24
rent: income-related 183; paying 161; receiving 86, **87**, 89, 116 88, 89, 90, 161

rental property, repairs and maintenance 161-62
renting a home 146-147, 159-62
repairs, and tax 128
repayment of debt 31, 68
repossession **56**, 57, 111-12
Reserve Bank 74
reserve price 151
Residential Tenancies Act 160
residential care subsidies 200-02
residential property investment: management of **87**, pros and cons of 86
Residents Withholding Tax 74, 119
residual tax 123
resignation 176
rest-home care subsidy 199, 200-02
retail property investment, pros and cons of 86
retailers' finance companies *see* finance companies, retailers'
Retirement Commissioner 95, 96; web site 96
retirement 95, 96, 178, 191-204; saving for 71, 97-98
retirement villages 202-04
revolving credit facility *see* line of credit
right to sue 188
rights as a borrower **50**
'ripping off' 182
risk (insurance) 37-38
risk, investment: **70**, 71, 74, 76 79
Romalpa clause 211
RWT *see* Residents Withholding Tax

sale and purchase agreement 156
sales commission *see* commission
same-sex couples 131
saving 20, **22**, 68, 69, 70, 71, 95, 96, 146. *See also* investment
saving money on your mortgage 63-65
savings account, spare cash in 62
scams **70**, 91, **126**
'Scamwatch' 70
school fees 163-64
school uniforms 164
second-hand goods 106-07, 164
secondary markets for bonds 77
secondary school system **163**
secured creditors 206, 210
secured deposits 75
secured loans 56
Securities Commission **70**
security: houses as 58, **64**, **207**; on loan 55-56; provided by guarantor **57**, **207**
self-employed contractor **126**
self-employment, security of income 55
separate property 131, 132, 135, 136, 140
separation *see* relationship, failure of
service level agreement 24
servicing income, agents **26**
settlement conference 140
sexual abuse 188
share certificates 79
share contracts 79
share index 80, 81-82
share registration 79

share traders 120; and tax 82
sharebrokers 78
sharemarket crash 84
sharemarket managed funds 79-82
shares 69, 70, 71, 72, 77-84; tax on 120
Sickness Benefit 183
Small Claims Court 113
smoke alarms 38, 40
smoking, and insurance costs 42, 43
Social Security Appeals Authority **187**
sole agency (real estate) 156-57
sole trader 124
special benefits 192
special leave 174-75
special needs grants 185
special offers 101
speculation 69
split loans 11, **61**, 64
stagging 82
stand-down period: health insurance 43-44; loss of income insurance 38
Steel & Tube 81
stock, government 74; local authority 74
stress from budgeting **21**
Student Allowance 141, 165-66, 167
Student Job Seeker Contract 166
Student Loan Scheme 11, 118, 143, 147, 167-70
subsidised work schemes 185-86
succession planning 195-200
Summary Instalment Order 208
superannuation scheme **118**
superannuation 73, 94-98, 102
surcharge, superannuation 94-95
surrender value of insurance policy 41
survivors' grant 189
suspension from school 163

table loans 61, 62
talent bank 186
taonga 132
Taranaki Savings Bank 194
Taskforce Green 186
tax 18, 85, 116-129; audit 24; avoidance **129**; on bonds 77; on capital gains 72, 77, 80, 82, 92, 120; efficiency 72, 77, 89, 118, 120, 121, **129**; evasion **129**; imputation credits 82-83, 91, 120; on interest 119, 127; minimising 118, **129**; on offshore investments 90-91; on property investment 89-90, 120, 128; refunds 64, 83, 88, 117, 121, 122, 123; returns 117-18; on shares 82-83, , 91, 118, 120; terminal 123
tax imputation credits 82, 83, 91, 120
tax-deductible expenses 127-28
taxation, double 82-82, 91, 120
Telecom 81, 84
telephone banking 35, 53
Tenancy Services 159, 160
Tenancy Tribunal 100, 114
tenancy 160-61
tenancy agreement 160, 162
tenants in common 154, 198, 202
tender, buying house by 151

TeNZ 72, 80
term deposits 74
term insurance *see* insurance, life
terminal tax 123
tertiary education 165; funding 165-70
testamentary promise 196, 199
testamentary trust 133, **143**
third-party cover **38**, 40
time payment *see* hire purchase
tip-off to IRD 129
Torrens system 57-58
trail fees 26, 27, 30
Training Incentive Allowance 184
training, occupational 175-76
transaction accounts 35-36
Transitional Retirement Benefit 183
trauma insurance *see* insurance
travellers cheques, charges for 36
trust account 28, **31**
trust companies 196, 197, 198
trust deed (managed funds) 72
trust, educational 143, 169
trust, family *see* family trusts
trustee company (managed funds) 72
trustees (family trust) 135
trustees (of estate) 198

UDC 75
unconditional contract 153, 158
unconditional offer 151
under-insurance 37, 38
Unemployment Benefit 182
Unemployment Benefit Student Hardship 166-67
unit title, definition of **154**
unit trusts 75, 79, 80
unsecured creditors 207
unsecured deposits 75
unsecured loans 56
up-front costs, retirement villages 203-04
up-front fees 30, **49**, 50, 52, 53, 72, 75
use-of-money interest 119, 123

value builders, borrowing to buy 46
value losers, borrowing to buy 46
valuing: businesses **17**; real estate **17**
variable-rate loans *see* floating-rate loans
verbal contracts 107
vesting date 97
volatility 69, 70, 71, 74, 79
volcanic activity, insurance against *see* Earthquake Commission
voluntary agreement (child support) 141
voluntary petition for bankruptcy 208

wages, minimum 173
warrant of fitness 104
warranties, car 105-06
warrants 84
web-based budgeting 11, 21, 22
whole-of-life insurance policies *see* insurance, life
wholesale money market 75
Widow's Benefit 184

223

wills 143, 195-98, 200
wills kits 196
windfalls 61, 64, 68, 134, 135, **143**
windscreen, insurance for 39
WINZ *see* Work and Income New Zealand
WiNZ 72, 90
women, financially disadvantaged 140
Work and Income New Zealand (WINZ) 164, 167, 181, 182, 186, 200, 201; appeals **187**

work experience 185
working: after retirement age **192**; while on a benefit 186
World Index 81, 90

yield 87-88

zero-rated supplies (GST) 122